LAW AND THE PARTY IN CHINA

In the Xi Jinping era, it has become clear that the rule of law, as understood in the West, will not appear in China soon. But was this ever a likely option? This book argues that China's legal system needs to be studied from an internal perspective, to take into account the characteristic architecture of China's Party-state. To do so, it addresses two key elements: ideology and organisation. Part One of the book discusses ideology and the law, exploring how the Chinese Communist Party conceives of the nature of law and its position within its broader range of policy tools. Part Two, on organisation and the law, reviews how these ideological principles manifest themselves in the application of law, as well as the reform of the Party-state. As such, it highlights how the Party's plans and approaches run counter to mainstream theoretical expectations, and advocates a greater attention to the inherent logic of the system itself.

ROGIER CREEMERS is Assistant Professor of the Law and Governance of China at the Leiden Institute for Area Studies, Leiden University. His research explores how the Chinese Communist Party views its role in governance and uses technology to further its project. With a VIDI grant from the Netherlands Organisation for Scientific Research, he leads a project to chart the development of a tech-enabled 'smart state' in China. He is also preparing a book on China in global cyberspace. His previous research has been published in, amongst others, *The China Journal, The Journal of Contemporary China* and *Asiascape: Digital Asia.*

SUSAN TREVASKES is a professor of Chinese Studies at Griffith University, Australia. Her research has resulted in over sixty publications, including the first books in English on the criminal courts in contemporary China (2007), policing serious crime in China (2010) and the death penalty reform in China (2012). She has published papers on Chinese justice in a number of journals, including *The China Journal, The British Journal of Criminology, The China Quarterly* and *Modern China.* Her latest co-edited volumes are *The Politics of Law and Stability in China* (2014), *Legal Reforms and Deprivation of Liberty in Contemporary China* (2016) and *Justice: the China Experience* (2017).

LAW AND THE PARTY IN CHINA

Ideology and Organisation

Edited by

ROGIER CREEMERS

Leiden University

SUSAN TREVASKES

Griffith University

CAMBRIDGE
UNIVERSITY PRESS

CAMBRIDGE
UNIVERSITY PRESS

University Printing House, Cambridge CB2 8BS, United Kingdom

One Liberty Plaza, 20th Floor, New York, NY 10006, USA

477 Williamstown Road, Port Melbourne, VIC 3207, Australia

314-321, 3rd Floor, Plot 3, Splendor Forum, Jasola District Centre, New Delhi - 110025, India

103 Penang Road, #05-06/07, Visioncrest Commercial, Singapore 238467

Cambridge University Press is part of the University of Cambridge.

It furthers the University's mission by disseminating knowledge in the pursuit of education, learning and research at the highest international levels of excellence.

www.cambridge.org
Information on this title: www.cambridge.org/9781108818919
DOI: 10.1017/9781108864596

First published 2020
First paperback edition 2022

A catalogue record for this publication is available from the British Library

Library of Congress Cataloging in Publication data
Names: Creemers, Rogier, 1982– editor. | Trevaskes, Susan, 1964– editor.
Title: Law and the party in China : ideology and organisation / edited by Rogier Creemers, Universiteit Leiden [and] Susan Trevaskes, Griffith University, Queensland.
Description: Cambridge, United Kingdom ; New York, NY, USA : Cambridge University Press, 2020. | Includes bibliographical references and index.
Identifiers: LCCN 2020012539 (print) | LCCN 2020012540 (ebook) | ISBN 9781108836357 (hardback) | ISBN 9781108818919 (paperback) | ISBN 9781108864596 (epub)
Subjects: LCSH: Zhongguo gong chan dang. | Political parties–Law and legislation–China. | Law–Political aspects–China.
Classification: LCC KNQ2488 .L39 2020 (print) | LCC KNQ2488 (ebook) | DDC 342.51/07–dc23
LC record available at https://lccn.loc.gov/2020012539
LC ebook record available at https://lccn.loc.gov/2020012540

ISBN 978-1-108-83635-7 Hardback
ISBN 978-1-108-81891-9 Paperback

CONTENTS

CONTRIBUTORS

ROGIER CREEMERS Leiden Institute for Area Studies
Leiden University

GLORIA DAVIES Faculty of Arts
Monash University

ADAM KNIGHT Leiden Institute for Area Studies
Leiden University

MARGARET K. LEWIS Seton Hall Law School
Seton Hall University

LING LI Department of East Asian Studies
University of Vienna

DELIA LIN Asia Institute
University of Melbourne

SAMULI SEPPÄNEN Faculty of Law
The Chinese University of Hong Kong

EWAN SMITH Christ Church
University of Oxford

SUSAN TREVASKES School of Humanities, Languages and Social Science
Griffith University

ABBREVIATIONS

BRICS	Brazil, Russia, India, China and South Africa
CASS	Chinese Academy of Social Sciences
CCDI	Central Commission for Discipline Inspection
CCP	Chinese Communist Party
CDA	critical discourse analysis
CDI	Commission of Discipline and Inspection
CGTN	China Global Television Network
CJFD	China Journal Articles Full-text Database
CPPCC	Committee of the Chinese People's Political Consultative Conference
CPSC	Central Party Supervision Commission
CPSU	Communist Party of the Soviet Union
DNA	deoxyribonucleic acid
GMD	Guomindang
MoS	Ministry of Supervision
MoU	memorandum of understanding
NDRC	National Development and Reform Commission
NGO	non-governmental organisation
NPC	National People's Congress
NSC	National Supervision Commission
PBoC	People's Bank of China
PeoSC	People's Supervision Commissions
PRC	People's Republic of China
PSC	Party Supervision Commission
SA	Sturmabteilung
SPC	Supreme People's Court
SPP	Supreme People's Procuratorate
USSR	Union of Soviet Socialist Republics
WTO	World Trade Organization

1

Ideology and Organisation in Chinese Law

Towards a New Paradigm for Legality

ROGIER CREEMERS AND SUSAN TREVASKES

1.1 Introduction

In decades past, in their analysis of the objective of post-Mao legal reform, Chinese and foreign observers generally agreed: the country was on its way to some form of the rule of law, or *fazhi* (法治). Throughout the 1990s and the early 2000s, it even seemed that both sides shared broad agreement on the fundamental elements of this term. Legal education and the legal profession were given considerable support, legislative and judicial processes became increasingly professionalised, and rule of law-related concepts entered the meticulously curated jargon of Chinese Communist Party (CCP or Party) ideology. Yet by the second half of the Hu Jintao administration, the momentum of reform gradually changed direction. Hu's security czar, Zhou Yongkang, presided over the rapid expansion of a security apparatus (Wang and Minzner 2015). Formal litigation increasingly made way for non-judicial conflict resolution methods such as mediation and arbitration (Liebman 2011; Minzner 2013), manifested in a renewed attention to the 'Ma Xiwu' method of dispute settlement (Zang 2010; Liebman 2011). While Zhou Yongkang himself was politically disgraced and imprisoned, the security state continued to grow from strength to strength in the new Xi Jinping period. Early on in the new Xi Jinping era, a prominent public debate concerning the role of the Constitution in governing the country (Creemers 2015) heralded successively a far-reaching anti-corruption campaign (Li 2018), a growing crackdown against activist lawyers and, perhaps most importantly, an authoritative decision on the role of law at the historic Fourth Plenum of the 18th CCP Congress in 2014 (hereafter 'the 2014 Decision').

The 2014 Decision, for the first time in Party history, made rule of law its central theme, heralding a new interpretation of the Jiang Zemin-era concept of 'governing the nation according to law' (*yifa zhiguo* 依法治国). Its top billing in this historic Congress signalled sharp rhetorical change in socialist rule of law theory, which now claims that supremacy of the Party over all areas of the state is a fundamental requirement of the rule of law. Crucially, the 2014 Decision made a novel claim about the value of *yifa zhiguo* in terms of the Party's governance ambitions: the CCP must exercise its leadership *through all processes* of 'governing the nation according to law' (Trevaskes 2018). This means that Party rule through the conduit of the law is the central organising principle for changes in Xi-era governance, in particular, for reforms that seek to enhance accountability and professionalisation.

The 2014 Decision thus put paid to any lingering doubts that the law itself can act as the ultimate constraint on power in China. Since the Party exercises its leadership through all processes of *yifa zhiguo*, law cannot be the ultimate constrainer of Party power. While the 2014 Decision enabled the Party to 'come out of the shadows' (Chen 2016) to be loud and proud about its authority over and above the law, the question of law–Party supremacy was in fact dealt with ideologically a few years earlier. During the Hu Jintao era (2002–2012), the Politburo initially considered the possibility that it might have to change its leadership style to accommodate the rule of law. It conducted a series of study sessions to debate the precise configuration of the rule of law–Party nexus. By 2014, the meaning given to the rule of law had come to accommodate the primacy of Party leadership. As Ewan Smith says, this change highlighted a shift in emphasis from institutions to individuals: the rule of law came to be recast as a theory of individual obedience to the Party-state, rather than a theory of how Party power could be constrained through institutions, standards and procedures (Smith 2018).

As a result, from a rule of law perspective, the 2014 Decision comes across as almost self-contradictory. On the one hand, it explicitly supported the further professionalisation of the judiciary and the enhancement of accountability rules and regulations through a series of impressive reforms that sought to build into the system meaningful constraints on the power of police, prosecutors and judges (Zhang 2016; Biddulph et al. 2017). Trials and not mediation were to become the centre of the judicial process, measures were put in place to reduce the oft-abused discretion of courts to reject cases at the filing stage, and cross-jurisdictional circuit courts were introduced in a bid to reduce the influence of local governments on court proceedings. Yet at the same time, the 2014 Decision clearly asserted the Party's authority over the legal process, as well as the fact that virtue and morality enjoy equal standing to law in terms of normative power. The 2014 document called for more effective mechanisms to implement the Constitution and sanction unconstitutional conduct, but it also underlined the role of Marxist and socialist doctrine.

How can these seemingly mutually exclusive points be reconciled? The central argument of this book is that to understand how law operates in China, particularly how law relates to 'reform' and 'development', we need first to appreciate the nature of ideology and its relationship to law. We argue that ideology is not merely an external device that sits outside the law to justify or rationalise legal rules, actions and decisions of Party-state actors. Rather, ideology is intrinsic to the logic of legal rules, actions and decisions: therefore it permeates all aspects of law and is in essence the architectural scaffolding within which law operates. Second, we need to appreciate the role that law (and more broadly, rule-based governance) is granted within the overall organisational framework of the Party-state. This framework existed for decades before the development of law was given consistent attention and priority, and this conditions the manner in which legal rationality has been introduced.

To tease out this two-pronged argument in more detail, it is necessary to study in greater depth the 'top-level design' (*dingceng sheji* 顶层设计) the Party envisages for its governing architecture; doing so will reveal the logic by which the CCP has made law into a pillar of this overarching political project. Indeed, the Fourth Plenum Decision itself explicitly indicates that although 'legal construction' may be a centrally planned project of considerable importance, it nevertheless serves as a mere subassembly in a much greater system of political thought and action. As such, the leadership does not pursue any specific legal arrangement for its own sake or merit, but for the utility it has in the grander scheme of national 'grand rejuvenation' (*weida fuxing* 伟大复兴).

Ideological visions frame the exercise and constraints of law's role in China's development. Deng Xiaoping's ideological vision was to achieve 'moderate prosperity' (*xiaokang* 小康) through the Four Modernisations. Xi Jinping's version of this is the 'Chinese Dream', which the Party leadership intends to realise through the Four Comprehensives (*sige quanmian* 四个全面). These comprehensives comprise one overall goal of 'comprehensively building a well-off society', and three organisationally based implementing tools that are to be put to use to realise that goal – 'comprehensively deepening reform', 'comprehensively implementing the rule of law' and 'comprehensively strengthening Party discipline' (Song 2017). This approach clearly expresses the relationship between the Party's ideological goal (national rejuvenation through the building of a well-off society) and the instrumental mechanisms through which it is to be achieved (reform, rule of law and Party discipline). Articulation of this law–ideology relationship contrasts with two lines of inquiry that have dominated Chinese law studies in the past: teleological, 'rule of law'-oriented research and bottom-up law and society approaches.[1] While the question of China's trajectory towards the rule of law was an attractive one both from Chinese domestic developmental perspectives and modernisation theory-influenced ideas concerning convergence with liberal democratic forms of governance, Donald Clarke long ago warned that such normative approaches risk obviating elements characteristic to the nature of Chinese law. Phenomena incongruent with a commonsensical reading of the rule of law would thus be considered aberrations, even though they would be eminently logical or functional within the Chinese context (Clarke 2003). Heeding his warning, this book will focus on the distinctive ideological, substantive and structural elements that make Chinese law what it is, and the dispositions for future change this entails. Consequently, this book will primarily investigate how the legal system is conceptualised, designed and reformed from the top down, and to a lesser extent how it functions in reality. This is not to belittle the great contributions that, for instance, legal sociology has made to academic insights of Chinese law in action, the functioning of legal institutions and legal consciousness among officials and citizens. Rather, it is to say that law on the books, or more abstractly, central beliefs, ideas and policies about how law should operate, are equally important. To be sure, particularly as the Xi leadership seeks to impose greater central control over all elements of the Party and the state, the official playbook forms the context within which the law is acted out in specific cases. Moreover, in China's Leninist system, with increasing limits to participation and external input, the Party-state remains the single venue where politically salient decisions can be negotiated and made.

Therefore, this book will build on a classic paradigm to study the Chinese Party-state: that of ideology and organisation (Schurmann 1968). Briefly put, this framework holds that Party ideology, consisting of both consistent and changing elements, informs the way the Party structures and governs itself, the state and society. Developed on the eve

[1] For an example of a bottom-up law and society approach, see Ng and He 2017.

of the Cultural Revolution, this paradigm has been rightly accused of 'mistaking myth for operational reality' and excessive state-centredness (Johnson 1982). We do not dispute this criticism if the purpose of inquiry is to better understand the actual daily conduct of social actors. Yet within law, particularly if the purpose is to better understand the framing and intention of ongoing legal reforms, we propose to turn the criticism on its head. In the manner in which the CCP governs China, myth and reality interact continuously. Building on a long imperial tradition in which the sacred and the profane were not institutionally or structurally separated, current-day Party leaders concurrently attempt to weave narratives about a transcendent cause, to reorient the functioning of political and legal structures in pursuit of that cause, and to manage the daily acts of officials and citizens. Law is one of the prime means used for these purposes, and the interactions, tensions and incompatibilities between them condition outcomes to a significant degree. In other words, we do not argue that operational reality is unimportant, nor do we wish to imply that the content of Party documents accurately describes actuality on the ground. Our claim is that both myth and reality are indispensable in building a correct and informative picture of Chinese law that assists observers in gaining a better understanding of the elements and logic of legal reform, instead of seeing Chinese law primarily as an incompletely developed system or, at worst, an aberration.

1.2 Bringing Ideology Back In

Ideology, defined in this book as a complex arrangement of ideas and assumptions that explains the world as it is and provides normative recommendations for political action, has been central to Chinese politics for centuries. The Confucian project of imperial rule survived with a remarkable degree of continuity for the better part of two millennia. At its core lay the idea that the primary task of governance is to ensure social order and cosmological harmony, with moral virtue being a prime enabling condition. A purported past golden age, exemplified by highly virtuous rulers such as Yao and Shun, could be recreated if all knew their place in society and conducted themselves accordingly. The Emperor, dubbed the Son of Heaven, ruled on the basis of a Heavenly Mandate. Yet this mandate was conditional: Heaven would allow an immoral ruler to be overthrown, for instance, through rebellion or foreign invasion. Ritual (*li*) was the external manifestation of this ideology, and the correct performance of ritual would ensure harmony, or the absence of social conflict.

As the Empire waned and disappeared, many of the supernatural and cosmological elements of imperial doctrine went with it. Instead, the nation (*minzu* 民族) became the primary locus for ideological allegiance, and restoration of its historical position of wealth and strength took centre stage in Chinese political thought (Schell and DeLury 2013). Now that China is wealthier and stronger than it has been for at least two centuries, Xi Jinping has reiterated that narrative as the 'Chinese Dream of the Great Rejuvenation of the Chinese Nation' (*Zhonghua minzu weida fuxing de Zhongguo meng* 中华民伟大族复兴的中国梦). In one of his first speeches as General Secretary, current president Xi Jinping claimed that '[s]ince 1840, we have struggled continuously, and have unfolded a brilliant prospect for the great rejuvenation of the Chinese nation in the territory of China. All of us can feel that we are closer to this objective of the great rejuvenation of the Chinese nation than at any other time in history, and we have more confidence and more ability to realise this objective than at any time in history' (Xi 2012). Nevertheless, Xi warned,

> [l]ooking back at the past, comrades in our entire Party must keep firmly in mind: if we are backward, we will take a beating, only development enables self-strengthening. If we look at the present, the entire Party must keep firmly in mind that the path decides destiny, and looking for a correct path is not easy at all. . . . History tells us, the historical destiny of every person is closely connected to the future destiny of the entire country, and with the future destiny of this nation. Only when the country does well, and the nation does well, can everyone do well. Our historical task of fighting for the great rejuvenation of the Chinese nation is glorious and arduous, and requires generation after generation of us Chinese to unwaveringly make common efforts.
>
> (Xi 2012)

In Xi Jinping's world, ideological faith, encapsulated in coded words and slogans, has become the bricks and mortar of a construction process to renew the CCP's central role in Chinese state and society, and bring about the intended rejuvenation of the nation. This process is aimed at fashioning a new-type political system (Lewis Chapter 6) in which, in the words of the CCP Constitution, amended in 2017, the Party 'leads over everything' (Brødsgaard 2018; Fewsmith 2018). Law, in turn, is to be mobilised as a key conduit to realise this leadership, raising important questions concerning the direction of future legal reform.

In tenor and approach, Xi Jinping represents a shift in tone and emphasis from his predecessors. The Deng, Jiang and Hu generations unfolded in the aftermath of the Cultural Revolution. Wary of repeating the catastrophes of the Maoist era, they toned down the romantic, heroic narrative of the revolution and replaced it with stolid technocracy, pragmatism and the promise of economic growth. The volume on ideological campaigns was turned down. Yet by the end of the Hu Jintao leadership, even though China had seen explosive economic growth, complaints grew about a moral vacuum in Chinese society, while the Party itself was increasingly battered by corruption scandals and protests. Burgeoning social media, in particular, made these political discussions much more visible. Xi's answer to this has been to emphasise the supremacy of the Party over all matters. This claim necessarily stresses the moral rectitude and discipline required of Party cadres, as well as stepping up propaganda and control efforts online, often with language that sounds as much religious as political. Building on the theme of the 'Chinese Dream', official propaganda now emphasises faith and confidence in the Party (cf., Xi 2015) – of which Xi Jinping is now the 'core' (*hexin* 核心).

There are two major elements to this notion of faith: a claim to legitimate authority and a claim to moral authority. With regard to legitimacy, Xi's new doctrine of 'Socialism with Chinese characteristics for a new era' moves away from the priority given to economic growth, in favour of a more diverse set of requirements that are to bring about a state of national rejuvenation. These range from the rule of law and social values to green development and international harmony. Yet the most important one is ensuring Party leadership over 'all forms of work in China' (Xue 2018). The Party is not perfect: the need for greater discipline is one of the central points of Xi's ideology, and the fight against corruption must remain a top priority. Nonetheless, only the Communist Party of China, it is held, possesses the intellectual resources necessary to steward the deified nation's future progress. These resources remain strongly rooted in Marxism, while instrumentally, selectively and creatively absorbing eclectic building blocks of language, meanings and methods inspired by traditional Chinese custom, republican and Communist history, as well as contemporary social science. Therefore, Party members and cadres are required to have confidence in the path, the system, the theory and the culture proposed by the CCP. The fundamental righteousness of the Party's belief system also invests it with moral authority: one of its tasks is to – paternalistically – define the good life.

This is expressed in ideological notions, such as the 'socialist core values system' (*shehui zhuyi hexin jiazhi tixi* 社会主义核心价值体系), as well as the increasing attention paid to 'honesty and credibility' (*chengxin* 诚信) in social and economic life. Morality is not merely seen as a guideline for individual conduct; it is also explicitly connected to the overall prosperity and welfare of the nation, for instance in the documents outlining the social credit system (State Council Notice 2014; Creemers 2018b; also see Chapter 9). In other words, the Party's role as moral guardian is a crucial aspect of its overall programme for social and economic change (Lin and Trevaskes 2019).

The goal of the ideological project in Xi's world is thus not to create primarily actionable ideas or political debate but a liturgy that assists in maintaining discipline and assessing the performed loyalty of officials. At the same time, ideology also creates a straitjacket for the single-party system. It is bound by the foundational premises of its various strands of belief, no matter how incongruous they might be.

Language, often in the form of '*tifa*', or slogans and imagery, has been central in this myth-building project and is meticulously manicured, revised and renewed by institutions such as the Central Propaganda Department and the Central Party School (Schoenhals 1992). Nonetheless, despite all efforts to maintain an external appearance of systemic integrity, which is in itself meant as a display of the fundamental correctness of its theory, the myth often remains somewhat of a patchwork. In order to protect its external integrity and authority, tensions between various objectives or beliefs are elided or ignored, deeper inquiry is often eschewed, many political issues are simply ignored, and empirics are not allowed to get in the way.[2]

[2] As Shue and Thornton argue, it is not helpful in understanding the governance of China to ascribe to it an order or structure it does not have. In particular, they take issue with the theatrical metaphors often used in this context, such as the Party's repertoire or playbook. In their view, this metaphor suggests Chinese leaders dispose of rehearsed scenarios acted out under specific circumstances, where society is reduced to a mere audience. This would pay insufficient regard to fragmentation within the leadership, the agency of individual political actors and the uncertain circumstances under which they operate. Instead, they propose the notion of a fairground, where various acts are played out at the same time, with only a limited degree of central coordination and with continuous interplay between the various tents (Shue and Thornthon 2017). On a similar basis, Jonathan Benney proposes the notion of bricolage as a characteristic of the use of aesthetic resources in Chinese politics. Under this conception, Chinese leaders use discrete 'bricks', or units of information in a way similar to Lego pieces: they can be disassembled and reassembled on the go, creating new intellectual structures suited to the political needs of the time.

As the Party claims legitimacy on the basis of the power of its ideology, it can only admit ignorance in highly constrained ways, such as the idea of a 'learning party' (*xuexixing zhengdang* 学习型政党). Brooking no political competitors, the CCP is obliged to either comprehensively deal with socio-economic claims or ignore them at the risk of fomenting dissent. In short, the lofty ideals and aspirations of the myth create the benchmarks by which the Party is evaluated, and failure to meet these benchmarks therefore can only be the Party's responsibility.

1.3 Ideology in Disciplining the Party-State

Within the context described above, ideology is thus the corpus of belief that, at least in the Party's view, animates how it governs itself and society. This book will argue that ideology shapes beliefs about approaches to governance and organisation that occur on three levels. First, it informs how the Party attempts to restructure itself to counter new challenges; second, it provides a methodology for the creation of policy; and, third, it provides the justification for the state to intervene in individuals' lives.

It is tempting to ascribe the Party's modus operandi, with its focus on internal discipline and obedience, exclusively to its Leninist heritage. It is, perhaps, slightly more accurate to suggest that this Leninist form of organisation slotted relatively easily into a historical context that shared many of its essential traits: both Leninism and the Chinese empire were founded on a form of elite rule based on the understanding of a specific corpus of knowledge, where paramount leaders held near-absolute power and space for contestation was highly limited. Equally, as Patricia Thornton has suggested, there is a tradition of mobilising morality to justify top-down political intervention and strengthen discipline (Thornton 2007). It is no coincidence that the Xi leadership has supported greater study of topics such as the Ming dynasty imperial censorate to provide inspiration for the reform of internal supervision structures (Xu 2019). As a result, they face similar tensions: it is difficult to reconcile strict discipline with the policy innovations necessary for economic growth and social adaptation; it is difficult for the centre to obtain accurate information about the functioning of government (the mountains are

Moreover, Benney (2020) suggests, this process turns concepts or actual meanings into mere signs and slogans in a process he refers to as 'mystification', removing it from critical analysis or its adoption by contrary voices.

high and the emperor is far away); and inadequate oversight encourages rule-breaking and corruption. Nonetheless, basing itself on both its own experiences and that of foreign precedents – most notably the Soviet Union (USSR) – the Party has nailed its colours to the mast when it comes to the foundations of its structure. No factionalism is permitted; the Party must retain authority over the military; and the doctrine of the Six Nos precludes multi-party governance, federalism, multi-cameralism, the separation of powers, the full privatisation of the economy and ideological pluralism. To address these issues within these sharp political boundaries, the Party continues to experiment with new organisational approaches. An old one is the Party School system, where for decades aspiring officials have become socialised in the Party's mode of operation and still return there when they are promoted, or for regular brushing up. The Party School system remains one of the key channels for the inculcation of official ideology into the cadre corps (Pieke 2009). More recently, technology has provided new ways for disciplining and oversight. It is no coincidence that the first section of the plan for the development of the social credit system is dedicated to monitoring officials' conduct (State Council Notice 2014; Creemers 2018a; 2018b).

A logical subsequent question in this discussion of ideology is to what extent officials actually believe in official ideology. The importance of acts of performative loyalty (*biaotai* 表态) means it is easy to mistake outward compliance with internalisation, which means demonstrated conduct is not necessarily a reliable guide to deeply shared belief. This, in turn, goes some way towards explaining the remarkably low level of internal opposition to the profound twists and turns the Party has taken in its seven decades in power. Yet at the same time those performative acts also indicate the importance of at least a certain degree of compliance with the myth. Moreover, the myth may operate at different cognitive levels: a particular official may be sceptical about Xi Jinping's specific modus operandi yet broadly agree with the leadership on economic policy. Lastly, the CCP now has greater technological, cognitive and organisational resources at its disposal than it did even in the recent revolutionary past. Instead of the exegesis of the Maoist canon that dominated Party life under the Cultural Revolution, the Party declares itself to be a 'learning party' (Tsai and Dean 2013). Mass campaigns have made way for controlled policy experimentation. Digital technologies provide new and more reliable ways for the centre to obtain knowledge about local conditions (Social Credit Plan 2014; Creemers 2018a).

Regardless of whether it involves campaigns or technology-enhanced authoritarianism, ideology is a framing device that explains the process of building the programme of national development needed to bring about a moderately prosperous society under the banner of national rejuvenation. Ideology articulates the method espoused for realising the Party's programme. We see this in Mao's doctrine of contradictions, which builds on Marx's theory of historical progress towards communism. Under this doctrine, history is divided in stages, each characterised by a principal contradiction that manifests itself in smaller, subordinate contradictions. The principal contradiction can be resolved by addressing the smaller ones, after which a new era will begin. After the death of Mao, the principal contradiction has been redefined twice: once by Deng Xiaoping, who declared it to be the contradiction between China's high material needs and low productivity, and once by Xi Jinping. At the 19th Party Congress, Xi declared that the contradiction between 'unbalanced and inadequate development and the people's ever-growing needs for a better life' characterises the current era (Xinhua 2017).

Critical in marshalling the resources and social forces necessary to address these contradictions is the notion of social management. Scientific planning, deeply influenced by the USSR, had been part and parcel of Chinese governance even during the Mao era but was often frustrated or even persecuted during the political turbulence of mass campaigns and the Cultural Revolution. After Mao's demise, Deng Xiaoping oversaw the broad introduction of particular social management approaches, often derived from systems engineering perspectives (Bakken 2000; Hoffman 2017). The leadership started borrowing from Western scholarship eclectically (Pieke 2012), but always with an instrumental perspective. What mattered was not academic validity but political utility. These new approaches were melded together in a comprehensive planning approach that primarily considers the task of reform as an engineering project, which must be broken down in tiered sub-assemblies across departmental and local boundaries. Consequently, Chinese policy has taken the form of a nested hierarchy of documents that, in the end, all refer back to the central Party programme, as laid down in its Constitution and the reports of the five-yearly Congresses. On this basis, policy is gradually made more detailed and specific as one moves from the central leadership to more specific leading groups, ministries and commissions – from the centre to the localities. To make matters easier, priorities are recast as slogans that are associated with particular leaders, but are often not substantially different.[3]

To summarise, the ideological and organisational elements that lie at the heart of China's governing architecture are hybrid in their functioning. On the one hand, they clearly serve to achieve policy outcomes. Yet at the same time they also serve to communicate unity of form and purpose through the related notions of harmony and discipline. However they are termed, they refer to a political and social order largely defined as the absence of conflict and opposition. In fact, Mao's doctrine of contradictions defines progress as the resolution of various kinds of social, economic and political conflicts, implying that the existence of any such conflict is undesirable in the long run. Understanding this point by itself may be helpful for China observers to refine their expectations. For instance, it assists in redefining the meaning of the word 'reform' (*gaige* 改革). For the CCP, this does not mean progression towards democracy, as is often believed, but being better able to achieve the goals of order, discipline and harmony as they are defined at a particular stage of history. This book intends to go further, by exploring the insoluble tension between the CCP's idealised vision of the future and the messiness inherent in daily human activities. Law, which serves equally to uphold this vision, as well as to manage everyday life, is the prime lens through which to study this juxtaposition.

1.4 The Role of Ideology in Law

The opposition between myth and reality is not new in Chinese law. There is a long-standing, if slightly tired, argument that the imperial legal system emerged as a backstop to punish through law (*fa* 法) those individuals who did not comply with the requirements of ritual and proper custom (*li* 礼) and thus endangered not just the social order but the order of the entire cosmos. This argument overlooks the complex reality of legal practice on the ground, and scholars such as Philip Huang and Perry Keller have discussed the discursive acrobatics and sleights of hand used by imperial officials to manage legal processes in a framework where the sacred legal codes often offered little guidance or assistance

3 As noted above, while Deng Xiaoping intended to achieve 'moderate prosperity' through the Four Modernisations, Xi Jinping seeks to realise the 'Chinese Dream' through the Four Comprehensives, the first comprehensive of which is a 'well-off society'.

(Huang 1993; Keller 1994). Yet the argument is salient in one very important sense: the conception of law as an element of the imperial cosmology constrained the space available for it to develop into an autonomous epistemic space. As a result, law in China did not develop many of the functions central in Western legal systems, particularly with regard to public affairs. To a considerable degree, the same remains true in today's People's Republic (PRC or China). Although the CCP did not take over the supernatural or cosmological claims of the imperial order, it reified its ideological cocktail of Marxist, Leninist, Maoist and traditional ingredients into a religion-like doctrine that is sometimes better understood through theology than through legal theory. Creemers (Chapter 2) summarises the essence of the CCP's theological construct using the following sequence of ideological logic:

> (1) The task of rulers is to lead China towards a predetermined, utopian future. (2) The rulers should be those who have the correct knowledge to realise this process, i.e., the CCP. (3) The CCP identifies and resolves its task by way of its correct political theory. The foundations of this are known, but it needs to be researched how these foundations should be turned into action. (4) This question depends on correctly identifying the primary contradiction defining a particular historical period, as well as all its subordinate contradictions. (5) Once these contradictions are identified, they can be tackled by researching the applicable objective *guilü*. (6) This requires experimentation and political flexibility, and, when solutions are found, they crystallise into doctrine, as well as stronger legal and policy norms.
>
> (p. 44)

In Xi Jinping's China today, there is still is no clear-cut separation between the sacred and the profane: the Fourth Plenum Decision combines 'governing the nation according to law' with 'governing the nation through moral virtue' (*yide zhiguo* 以德治国). Instead, they form a complex and continuously shifting ecosystem in which the sacred justifies the profane, and the profane is seen as having an important impact on the sacred. It is no coincidence that many legal and policy documents state that relatively minor misdemeanours may have a destructive impact on the social order. As a result, PRC law cannot be studied as most Western systems can. While legal scholarship does have a role to play, in some areas it may be more fruitful to understand the CCP as an institution akin to the Roman Catholic church in the heyday of its power. These are both organisations with purchase both on spiritual and temporal matters, plagued with corruption and hypocrisy arising from the clash between intended sanctity and the crooked timber of human nature.[4] Therefore, an accurate understanding of Chinese law requires an account of how doctrine is created and distributed throughout the system, how the system seeks to maintain internal discipline and coherence, how it searches for means to organise society and the economy in ways that can fit Procrustean ideological demands, and how it engages with calls for change from outside. This understanding can provide the theoretical tools to combine with empirical legal studies to illuminate the central tensions and driving forces of Chinese law.

1.5 Party Leadership through Law and Organisation

Since the beginning of the reform era, one of the enduring tensions impacting legal development has been the ongoing friction between the Party's penchant for encouraging 'flexible' local governance practices used to facilitate breakneck economic growth and the requirement of a stable system of routinised law used to regulate that growth. Gradually over the forty-year period of reform and opening up, a system of increasingly effective legal regulation created a demand to expand the state in order to administratively and legally regulate that growth. In turn, as legal and governmental organs expanded, so too did the need for the Party to more effectively regulate society, state and itself. But, notwithstanding this growth of legal regulation, for the economy to expand at the speed required of it to bring about an acceptable level of moderate prosperity, Party leaders deemed it necessary to maintain a high level of flexibility and discretion in policy implementation at local levels of government. Ongoing 'monopolistic and discretionary power' (Chen 2017: 33) exercised at local levels, coupled with the abuse of *guanxi* networks (Broadhurst and Wang 2014), produced decades of ongoing widespread corruption (Gong 2006). Rampant abuse of power together with the ongoing use of flexible 'campaign-style governance' (*yundongshi zhili* 运动式治理) (Biddulph et al. 2012; van Rooji 2014; Qi 2015; Sun 2018) hampered the development of a credible and routinised system of legal regulation, further exacerbating runaway mismanagement, non-compliance and inertia in local government offices across the nation.

To tackle corruption and the related legitimacy crisis, in 2014, the Xi leadership proposed a program of good governance-building based on

[4] One critical difference may be that Catholic doctrine calls for the forgiveness of sins, whereas Party doctrine requires the re-engineering of the human soul.

centralisation reforms and on assuming greater direct Party leadership over all facets of governance. This new program did not attempt to eliminate flexible policy implementation and campaign-style governance, nor did it turn to Western models of dispersed power arrangements for inspiration. Rather, Party leaders began constructing a tighter system of centralised Party supervision and discipline to build the Party's governance capacity (*zhili nengli* 治理能力) into state organs. The Xi leadership understood that this new program of improving governance capacity would require not dispersing power relationships to create independent accountability checks and balances but the opposite: a fully integrated system of central Party-managed discipline and supervision controls. By March 2018 the Party announced this construction project as a 'new-type political-party system' (*xinxing zhengdang zhidu* 新型政党制度) (Lewis Chapter 6). Major constitutional amendments announced on 11 March 2018 require that in order to intensify reform, 'comprehensive Party leadership' must now be exercised in and over all state organisations. The Fourth Plenum of the 19th Party Congress in October 2019 consolidates these tenets (Xinhua News 2019).

Comprehensively embedding the 'leadership of the Party' into the state did not begin at the time of the March 2018 constitutional amendment. Rather it progressively developed over a five-year period from the 2014 Fourth Plenum onwards and through four key organisational changes. The Xi leadership's governance ambition was to create a sui generis model of governance based on supervision and discipline as key instruments of perfecting the Party's governance capacity. First, the Party progressively developed tighter intraparty regulations in order for senior Party members to more effectively control the decision-making capacities of lower local Party functionaries, promoting these Party rules as integral to the overall *yifa zhiguo* rule of law system (Zhang X. 2019; Seppänen Chapter 8). Second, Party authorities developed a social credit system as an amplification device for law enforcement, as well as government information integration (Creemers 2018b; Knight Chapter 9). Third, Central Party authorities reinvigorated the role of Party cells within state organs and state-owned enterprises and merged a number of functions between Party and government (Brødsgaard 2018; Fewsmith 2018; D. Zhang 2019). Fourth, the Party greatly expanded its state supervisory processes by establishing a National Supervision Commission (NSC) in 2017, cementing it in law through NSC legislation in 2018 (Li Chapter 7). This state-based anti-corruption and national surveillance entity is now run directly by Party authorities.

To make ideological sense of this sui generis model of authoritarian governance, the Party reframed its concept of governing the country according to law and promoted it in the media and through Party propaganda organs progressively from 2013 onwards (Trevaskes 2017; 2018). *Yifa zhiguo* was thus 'weaponised' as a new legal framework for Xi-style governance, transformed now into a term that ideologically houses a constellation of not only state laws but also Party regulations and supervisory mechanisms. And along with *yifa zhiguo*, the Party revitalised morality politics, making 'governing the country by moral virtue' a key governance objective of its virtuous Leviathan (Lin and Trevaskes 2019).

Improving prospects for greater accountability and compliance within Party-state institutions was one reason for deepening centralised Party control over the Party-state in the post-2014 period. Gaining more direct control over the levers of security in China was another.[5] The expanding opportunities for corruption, non-compliance and inertia created a decade of social unrest in the 2000s. After 2013, given the continuing potential for social unrest to threaten China's economic miracle, the Party leadership progressively proceeded to directly take over key security, judicial and policing arrangements. This, too, was initiated through legislative means. The first signs of furthering Party integration into state security through law came in 2015 with the legislative embedding of Party control over the National Security Law. This 2015 law gave the Party the authority to directly exercise state powers, a practice, legal scholar Chen Jianfu notes, that 'only existed during the Cultural Revolution in the PRC' (Chen 2016: 200). Other laws, including the Counterterrorism Law (2015), the Foreign NGO Management Law (2016), the National Intelligence Law (2017), revision of the People's Armed Police Law (2016) and other legislation, further deepened direct Party securitisation of the state. Within this new legislative context, we are now witnessing the ever-expanding use of technology to enforce these new laws and to monitor Party-state officials and citizens alike, bringing about a new era of what some scholars describe as digital

[5] Demotion of the *zhengfa* (politico-legal) portfolio within the Politburo Standing Committee occurred in late 2012 as a result of Security Czar Zhou Yongkang's demise. For more discussion of the abuse of power under Czar Zhou Yongkang and political networks, see Broadhurst and Wang 2014. For a discussion of changes in the security sphere in the early Xi period, see Wang 2014.

authoritarianism or technology-enhanced, 'networked authoritarianism' (Creemers 2017; 2018a).

Within this tripartite law–ideology–organisation context that we have described above, this book explores the ideological nature of the law and its impact on Party-state organisation in the following manner. It is structured in two parts: the first four chapters focus on the nature of the law–ideology relationship and discursive shifts under Xi, and the second half examines changes to the structures of power that aim to realise the Party's ambitions to create a high-functioning disciplinary regime. The first half explores ideological and discursive qualities of law, particularly in the current Xi Jinping period. The second half examines how law and legal regulation have come to support the disciplinary ambitions of the Party today.

1.6 Writing on Law and Ideology

Our first contributor, Rogier Creemers, explores the importance of ideology in both delineating the space law occupies in China's governing order and shaping some of its fundamental substantive aspects. Through studying the evolution of three aspects of statecraft – what is the purpose of politics? who should be in charge? and by what method should they govern to achieve that purpose? – it sketches the epistemological framework that structures the CCP's worldview. First, this worldview is teleological: the purpose of politics is to achieve the utopian promises made by Marxist doctrine and to echo concepts of harmony predominant in the imperial age. Moreover, this teleology is aimed at the level of the nation; the individual is of little importance and is subordinate to the needs of the collective. Second, it requires rule by a knowledge elite. The CCP's Leninist tradition justifies single-party rule by holding that the CCP alone possesses the wisdom and knowledge required to enable national progress. It remains the vanguard of the entire nation. This, also, echoes imperial practices, most notably the meritocratic examination system. Lastly, the CCP has developed a methodology by which it claims to be able to set the agenda, identify circumstances and tasks, and guide implementation. This is based on Marxist and Maoist elements, such as dialectics and the doctrine of contradictions, but it has also incorporated elements of social science, particularly complex systems theory. This worldview is essentially monist: it holds that there is one single correct approach to reality, which contains (and, indeed, integrates) moral and factual truth. Under this conception, and in line with the requirements of harmony, any social conflict or contradiction is, *in se*, illegitimate and needs to be resolved. This has considerable implications for the space law is given, as well as for some of its substantive aspects. First, there are many areas of public life where law (as opposed to administration) plays no meaningful role, particularly in the area of constitutional law. Second, ideology infuses the language in which legal issues are framed and discussed, co-opting it as a political tool, rather than an autonomous epistemic space. Lastly, ideology creates benchmarks for meritocratic progression and Party discipline, influencing legal actors' conduct and limiting the extent to which legal rationality is applied.

In Chapter 3, Gloria Davies focuses on two aspects of ideology that help to determine how we can look at law in China. She contrasts two different ways of thinking about ideology, engaging with the question of ideology in two distinct sites, one implicit and the other explicit. She first considers how the disciplinary rules and conventions of academic work – ideas such as academic freedom – sustain the discursive dominance of certain patterns of understanding. Second she looks at the dominance of ideology under Xi Jinping, particularly how it has worked to undermine academic inquiry in China in some areas and to produce a more explicitly political understanding of China's 'socialist rule of law' in others. In the first part of the chapter, she observes that to critically engage with 'ideology' is to encounter an always-expanding spectrum of connotations. At one end there remain simplistic equations of ideology with 'doctrine' or 'dogma'. At the other, we find ever more refined arguments (and problematising of these arguments) about how the ideologically structured nature of upbringing, education and socialisation shapes and constrains people's understanding of themselves and the world. She recognises that one particularly productive outcome of ideology's semantic and theoretical overload is that it has encouraged scholars to attend to both rhetorical and actual aspects of ideology. She argues that to the extent that ideology is shaped by spoken and written communications, texts and images, its imprint as a dominant pattern of understanding, whether religious or secular, is contingent as much on the persuasiveness of what it promises and represents as on its institutional entrenchment. Formal ideology, such as that of the CCP, succeeds when people make sense of their lives using its language. This was demonstrably the case in the first three decades of CCP rule when the Party leadership made Mao Zedong Thought virtually synonymous with the Party to secure the Party's authority.

Until recently, their wordings and formulations of Mao's 'Socialism with Chinese Characteristics' as a label for Party and national ideology have sought to reflect a collective-style leadership. The challenge for these Party leaders has been that as China has become more cosmopolitan and culturally diverse, the popular authority of Party ideology has greatly diminished, even as it remains integral to China's political culture. With these issues in mind, Davies' chapter explores Party ideology as a cultural and linguistic phenomenon of China's Party-state system. Under consideration are recent developments under Xi Jinping's administration to re-fortify Party authority, such as intensification of the ideological management of schools and universities, the imposition of increasingly harsh penalties for dissent and the inauguration in October 2017 of 'Xi Jinping Thought on Socialism with Chinese Characteristics for a New Era'.

Our third contributor, Ewan Smith, introduces a persuasive argument about the functioning of rule of law in China under Xi Jinping. Smith argues that Party leadership has shifted the dominant understanding that rule of law functions to rectify institutions to understanding that it 'rectifies' or disciplines individuals, as state and as non-state actors. Here he reframes the argument he introduced in an earlier article (2018) on rule of law discourse-building in the Hu Jintao era and up until the Fourth Plenum, amplifying that account in light of both developments in Party doctrine under Xi Jinping and the broader themes in this volume. The original article charted the evolution of Party doctrine on rule of law from the 16th Party Congress to Fourth Plenum of the 18th Central Committee, using reported content of Politburo study sessions to shed light on the leadership's deliberations. In particular, it explained two developments: how the concept of governing the nation according to law or 'rule of law' in China was reconciled with the concept of 'Party leadership' by presenting the two as parts of an 'organic unity', and how the rule of law evolved from a system or process that rectifies institutions into a system or process that rectifies cadres. Under Xi Jinping, these ideas have been developed further. The result of these two movements is that the rule of law has been explicitly subordinated to 'Party Leadership', and the law has been recast as one form of social control among many. Moreover, the rule of law under Xi is explicitly superstructural. It yields to basic economic changes, including China's development needs. Finally, whereas earlier accounts suggest a foreign idea under cautious inspection, CCP doctrine under Xi identifies rule of law in China as indigenous and unrelated to Western accounts. These shifts in the Party's frame of reference in relation to rule of law see it now, under Xi Jinping, as 'not merely an ephemeral concept, but a superstructural concept', relativised as 'socialist rule of law with Chinese characteristics' in the new era.

Delia Lin and Susan Trevaskes continue this discussion of Party leadership through an examination of key assertions about the nature of law and morality under the Xi administration, identifying that these assertions have been to frame and embed the Xi leadership's ambitions 'to lead over everything' through greater supervision and discipline, including promoting morality-based 'self-discipline'. They first look at rule of law discourse in the Xi era: how it has come to describe not only state law but also Party rules, regulations and modes of governance including 'governing the nation through moral virtue'. Xi-era discursive emphasis on Party leadership has sought to bring ideological coherence to this sui generis framework of rule of law by claiming that the Party, by dint of its leadership status, has moral supremacy to rule. Its ubiquitous power gives it not only built-in moral authority to govern but also the authority to ideologically interpret the nature of social conflict and disputes amongst the people it governs. Lin and Trevaskes identify how the current discourse has reignited the ideological import of morality from the Mao and pre-Mao eras to affirm the Party's contemporary moral supremacy to 'govern the nation according to law' through core socialist values. Thus, in China today a particular brand of it socialist morality is integrated into the overall ideological mix to justify and explain how and why the Party needs to bring about a rejuvenated and spiritually civilised well-off society. The upshot of this is that the Party intends for both state functionaries (including judges) and society at large to reinterpret the way that they understand social conflict and dispute: that is, to see conflict and dispute and illegal behaviour as a moral issue first and foremost that needs to be solved through the conduit of the law (as opposed to seeing these as legal disputes that have a secondary moral dimension).

1.7 Writing on Law, Ideology and Organisation

The chapters in the first half of the book, discussed above, concern changes in the ideological makeup of Party rule under Xi Jinping. Those changes have presaged shifts in the structural makeup of the Party's governance over the state and its citizens. In the second half of the book we refract the lens from the language of legal ideology to the structures of Party-state power and, in particular, the structures of power which exist to constrain, supervise and, when necessary, discipline and punish behaviour.

In Chapter 6, Margaret K. Lewis looks at the 'new-type political-party system' (*xinxing zhengdang zhidu* 新型政党制度) announced in 2018 and at related attempts by the Party-state to export its governance ethos to international contexts. In the first part of the chapter, she provides readers with a fine-grained outline of the internal power structures that explain the relationship between state and Party both in an historical context and under Xi Jinping. Analysing movements in the Party-state relationship in recent years, she notes that under Xi Jinping, the official position towards permitting constraints on the concentration of power has shifted from quiet rejection in the pre-Xi period to overt hostility today, a phenomenon with implications beyond China's borders. Since China's projection of its governance strengths are nowadays propagated not only domestically but across the globe, the words that the Party uses to describe its structure of governance matter, as it reaches beyond borders 'with money, surveillance technology, and military hardware' and into international organisations where it takes each available opportunity to celebrate the authoritarian ideal that consolidation of power is a superior form of government.

She cautions against validating some of the discourse of the current Party approach to governance in international arenas such as the UN Human Rights Council, as an attractive alternative to traditional understandings of government based on a separation of powers.

In Chapter 7, Ling Li focuses on how the Party operates in the governance space in China, using the evolution of the disciplinary regime of the Party to demonstrate what she sees as the defining feature of China's single-party state: two separate seats of power and sources of legitimation which enable the Party to use a variety of ways to impose authoritarian control over state affairs. She begins with an analysis of the conceptual qualities of the Party-state and then, through a historical examination of the evolution of the disciplinary regime of the Party-state, she demonstrates how the dual seats of power operate to sustain authoritarian governance in China.

Her study explores supervision and discipline in the context of the structure of China's Party-state. In China these have evolved through the development of a particular structure of Party-state power that enables the Party to claim it can effectively supervise state actors in the absence of a western–liberal system of accountability and checks and balances. Li examines the establishment and preservation of dualism – two separate seats of power and sources of legitimacy – that she argues is the defining characteristic of the mode of operation of the type of single-party state that China represents. Her analysis of the particular organisational features of China's Party-state draws on a description of the evolution of this dualism and the historical development of anti-corruption institutions as an exemplar of how the Party governs through supervision and discipline in China. She connects this discussion in the latter part of the chapter with the contemporary development of the NSC. In this way, the chapter presents an historical evolution that can explain the establishment of the Commission, which represents the apex of Party-state disciplinary and supervisory ambitions in China today.

In Chapter 8 by Samuli Seppänen we move to a discussion about another aspect of the architecture of Party-state power: the issue of Party rules in the organisation of the Party-state and their relationship to the overall *yifa zhiguo* system. Seppänen examines arguments around how we are to understand how the Party governs itself and society, and, in doing so, he explores a curious political and cultural moment in contemporary China, a paradox in current rule of law thinking. Curiously, institutional reforms have coincided with equally prominent efforts to establish a 'rational' system of intraparty regulations within the CCP. Xi Jinping describes intraparty regulations as a 'cage' which must constrain the Party cadres' uses of power. Intraparty regulations are also constitutionally important for the Party, since they determine – at least formally – whether an act of an individual Party member is an act of the Party itself. This dual posture produces a number of anomalies which illustrate how fraught is the Party's governance project (and illiberal legal thought more generally). Under Xi Jinping, Central Party authorities have further developed Party rules, but they have done so under the rubric of what they describe as 'rule of law reform' in order to better constrain Party members' power. Rule of law reform in this era has also seen the limiting of law-based governance in line with the expansion of the Party's extra-legal disciplinary rules and supervision regime to better control the actions of Party and state officials. But why continue promoting law-based governance while seemingly working to undermine that governance through the expansion of a Party disciplinary and supervision regime? The expansion of the Party's disciplinary and regulatory regime into spheres that were once the preserve of the state legal system has prompted many legal and political scholars to take on a 'commonsense' approach: to assume, following an instrumentalist tradition, that the 'political' and the 'legal' are not necessarily in tension with each other since they both sit under a system of 'rule by regulations'. Seppänen problematises the commonsense narrative of understanding the Party rules–law nexus in China and, in doing so, describes an alternative way of understanding 'the political' in China. He explores such anomalies through texts of both the Chinese leadership and legal scholars on intraparty regulations, particularly in the context of the newly established National Supervisory Commission.

The focus of the final chapter moves from internal Party governance and discipline to disciplining and controlling both state actors and the general populace alike through the mechanism of social credit. Adam Knight in his study on China's social credit system (*shehui xinyong tixi* 社会信用体系) examines how the Party-state is harnessing modern technology to automate processes for consolidating and expanding its power both organisationally and ideologically. Knight begins with a short history of the social credit system, from its origins as a 'technology of risk' in the financial services market to its current role as a disciplinary 'technology of regulation'. This technology of regulation today has expanded into measures to enforce judicial decisions and, more widely at the local level, to enforce model behaviour on a wide range of fronts, 'in the pursuit of a state-arbitered moral ideal'. In this shift from a technology of managing financial risk to a technology of social regulation, the Party-state has applied advances in automation to augment existing social and political control strategies through a punishments and rewards system. It is, as Knight describes it, as a model of '"divide and conquer" governance', part of the overall ideological repertoire of *suzhi* ('human quality') behavioural management techniques.

A shift has occurred on two fronts, organisationally and conceptually. As Knight notes, organisationally, social credit's evolution reflects a movement in policy innovation and implementation from the centre to the periphery, promoting the localisation of social credit experimentation. At the centre, development of policy in relation to social credit has been scarce on detail to allow not only local jurisdictions but also national state ministries to fill the void through customised policy innovation. Social credit's development and roll out has been a prime example of the importance of what Heilman and Perry have described as adaptive governance; localised piloting and experimentation in Chinese policy-making through campaign-style policy innovation (Heilmann and Perry 2011). The space left for interpretation of policy has enabled both local and national authorities to employ social credit systems to a wide range of issues that go far beyond its original purpose of social credit introduced in decades past.

Conceptually, social credit's development from a narrow policy goal to an increasingly broad array of punishment and reward initiatives is part of a political move by the Party to promote the ideological spread of what Knight calls *chengxin* (诚信) culture ('honesty and credibility' culture) under Xi Jinping. Knight attributes this conceptual shift to a *chengxin* culture as integral to the Party-state's broader paternalistic aspirations in China today.

1.8 Conclusion

Ideology is indeed foundational to law and its operation in China. It is not simply an external veneer to justify the actions of legal and Party-state actors but the discursive underpinning of legal rules – framing actions and decisions that permeate all aspects of law and organisation in China. This volume is the first study of its kind to interrogate the relationship between law, ideology and organisation in contemporary China. Particularly in the current Xi Jinping era, ideology is not merely a branding exercise but a framing mechanism to articulate the CCP's endeavour to reach its end goal of national rejuvenation. The blueprint of this end goal is manifest in the 'Four Comprehensives' ideological goal of '(1) comprehensively building a well-off society' through the ideologically-inspired mechanisms of (2) comprehensively deepening reform, (3) comprehensively implementing the rule of law and (4) comprehensively strengthening Party discipline. Politically-charged words and slogans have become the bricks and mortar of a construction process to renew the Party's central role in Chinese state and society. This process is aimed at fashioning a new-style political system in which, in the words of the newly amended CCP Constitution, the Party 'leads over everything'. Law, in turn, is to be mobilised as a key, but not the sole, conduit to realise this leadership, raising important questions concerning the direction of future legal reform. This book seeks therefore to address two major points of discussion to illuminate scholarship and policy on law in China: how ideology has come to shape and reshape the law and the legal system in China today, and how law has become an integral tool to uphold the Party's ambitions to govern itself, society and the economy.

The contributors examine the ideological underpinnings of socialist law, how they have shifted in recent years under Xi Jinping, and the way that they have reshaped the structure and organisation of political and legal power in China today. This reshaping has been achieved in ways that allowed the Party to more closely supervise and discipline both everyday citizens and Party members through laws and regulations and innovative governance approaches and technologies in order to achieve the goals of order, discipline and harmony. These goals are the foundational pillars upon which the Party seeks to achieve its much lauded endgame goal of a great national rejuvenation.

References

Bakken, B. 2000. *The Exemplary Society: Human Improvement, Social Control and the Dangers of Modernity in China*. New York: Oxford University Press.

Benney, J. 2020. Aesthetic resources in contemporary Chinese politics. *Critical Inquiry* 46(3), 605–626.

Biddulph, S., Cooney, S. and Zhu, Y. 2012. Rule of law with Chinese characteristics: the role of campaigns in law-making 34(4), 374–401.

Biddulph, S., Nesossi, E. and Trevaskes, S. 2017. Criminal justice reform in Xi Jinping's China. *China Law & Society Review* 2, 63–128.

Broadhurst, R. and Wang, P. 2014. After the Bo Xilai trial: does corruption threaten China's future? *Survival* 56(3), 157–78.

Brødsgaard, K. E. 2018. China's political order under Xi Jinping: concepts and perspectives. *China: An International Journal* 16(3), 1–17.

Chen, G. 2017. Reinforcing Leninist means of corruption control: centralization, regulatory changes and party-state integration. *The Copenhagen Journal of Asian Studies* 35(2), 30–51.

Chen, J. 2016. Out of the shadows and back to the future: CPC and the law in China. *Asia-Pacific Law Review* 24(2), 176–201.

Clarke, D. 2003. Puzzling observations in Chinese law: when is a riddle just a mistake? In S. Hsu, ed., *Understanding China's Legal System: Essays in Honour of Jerome A. Cohen*. New York: New York University Press, pp. 93–121.

Creemers, R. 2015. China's constitutionalism debate: content, context and implications. *The China Journal* 74, 91–109.

2017. Cyber China: upgrading propaganda, public opinion work and social management for the twenty-first century. *Journal of Contemporary China* 26(10), 85–100.

2018a. Disrupting the Chinese state: new actors and new factors. *Asiascape: Digital Asia* 5(3), 169–97.

2018b. China's social credit system: an evolving practice of control. Available from: https://papers.ssrn.com/sol3/papers.cfm?abstract_id=3175792.

Fewsmith, J. 2018. The 19th party congress: ringing in Xi Jinping's new age. *China Leadership Monitor*, 55. Available from: www.hoover.org/research/19th-party-congress-ringing-xi-jinpings-new-age.

Fourth Plenum Decision. 2014. Central committee decision on some major questions in comprehensively moving forward governing the country according to law, issued October 2014. English translation available from: http://chinalawtranslate.com/fourth-plenum-decision/?lang=en/).

Gong, T. 2006. Corruption and local governance: the double identity of Chinese local governments in market reform. *The Pacific Review* 19(1), 85–102.

Heilmann, S. and Perry, E. 2011. *Mao's Invisible Hand: The Political Foundations of Adaptive Governance in China*. Cambridge: Harvard University Press.

Hoffman, S. 2017. *Programming China: the communist party's autonomic approach to managing state security*. Ph.D. Dissertation, University of Nottingham. Available from: http://eprints.nottingham.ac.uk/48547/1/Hoffman%2C%20Samantha%20Student%20ID.

Huang, P. 1993. 'Public sphere'/civil society' in China? the third realm between state and society. *Modern China* 19(2), 216–40.

Johnson, C. 1982. What's wrong with Chinese political studies? *Asian Survey* 22(10), 919–33.

Keller, P. 1994. Sources of order in Chinese law. *The American Journal of Comparative Law* 42(4), 711–59.

Li, L. 2018. Politics of anticorruption in China: paradigm change of the party's disciplinary regime 2012–2017. *Journal of Contemporary China* 28(115), 47–63.

Liebman, B. L. 2011. A populist threat to China's courts?. In M. Y. K. Woo and M. E. Gallagher, eds., *Chinese Justice: Civil Dispute Resolution in Contemporary China*. Cambridge: Cambridge University Press, pp. 269–313.

Lin, D. and Trevaskes, S. 2019. Creating a virtuous leviathan: the party, law, and socialist core values. *Asian Journal of Law and Society* 6(1), 41–66.

Minzner, C. 2013. China at the tipping point? the turn against legal reform. *Journal of Democracy* 24(1), 65–72.

Ng, K. and He, X. 2017. *Embedded Court: Judicial Decision Making in China*. New York: Cambridge University Press.

Pieke, F. N. 2009. *The Good Communist: Elite Training and State Building in Today's China*. New York and Cambridge: Cambridge University Press.

2012. The communist party and social management in China. *China Information* 26(2), 149–65.

Qi, Fanhua. 2015. Fazhi: bixu gaobie 'yundongshi zhili' (For the sake of the rule of law, we must say farewell to campaign-style governance). *Zhonghua huanjing* (Environment in China), 6, 29–31.

Schell, O. and DeLury, J. 2013. *Wealth and Power: China's Long March to the Twenty-First Century*. New York: Random House.

Schoenhals, M. 1992. *Doing Things with Words in Chinese Politics: Five Studies*. Vol. 41. Institute of East Asian Studies. Berkeley: University of California Press.

Schurmann, F. 1968. *Ideology and Organisation in Communist China*. Berkeley: University of California Press.

Shue, V. and Thornton, P. M. 2017. Introduction: beyond implicit political dichotomies and linear models of change in China. In V. Shue and P. M. Thornton, eds., *To Govern China: Evolving Practices of Power*. London and New York: Cambridge University Press, pp. 1–26.

Smith, E. 2018. The rule of law doctrine of the politburo. *The China Journal* 79(1), 40–61.

Song, W. 2017. Four comprehensives light up the future. *China Daily*, 10 July. Available from: www.chinadaily.com.cn/opinion/2017-07/10/content_30050292.htm.

State Council Notice. 2014. Planning Outline for the Construction of a Social Credit System (2014–2019). Available from: https://chinacopyrightandmedia.wordpress.com/2014/06/14/planning-outline-for-the-construction-of-a-social-credit-system-2014-2020/.

Sun, L. 2018. Movement, movement, movement. *China Media Project*. Available from: https://chinamediaproject.org/2018/02/13/mobilizing-for-the-china-solution/.

Thornton, P. M. 2007. *Disciplining the State: Virtue Violence and State-Making in Modern China*. Cambridge: Harvard University Asia Center.

Trevaskes, S. 2017. Weaponising the rule of law in China. In F. Sapio, S. Trevaskes, S. Biddulph and E. Nesossi, eds., *Justice: The China Experience*. Cambridge: Cambridge University Press, pp. 113–40.

2018. A law unto itself: Chinese communist party leadership and *yifa zhiguo* in the Xi era. *Modern China* 44(4), 347–73.

Tsai, W. and Dean, N. 2013. The CCP's learning system: thought unification and regime adaptation. *The China Journal* 69, 87–107.

van Rooij, B. 2014. Regulation by escalation: unrest, lawmaking and law enforcement in China. In S. Trevaskes, E. Nesossi, S. Biddulph and F. Sapio eds., *The Politics of Law and Stability in China*. Cheltenham: Edward Elgar, pp. 83–106.

Wang, Y. 2014. Empowering the police: how the Chinese communist party manages its coercive leaders. *The China Quarterly* 219, 625–48.

Wang, Y. and Minzner, C. 2015. The rise of the Chinese security state. *The China Quarterly* 222, 339–59.

Xi, J. 2012. Speech at 'the road to rejuvenation'. 29 November. Translation available from: https://chinacopyrightandmedia.wordpress.com/2012/11/29/speech-at-the-road-to-rejuvenation/.

Xi, Jinping. 2015. Xi Jinping: renmin you xinyang minzu you xiwang guojia you liliang (Xi Jinping says: the people have faith in the nationalities and have hope in the nation). *Xinhuawang* (Xinhua Net), 28 February. Available from: http://news.xinhuanet.com/politics/2015-02/28/c_1114474084.htm.

Xinhua. 2017. Xinhua insight: China embraces new 'principal contradiction' when embarking on new journey. Xinhua news, 20 October. Available from: www.xinhuanet.com/english/2017-10/20/c_136694592.htm.

2019. Shifang 'zhongguo zhi zhi' zui qiang xinhao: jiexi dang de shijiujie shizhong quanhui gongbao guanjianci (Give voice in the strongest terms to [the idea of] 'China-style governance': analysis of the fourth plenum of the 19th party congress keywords). *Xinhuawang* (Xinhua online), 1 November. Available from: www.xinhuanet.com/2019-11/01/c_1125178834.htm.

Xu, W. 2019. Xi Jinping calls on historians to improve research. *China Daily*, 4 January. www.chinadaily.com.cn/a/201901/04/WS5c2e4f2ca31068606745ec8e.html.

Xue, Wanbo. 2018. Zenyang renshi 'dangshi lingdao yiqie'de xieru dangzhang (How to understand the inclusion of the statement 'the party leads over everything' in the party constitution). *Zhongguo gongchandang xinwenwang* (CPC news), 25 January. Available from: http://cpc.people.com.cn/n1/2018/0125/c123889–29787340.html.

Zang, G. 2010. Rise of political populism and the trouble with the legal profession in China. *Harvard China Review* 6(1), 79–99.

Zhang, D. 2019. The leadership of the CCP: from the preamble to the main body of the constitution – what are its consequences for the Chinese socialist rule of law? *Hague Journal on the Rule of Law*. Advanced online publication: doi.org/10.1007/s40803–019-00100-7.

Zhang, Q. 2016. Judicial reform in China. In J. Garrick and Y. C. Benne, eds., *China's Socialist Rule of Law Reforms under Xi Jinping*. London: Routledge, pp. 17–29.

Zhang, X. 2019. The historical track of internal regulations of the communist party of China ruled by law. *China Legal Science* 7, 3–30.

PART I

Ideology and the Party in Law

2

Party Ideology and Chinese Law

ROGIER CREEMERS

2.1 Introduction

What is the importance of ideology in China's legal and political system? According to much recent academic literature, not much. The post-Deng turn away from Maoism ushered in an era in which many observers opined that China had become a 'post-ideological' state (Brown 2012), whose politics were guided by pragmatic concern or could be explained by more universal theoretical approaches. More broadly, ideology came to be seen as obsolete in the post-Cold War era, where the widely shared idea of the 'End of History' (Fukuyama 1989) posited that the world would converge to the forms of social organisation that had proved optimal: liberal democracy and free-market capitalism. Numerous academics and observers expected that the Chinese Communist Party (CCP or Party) would sooner or later follow the Soviet Union (USSR) and Eastern European socialist regimes into the dustbin of history (Chang 2001; Shambaugh 2015). The subsequent body of literature on 'authoritarian resilience' (Nathan 2003) has attempted to explain how CCP rule could hold off democratizing forces, but, nevertheless, often remains stuck in a paradigm that considers China's status quo as, at best, in flux and, at worst, an aberration. Consequently, academic interest in Party ideology has waned. In his survey of the field of Chinese politics, Lieberthal identifies ideological studies as perhaps the only topic to have disappeared from view (Lieberthal 2010).

In the study of Chinese law, the liberalising paradigm manifests itself in the discussion on the concept of 'rule of law', the usual translation for the Mandarin term *fazhi* (法治). Chinese and foreign scholars alike have discussed the post-Deng reconstruction of the legal system as the beginning of a path towards convergence with, or at least similarity to, the legal systems of developed liberal democracies (Pan 2003; Zou 2006; Cai 2010; He 2012), and the obstacles to achieving that goal (Turner et al. 2015). Even those critical to the narrative of full convergence confirm, at least, part of the paradigm. Peerenboom, for instance, argues that China would not converge with a 'thick' conception of rule of law, laden with liberal values, but a 'thin' one, focusing merely on procedural aspects of law (Peerenboom 2002).

However, this analysis seems to presume that China's legal development process is teleological towards some form of Weberian legal rationality or idealised Western order. Peerenboom's proposition of the thin rule of law, for instance, is unclear on the extent to which procedural elements themselves reflect particular values, or can indeed be fully separated from values at all. Moreover, it has not paid particular attention to the question concerning which values Chinese law would alternatively embody. He argues that Party interference and Socialist ideology are factors of secondary importance, or 'easily overstated' (Peerenboom 2002: 217), in the construction of a law-based order. Instead, he points to institutional and systemic issues, such as an incomplete legislative framework, a weak judiciary, the lack of a civil society, regional discrepancies and corruption (Peerenboom 2002: 11–12). Yet while these elements are undoubtedly of considerable importance, law is not merely a mechanistic or technical exercise. As a form of social practice and social control, it is imbued with meanings that, particularly in the public realm, largely originate from political practice and discourse.

As Clarke (2003) warned, the teleological question of what Chinese law *could* or *should be* in an idealised, often Westernised, future has overshadowed the analysis of the internal logic of Chinese law as it currently *is*.[1] For instance, deLisle (2017) argues that, under Xi Jinping, law in China remains 'narrowly instrumentalist, uneven across subject matter and region, and beset by both "supply-side" and "demand-side" challenges.' What remains unclear is the extent to which these phenomena are aberrant or intended. What elements, then, are necessary for a plausible account of the development of China's legal system? Perhaps the most salient of its characteristics is that it is essentially new. Although Chinese law has a long and sophisticated history, few institutions or legal rules in their current form predate the beginning of the reform era.[2] The People's Republic of China (PRC or China) didn't require a Constitution to constitute itself. As Ewan Smith discusses elsewhere in this volume, it took the Politburo until the 2000s to seriously consider the rule of law as

[1] One noteworthy exception is von Senger (2000).

[2] One important exception is the 1958 Household Registration Regulations (*Hukou dengji tiaoli* 户口登记条例), which institute the *hukou* system.

something that might have a profound impact on state structuring and the relationship between state and citizen. The Chinese legal order, much more than in most other systems, emerged only in secondary importance to political imperatives. Therefore, it is necessary to explore the political and institutional context in which this system was created.

This chapter argues that Party ideology provides an important part of an account of the development of China's legal system as intended by those in charge. Ideology does more than simply provide a convenient cover or justification for pragmatic political manoeuvring or the exercise of power. It constitutes an important part of the very definition of legality and legitimacy. Yet this claim requires clarification of what 'ideology' means. Often, the term is used pejoratively to refer to political beliefs that distort reality, for instance, for autocratic, dictatorial or irrational purposes. In that sense, it is juxtaposed with pragmatism or rationalism. However, this paper will use a more neutral definition, developed by Freeden. In this definition, ideology is an interrelated set of concepts, assumptions, norms, values and ideas that (1) provides an explanatory account of reality and (2) outlines a path for political action and change. This, in turn, requires ideological systems to contain programmatic elements, such as claims about the role of the state or socio-economic arrangements on the one hand and epistemological elements, such as assumptions about the nature of truth, knowledge or human nature, on the other. Moreover, as Freeden argues, this definition sees ideology as a crucial part of any political structure and practice. Studying it thus assists us in 'the laying bare of the thought-processes and thought-practices that societies exhibit' (Freeden 2006:16). When it comes to CCP ideology, this means we must look beyond the standard thesaurus of classical socialist terminology, explore how the CCP has created a doctrinal worldview imparted on all its members and inquire what role the phenomenon of law has been given in that worldview.

For its part, CCP has consistently been explicit about the prominence it attaches to ideological affairs. In its near-century of existence, the Party has meticulously built up and continuously revised a sophisticated ideological edifice that is contained within its foundational documents, such as the CCP Constitution and the state Constitution. This edifice is explicitly reflected in its structures, processes and policies: the first substantive section of most important policy documents is usually titled 'guiding ideology'. The importance of ideology is repeated regularly in prominent Party publications, such as the journal *Qiushi* ('Seeking Truth' – 2013, 2014). With regard to law, Smith (2018) suggests, the consequence is that doctrine about the role and nature of law must be seen as a larger project to formulate doctrine that should be understood and reproduced by cadres.

This chapter will analyse this corpus in the light of the three questions presented above: what is the purpose of politics? who is entitled to political power? and by what method is the purpose to be achieved? To this end, this paper is divided into two further sections. Section 2.2 will review how the CCP has answered these three questions. It will argue, first, that the chief objective of China's political project has been denominated in teleological terms that, while different, share a considerable part of their ideological underpinnings. Second, it will discuss how the CCP uses the Leninist concept of a vanguard Party to legitimise its continued rule, as well as to organise its penetration of society. Lastly, it will analyse the Party's claim to scientific truth as the root of its method for governance. It will also reflect on the epistemological underpinnings of Party ideology. Section 2.3 will discuss how these insights might elucidate our understanding of Chinese law and influence future scholarly work.

2.2 Accreted Layers of Historical Meaning

2.2.1 Who Governs, and Why?

The roots of the CCP's political project must be traced back far before its foundation in the 1920s. As early as the eighteenth century, China faced a political crisis born of a combination of population growth and economic change and the failure of the state to keep up with the new needs this presented (Kuhn 2002). As the nineteenth century unfolded, the crisis deepened: imperialist powers threatened the empire from abroad, while domestic catastrophes such as the Taiping uprising (Platt 2012), as well as the inability of the Qing government to adapt to changing circumstances, eroded the dynasty's domestic authority (Dai 2013). As the crisis deepened, the major political question became how to save the nation (*jiuguo* 救国), and the nature of proposals for political reform escalated and radicalised, criticising in particular the dominant imperial ideology, which was based on Confucian tenets.[3]

[3] The term Confucianism has now become contested among historians of China. It gained currency due to the efforts of late nineteenth-century scholars such as James Legge, who projected onto Chinese tradition a view of religion in the mold of Christianity. Swain (2017) suggests the term 'the way of Ru' might be more apposite.

Successive generations of reformers developed new ideas concerning the purpose of rule. At first, these were incremental. Kang Youwei's Book of Great Unity (*Datong shu* 大同书) proposed a utopian model for world governance based on a syncretic integration of Confucian, Buddhist and Western ideas (Knight 2007: 123). As imperial rule waned, however, more transformative thinking emerged. Most notably, Sun Yat-sen, a Hong Kong-trained physician who had spent his formative years in Hawaii, devised the Three Principles of the People (*sanmin zhuyi* 三民主义), first outlined in 1905 (Sharman 1968: 94). The first of these principles, *minzu* (民族) or nationalism, called both for independence from imperial imposition and for the creation of an integrated 'Chinese nation' (*Zhonghua minzu* 中华民族). The second principle, *minquan* (民权) or popular power, entailed the creation of a representative form of government, as opposed to imperial-era elitism. The last principle, *minsheng* (民生) or popular welfare, described the way in which government was supposed to take care of its people.

The political malaise caused by the initial failure of the republic created space for other forms of political thought, the most historically significant of which turned out to be communism. The CCP was founded in 1921, inspired by both Marxist ideas of liberation and the actual success of the Bolshevik revolution. Since taking power in 1949, the CCP has defined as its ultimate objective the realisation in communism.[4] In classical Marxism, this is vaguely defined as a future state of material superabundance, in which no conflicts over material distribution will be necessary and in which the state (which is a reflection of oppressive class relationships) will wither away. It reflects Marx's assertion that history progresses along a predetermined path from capitalism, via an intermediate stage of socialism, to the promised Utopia, driven along by the incessant process of dialectic materialism (Kolakowski 2005; Brown 2010).

Successive generations of Chinese leaders have, however, had different ideas concerning how quickly that process could be realised. The revolutionary fervour of the Great Leap Forward, for instance, was a bid to

[4] The first iterations of the Party Charter primarily focused on organic and organisational matters. In 1945, at the 7th Party Congress, a section entitled 'General Programme' was added. This contains a provision, which has remained unchanged, stating that the establishment of a communist system is the CCP's ultimate objective (Zhongguo Gongchandang 1945).

leapfrog towards communism within a generation.[5] Under Deng, however, China's position on the ladder of history was revised. Official ideology now stated that China was at the 'primary stage of socialism', and would remain so for a long time.[6] Yet, while communism remains part of ideological doctrine, it came to be supplemented by other objectives, now sloganised as the 'Two Centenaries Struggle Objective' (*liangge yibainian douzheng mubiao* 两个一百年斗争目标). Having little to do with orthodox Marxism, this approach aims to realise two stages of development, respectively, by 2021 – the centenary of the CCP's foundation – and 2049 – the centenary of the PRC's establishment. The first, intermediary, objective is the realisation of a 'moderately prosperous society' (*xiaokang shehui*/小康社会), a concept derived from Confucian traditions.

To summarise, the driving purpose of Chinese political activity since the decline of the empire has been 'saving the nation' by restoring it to a position of material prosperity and political strength (often abbreviated as *fuqiang* 富强 [Shell and Delury 2013]). This political project has consistently been teleological and collectivist in nature. It focuses on a future to be achieved, rather than a present to be governed; it elevates the nation and its interests over the concerns of the individual, who is expected to perform continuous sacrifice in furtherance of national goals. As Xi Jinping stated, 'Only when the country does well, and the nation does well, can every individual do well' (Xi 2012).

Since 1949, the justification for Party leadership has been that only the CCP had the ability to realise this programme. As a popular revolutionary-era song proclaims: 'Without the CCP, there would be no New China' (*meiyou gongchandang jiu meiyou xin Zhongguo* 没有共产党就没有新中国). During the Second World War, the Party had been able to rectify itself organisationally and ideologically (Cheek 1984), and experiment with governance tools (Goodman 2002) that allowed it to vanquish the Guomindang (GMD) in 1949. Rhetorically, however, Party documents also ascribe this unique position to its identity as an intellectual vanguard that commands the fundamental truths necessary to generate progress. The Preamble of the PRC Constitution (1982)

[5] One of the key documents in the rural collectivisation process states in 1958 that the achievement of Communism 'is not a matter in the distant future anymore' (Central Committee 1958).

[6] This phrase entered into the Party Charter at the 13th Party Congress of 1987. On this process of reframing, see (Sun 1995).

enshrines 'the leadership of the Communist Party of China and the guidance of Marxism-Leninism and Mao Zedong Thought', as well as subsequent ideological contributions made by successive Party leaders. The Party Constitution squarely states,

> The Communist Party of China is the vanguard both of the Chinese working class and of the Chinese people and the Chinese nation. It is the core of leadership for the cause of socialism with Chinese characteristics and represents the development trend of China's advanced productive forces, the orientation of China's advanced culture and the fundamental interests of the overwhelming majority of the Chinese people.
>
> (Zhongguo Gongchandang 2017)

The basis for this claim is an intellectual one: only the CCP possesses the scientific knowledge, based on Marxism-Leninism, to achieve the aim of China's prosperity.

2.2.2 Science

The idea that political influence depends on intellectual accomplishments has profound roots in Chinese tradition. For centuries, the only institutionalised route to political power lay through the examination system, which tested knowledge of a defined canon of classical works.[7] Neither land ownership nor religious or military authority automatically entitled the holder to office – even if there have been ample historical examples of such figures, eunuchs or courtiers, wielding considerable influence over rulers. There was equally no notion of representation[8] or political validity of the popular will. Furthermore, this canon closely connected power with morality: the notion of the Mandate of Heaven implied that Emperors obtained and retained power through moral conduct and righteous governance.

As China's crisis deepened in the nineteenth century, increasingly radical voices called for the expunction of Confucian thought from public life, and began a search for new ideas and theories on how to achieve national salvation. Many sought inspiration from abroad: Yan Fu

[7] As Vivienne Shue (1990) argues, while there are considerable differences in actual policies and forms of interaction during various stages of the imperial period, the consistency throughout this very long period is remarkable.

[8] Representation, as defined by Martin Loughlin (2003: ch 4), refers to the notion that governing power is organised in the name of the people and the common interest, and that therefor the people need to be represented in the structures of power.

translated John Stuart Mill and Adam Smith into Chinese but became particularly influential through his interpretations of social Darwinist thinkers such as Thomas Huxley. Social Darwinism, with its focus on the survival of the fittest, was highly attractive for those intent to cast away 'backward' traditions. Some May Fourth movement thinkers turned towards Marxism. Others, such as Hu Shi, the figurehead of efforts to vernacularise written Chinese, were inspired by pragmatic theories. Hu would even go so far as to invite his old teacher John Dewey to lecture in Shanghai (Chan 1956). While these theoretical approaches vary wildly in their assumptions and implications, what they all share is that they conceive of governance primarily as an intellectual endeavour. It is no coincidence that 'Mr. Science' was supposed to join 'Mr. Democracy' in modernizing the nation (Sun 1999).

For Sun Yat-sen, however, imported social theory would not be helpful in establishing and consolidating a republic on its own. Having concluded that military power would be indispensible in obtaining power, the next question was how to build and maintain political authority. His response (Sun 1924), heavily influenced by Leninist organisational techniques, was a three-step scenario in which military rule was followed by a period of political tutelage, aimed at educating the citizenry about their new political environment. This, in turn, would pave the way for the final stage of constitutional government (*xianzheng* 宪政). Under Chiang Kai-shek, the GMD attempted, at least symbolically, to carry out this process. The GMD-led government promulgated a provisional constitution for the period of political tutelage in 1931 (Zhonghua Minguo 1931), as well as a full constitution in 1946 (Zhonghua Minguo 1946), which was supposed to signify China's entry into the *xianzheng* stage.

After its expulsion from urban China during the 1927 GMD takeover, the CCP was forced to develop new tools and tactics, not just for governance but for its very survival. By 1935, Mao had asserted himself as the Party's leader. Over the next ten years, Mao would create a body of writings that would become enshrined in Party constitutional documents as 'Mao Zedong Thought'. Eclectically borrowing from Marxism and Leninism, actual practice and traditional Chinese writers, Mao Zedong Thought included military and organisational tactics, as well as an epistemological approach to politics. The two related essays, *On Practice* (Mao 1937a) and *On Contradictions* (Mao 1937b) are of particular importance. In the former, Mao argued, with more than a whiff of Comtean positivism, that objective laws underpinned social development. In order to progress towards communism, it was necessary to both understand these laws and apply them for social change. This, in turn, required knowledge that could be gained through integrating observed practice with the essential truths of Marxism. Pragmatic experimentation was hailed as a crucial way to obtain practical experience.[9] The latter essay further elaborated on these conclusions by identifying contradictions between dialectical opposites as the starting point for action. According to Mao, history progressed through the correct identification and resolution of contradictions in society. More specifically, he argued that contradictions were universal, in the sense that 'there is nothing which does not contain contradictions' (Mao 1937b), and, in particular, in the sense that every contradiction was determined by its context. Furthermore, any historical phase was defined by a principal contradiction that determined the nature of other contradictions. Resolving this principal contradiction would thus enable a transition from one historical period to the next. Mao divided contradictions into antagonistic and non-antagonistic categories; the former could only be resolved by struggle, while the latter could be tackled through diligent thought and reform. Furthermore, organisational techniques such as democratic centralism and intraparty criticism were developed. In 1945, Mao Zedong Thought officially entered into canon through a Resolution on the history of the Party (Central Committee 1945), which imposed an orthodox reading of Party history and cemented the position of Maoist ideology (Saich 1995).

The doctrine of contradictions turned out to be a very flexible tool to justify nearly any measure later on. Mao used it to designate class struggle as the highest priority, with permanent revolution the necessary response. In 1957, a further speech by Mao on contradictions among the people, which seemed to advocate a more open climate for political criticism, resulted in an outpouring of severe criticism against Party rule. While it is still debated whether Mao deliberately lured his critics into the open or was genuinely surprised at the amount of intellectual discontent after eight years of Party rule (Schoenhals 1986), the Party rapidly embarked on a campaign against 'Rightist' intellectuals, followed by the voluntarism of the Great Leap Forward. Equally, the Cultural Revolution was ideologically justified by identifying the principal contradiction as 'the antagonistic one between, on the one hand, the broad masses of the workers, peasants, soldiers, revolutionary cadres and revolutionary

[9] In this regard, Mao seems to have been strongly influenced by Dewey (Heilmann 2008).

intellectuals, and, on the other hand, you the handful of anti-Party and anti-socialist representatives of the bourgeoisie. This is a contradiction between revolution and counter-revolution, an irreconcilable contradiction between the enemy and ourselves' (Peking Review 1966).

With all the attention paid to the discontinuity between the Mao era and the subsequent period of reform and opening up, the extent to which the latter had to be rooted in the context of the former is often overlooked. In the power struggle between Hua Guofeng and Deng Xiaoping after Mao's death, both sought to legitimise themselves by appropriating particular elements of Mao Zedong Thought. Hua was a provincial official from Hunan who lacked a strong powerbase of his own and derived his authority from the fact that Mao had appointed him. His slogan, 'Two Whatevers', implied that the Party would 'resolutely defend whatever policy decisions Chairman Mao made, [and] steadfastly abide by whatever Chairman Mao gave' (Schoenhals 1991). Deng, an ex-senior military commander, ex-senior bureaucrat and Vice-premier, countered by having associates publish newspaper articles proposing a more scientifically grounded approach, based on 'seeking truth from facts' (*shishi qiushi* 实事求是). This phrase, which originates from the *Book of Han*, was inscribed on a school building in Changsha, where Mao resided during his youth. Mao first used it in a speech to the 6th Plenum of the 6th Party Congress (Mao 1938), and the Dengist leadership made it into a central pillar for his pragmatic governance reforms (Hu 1979; Central Committee 1980).[10]

The new leadership issued a resolution on CCP history that passed the authoritative verdict on the previous three decades of Party rule. This resolution celebrated the theoretical contribution of Mao Zedong Thought and employed Mao's theory of history to both condemn the excesses of the Great Leap Forward and justify Deng's reforms: it argued that class struggle could not be the primary contradiction, as the exploiting classes had been eliminated in socialist China. Instead, it asserted that, since the full establishment of socialism, 'the principal contradiction our country has had to resolve is that between the growing material and cultural needs of the people and the backwardness of social production' (Central Committee 1981). In other words, Mao's continued focus on class struggle was deemed erroneous, and the task of the Chinese

[10] 'Seeking Truth' (*qiushi*) has, since 1988, also been the title of the Party's leading theoretical journal. Until then, it was titled 'Red Flag'.

government had always been to embark on the economic reforms that would now start.

Deng's ideological reset also had important consequences for intellectual life within the Party: policy precepts were no longer to be derived from exegesis of Mao's writings and aphorisms but generated through scholarly research. This led to the reinvigoration and expansion of the Party-state's intellectual branch, and the CCP designating itself as a 'learning-type party' (*xuexixing zhengdang* 学习型政党) (Tsai and Dean 2013). The Party School system was restructured to not only indoctrinate cadres with Party ideology, but with a broader curriculum increasingly based on social science research (Shambaugh 2008b). Marxism remains important, as a stated source of basic theory.[11] As the Party Constitution puts it: 'Marxism-Leninism brings to light the laws governing the development of the history of human society. Its basic tenets are correct and have tremendous vitality' (Zhongguo Gongchandang 2017). However, concerning governance and social management, the Party has adopted a complex systems engineering approach pioneered by physicist Qian Xuesen. In this view, complex systems thinking pioneered in the natural sciences applies to social management as well. Society, like nature, is considered to be an integral system that therefore must be managed holistically. Social development is governed by objective 'laws' (*guilü* 规律) that, similar to the laws of nature, are intelligible and can be used to forecast and control social reality (Bakken 2000; Hoffman 2017). On this basis, and echoing the wholesale introduction of foreign knowledge in the late nineteenth century, a new wave of Chinese researchers has also eclectically imported academic tools and approaches in support of the new development agenda.[12] Comprehensive research plans for social sciences and the humanities not only intend to foster policy-relevant inquiry but to cement a position for these disciplines at the same level as the natural sciences (Central Committee 2004).

The importance the Party attaches to its intellectual support is evidenced not only by the fact that both Hu Jintao and Xi Jinping headed the Central Party School before they became General Secretary, but also by the fact that one of the most important symbolic achievements of

11 Xi Jinping, for instance, underlined the importance of dialectical materialism at a Politburo study session (Xinhua 2015).

12 One example is the importation and indigenisation of public administration and public management theories (Pieke 2012).

every leader is to have their signature ideological contribution inscribed into the Party Constitution. In this way, it is possible to trace both continuity and change in top-line ideology: Deng Xiaoping Theory built on Mao Zedong Thought but added a focus on pragmatism, economic development and the Four Cardinal Principles.[13] Jiang Zemin's Three Represents (*sange daibiao* 三个代表) focused on opening up the Party to its traditional adversaries: businesspeople and entrepreneurs. Hu Jintao's 'scientific development view', in turn, focused on social harmony (Miller 2017). Wang Huning, the Party's leading ideologue and architect of both the Three Represents and the scientific development view (Patapan and Wang 2017), was promoted to the Standing Committee at the 19th Party Congress. This Congress also approved the addition to the Party Constitution of Xi's theoretical contribution, the verbosely named 'Xi Jinping Thought on Socialism with Chinese Characteristics for a New Era'. This new era referred to Xi's redesignation of the primary contradiction: Deng's prioritisation of economic growth was replaced by a focus on more equitable and balanced development (Xi 2017).

Basing Party ideology on externalised notions of objective and scientific truth simultaneously enables constancy and flexibility. On the one hand, the core assertion of unswerving loyalty to Marxism-Leninism and the accumulated (if sanitised) core of Party insight not only justifies the architecture of the Party-state, it also creates a durable basis for constitutional continuity and stability, even as particular policies change radically. Yet, at the same time, the doctrine of contradictions, and dividing history into phases, provides considerable flexibility for innovation and reform, as well as the ability to respond to changing circumstances. The assertion of truth also implies the depoliticisation of the policy process: if decisions result from the need to conform to historical imperative as understood through the lens of 'science', the people only need to be included or represented as far as that scientific approach requires. In other words, the notion that the CCP 'represents' (*daibiao* 代表) the population (which may be sovereign in name) does not imply or require a direct, institutionalised link between the popular will and policy, legal or regulatory outcomes.

[13] These are: persisting in (1) the socialist path, (2) the dictatorship of the proletariat, (3) the leadership of the CCP and (4) Marxism-Leninism and Mao Zedong Thought (Deng 1979).

2.2.3 *The Epistemological Chassis of CCP Ideology*

The teleological nature, primacy of Party rule and scientific characterisation of CCP ideology reflect a central epistemological assertion echoing Berlin's conception of monism, in which

> (1) All genuine questions must have a true answer, and one only; all other responses are errors. (2) There must be a dependable path to discovering the true answers, which is in principle knowable, even if currently unknown. (3) The true answers, when found, will be compatible with one another, forming a single whole; for one truth cannot be incompatible with another. This, in turn, is based on the assumption that the universe is harmonious and coherent.
>
> (Cherniss and Hardy 2013)

Again, this idea has profound roots in Chinese political history. In Kuhn's analysis of Qing-era politics, 'only one public interest existed, defined in a righteous rhetoric of personal ethics' (Kuhn 2002:13). Factionalism was abhorred in rhetoric, even if it was inevitably practiced extensively in reality. This had a considerable impact on political discourse and the resolution of political conflicts: factionalism was often associated with political instability and the fall of the Tang, Song and Ming dynasties. It was often used as a brush with which to tar political enemies, accusing them of sowing discord and threatening the stability of the regime. But this had major consequences for the institutionalisation of governance. As Ter Haar puts it, 'it is the tragedy of traditional China that it never succeeded in developing good mechanisms to foster a constructive political debate, which could also lead to good governance' (Ter Haar 2009: 310).

In Party ideology, monism entails that what is scientifically correct is also morally preferable and in the interest of the People (*renmin* 人民), who remain an undifferentiated mass. In some cases, there is recognition of diversity, but not of pluralism. In other words, Party ideology accepts that there are various groups in society who are different in objective terms (due to, for instance, age, class background, socio-economic position, educational attainment, gender or ethnic identity) and attempts to identify and address their special needs. However, any conflicts between those needs are identified as contradictions that need to be resolved, as opposed to legitimate but incommensurable interests that can only be mediated.

This assertion of fundamental harmony and coherence manifests itself in the manner in which CCP policy documents, such as Five-Year Plans, are composed and hierarchically interrelate. Usually, a first section outlines the status quo, situating the document within the systemic context of present circumstances, as well as the previously established policy direction (for instance, when ministries refer to State Council policies). A second section covers the 'guiding ideology', which lists the slogans and principles that have informed the drafting of the document. Subsequent sections then outline the various objectives and priorities of the plan, followed finally by the organisational and structural measures taken to realise this objective. Legal and regulatory documents nearly always identify explicitly which higher-level policy document they are supposed to execute and to which objective or slogan they contribute.

The essence of the Party's ideological construct can be summarised as follows. (1) The task of rulers is to lead China towards a predetermined, utopian future. (2) The rulers should be those who have the correct knowledge to realise this process, i.e., the CCP. (3) The CCP identifies and resolves its task by way of its correct political theory. The foundations of this are known, but it needs to be researched how these foundations should be turned into action. (4) This question depends on correctly identifying the primary contradiction defining a particular historical period, as well as all its subordinate contradictions. (5) Once these contradictions are identified, they can be tackled by researching the applicable objective *guilü*. (6) This requires experimentation and political flexibility, and, when solutions are found, they crystallise into doctrine, as well as stronger legal and policy norms.[14]

2.3 How Does Ideology Influence Law?

To understand how ideological norms and concepts influence China's political–legal structure, elucidating their substantive anatomy is merely a first step. It is also necessary to identify how these norms and concepts influence individuals within the systems in practice. In other words, we need to address questions about whether, when, why and how ideas matter. The assertion that they do seems commonsensical. Nevertheless, in the Chinese context, it is often held that the reform era heralded the end of ideology, or that deeply cynical cadres don't believe in socialist ideology anymore and merely play along with the melody for personal advancement.

[14] One example of this in the legal field is Smith's analysis of the evolution of the 'rule of law' concept elsewhere in this volume.

To a certain degree, these criticisms are valid. First, as indicated earlier, the territory for deductive ideological reasoning has been reduced by the re-recognition of the value of scientific and technological insights. The fervent drive to let willpower triumph over natural and social constraints present in the Great Leap Forward would be difficult to envisage in the China of the present. What that means for law is that one cannot accurately predict the substance of legal norms, or their specific application in cases, on the basis of a logical reasoning based on ideological first principles.[15] Yet it may be going too far to claim, as Shambaugh does, that ideology is merely a tool of post-hoc rationalisation or a coded language for legitimation, obeisance and political conflict (Shambaugh 2008b: 105–6). It isn't because ideology does not always matter, or is sometimes honoured more in the breach than the observance, that it never matters substantially. Hypocrisy, rule breaking, contestation and shirking are part and parcel of human polities everywhere. The huge divergences in outlook between ardent liberation theologians and firebrand evangelical preachers, the excesses of the Borgias or the child abuse scandals in the Catholic church today do not entail that the content of the Bible is of no value in studying Christianity. Instead, one must attempt to find the way in which ideology is consciously or subconsciously used, resisted, interpreted, followed or contested in a manner that shapes law-related conduct. Sections 2.3.1 through 2.3.3 discuss three ways in which further research could enlighten this question. First, evolving ideological tenets have delineated the sphere in which legal rationality, as generally understood, has been introduced. Second, ideology defines the nature and applicability of legal norms. Third, ideology creates incentives for legal actors' conduct.

2.3.1 Ideology Delineates the Spheres of Law

As Section 2.2 of this article argues, ideological conceptions of governance evolved in lockstep with changes in political practice, as successive generations of political leaders applied their ideas to ever-changing external circumstances. Each accorded a varying weight to the role of law. Late Qing and early republican reformers saw law as one of the most prominent manifestations of political modernity, and thus prioritised the drafting of constitutional texts, criminal law and civil codes (Hua 2013),

[15] The legal realist school would argue that this is equally true in Western legal systems. See, for instance, Llewellyn (1930).

largely based on foreign models (Chen 2008: 33). Human rights were actively explored in Beijing intellectual circles, even if primarily as an elite concept rather than a universal one (Svensson 2002). However, as Rankin (1997) argues, the legislative assemblies in which these processes took place were among the least well-rooted of political associations during the political transition. The subsequent failure of this early republic, and the descent of the Beijing government into factionalist squabbling (Nathan 1976), taught subsequent GMD and CCP leaders that effective control and authority were far more important than instituting a constitutional order founded on legal rules and rational authority. Moreover, the modernising ethos of both the republic and the People's Republic entailed a comprehensive repudiation of the past: the imperial legal system was cast away with the rest of the nine-dragoned trappings, while the CCP abolished GMD law wholesale, denouncing it as a 'sham' (Central Committee 1949). Yet the CCP didn't create a comprehensive new legal system to replace it: during the Mao era, social and economic processes were largely regulated through administrative and managerial means, while the brunt of judicial work was oriented towards class struggle and dealing with counterrevolutionary elements (Chen 2008: 39). It was only under the Dengist reforms that CCP leaders began consistent and durable efforts to introduce legal rationality in distinct spheres of activity. In other words, law as it exists in the CCP is a fairly recent introduction into an extant architecture of governance that had survived (although not thrived) without it. As a result, the question of where legal rationality has emerged can be restated as a question of where it has been tolerated, encouraged or intended.

This instrumental use of law is most obvious in the areas of public and criminal law. The CCP's Leninist structure entails that constituent power has been absorbed fully by the Party. Consequently, many of the elements and functions of constitutional and, more broadly, public law have been internalised into the Party system and thus often find no, or merely a subordinate, expression in law. As Smith argues in Chapter 4, many of the functions that in Western jurisdictions are governed by legal rules or conventions are in China subject to political rules that often seem less long-lived and less binding. The relationship between the state qua state and its citizens also does not brook judicial or legal scrutiny. The Constitution is not actionable; the National People's Congress (NPC) Standing Committee has yet to use its on-paper powers for the first time to revoke administrative regulations inconsistent with higher-level norms. Party processes, not legal rules, are primordial in the selection, appointment, promotion, dismissal and disciplining of cadres and officials, with law merely providing its imprimatur after substantive decisions have been taken. Political leaders and officials do not derive their position from explicitly granted consent of the governed but from the combination of asserting authority on the basis of Leninist tenets and the monopolisation of all significant resources of power within the ambit of the Party-state. In criminal law, Sapio has observed 'zones of lawlessness', where the normal operation of legal rules is suspended in favour of the exercise of sovereign power. Sapio describes these zones not as an aberration but as an integral component of the legal system (Sapio 2010: 3). For instance, the way in which criminal law is used to deal with ordinary thieves and murderers on the one hand and disgraced senior officials or high-profile dissidents on the other clearly illustrates the boundaries of such zones and can be seen as an illustration of where the requirements of Party unity and discipline override the rational functioning of the legal system.

This limited acceptance of legal rationality in the public law field clearly impedes and constrains not only the judiciary but also the development of China's legislative processes. In 2008, Supreme People's Court (SPC) president Wang Shengjun promoted the 'Three Supremes' (*sange zhishang* 三个至上) doctrine: in enforcing the law, judges should take into account first the supremacy of the Party's undertaking, second the supremacy of the popular interest and only third the supremacy of the law (Xinhua 2008). In a 2011 address to the NPC, then-Vice-premier Wu Bangguo ruled out rotational multi-party governance, ideological pluralisation, a tripartite separation of powers and a bicameral system, federalisation and privatisation (Standing Committee 2011). The 2014 Fourth Plenum rendered this reading explicit through the confirmation of Party leadership over legal processes, confirming a more doctrinal reading of institutional monism (Central Committee 2014).

Ideological imprints are less visible in many areas of economic and private law. Partly in order to comply with international regimes and the rules of the global trading system and partly in order to consolidate the gains from economic reform, China committed to a thorough overhaul of its legal and regulatory framework when it joined the World Trade Organization (WTO) (Qin 2007; Zhang 2013). Many technical international regimes, such as telecommunications and civil aviation, are less politically sensitive, and the value of compliance for interoperability is clear.[16] In the realm of family law, the existence of rules concerning marriage enables individuals to render the arrangements they

[16] Even if China emphasises national sovereignty in its engagement with such regimes, which is perhaps the most visible in the area of cyberspace. See, for instance, MFA 2017.

autonomously make legally valid, reducing administrative burdens on the state. Nevertheless, individual provisions in certain areas of law still evince traces of the close bond between law and morality, such as the obligation on children to visit their parents regularly (NPC 2012), while the Copyright Law denied protection to unapproved works until the measure was successfully challenged at the WTO (WTO 2009).

This observation challenges Peerenboom's argument that China would move towards some version of a thin conception of the rule of law, characterised by the presence of formal and procedural elements of legal rationality, but not normative elements such as constitutional rights or commitment to a particular economic system (Peerenboom 2002: 65). The notion that the Chinese state would commit to formal and procedural rationality across the board is irreconcilable with the concept of Party leadership over the law, and the flexibility (or arbitrariness) that the Party values. Instead, we might do better to build on the concept of 'zones of lawlessness'. While Sapio focuses her analysis largely on the area of criminal justice, it can be argued that similar pockets of unevenness exist across all areas of law. In other words, the ideological conception of legal rationality views it as having an important but bounded role in social management. The boundaries of that role vary across legal and policy areas, across regions and across time. Within these boundaries, it is the intention that law is a powerful and effective tool, yet they are meticulously policed to ensure the law stays within its box. In this sense, deLisle's (2017) assessment concerning the instrumentality and unevenness of law is perhaps better interpreted as being a feature of the legal system rather than a flaw.

A similar argument can be made specifically with regard to courts. In the 1990s, certain activist judges and scholars came to see courts as providing a judicial trajectory to sidestep the political imperatives of a single-party system (Fu and Zhai 2018). In the well-known Qi Yuling case, the SPC invoked the Constitution in its ruling, which had hitherto been treated as unjusticiable.[17] Very soon, however, the leadership began to curtail legal activism, leading the SPC to withdraw the Qi Yuling decision (Kellogg 2009). Since then, China's leadership has explicitly rejected a separation of powers in which courts have rule-making, checking or balancing roles. Zhou Qiang, the current head of the SPC, stated,

[17] The author of this decision called it China's '*Marbury* v. *Madison*' (Huang 2001).

> [China's courts] must firmly resist the western idea of 'constitutional democracy', 'separation of powers' and 'judicial independence'. These are erroneous western notions that threaten the leadership of the ruling Communist Party and defame the Chinese socialist path on the rule of law. We have to raise our flag and show our sword to struggle against such thoughts. We must not fall into the trap of western thoughts and judicial independence.
>
> (Xinhua 2017)

Courts do not, in principle, have jurisdiction over regulations issued by ministries or the State Council. Given the fact that many laws do not contain detailed substantive provisions but create mandates to be implemented by administrative agencies, this limits the role courts can play in clarifying law.[18] Courts do not have judicial review powers over laws or administrative regulations. Only the NPC Standing Committee can, officially, rescind administrative measures, but in practice these powers have never been used.[19]

The flipside of this containment of law can be found in the concept of benign constitutional violation (*liangxing weixian* 良性违宪) and, more broadly, in the condoning of legal violations in pursuit of progress (Clarke 2007). The notion of benign violation entails that the Constitution or the law often lags behind the needs of the time. Therefore, breaches should be condoned where they bring about desired social or economic effects. Indeed, some of Deng's core reforms, such as the household responsibility system that greatly improved agricultural productivity, were the result of illegal initiatives that were retroactively blessed and adopted later (Zhang 2012: 59–60). The tradition of experimentation that lies at the heart of the Party's policymaking approach requires the suspension of the existing legal order. Yet this example also displays the paradoxical consequences this notion might have, even to the detriment of Party discipline. As Clarke critiques, 'Taken seriously, this theory means reducing the entire constitution to two principles that can be stated in a single sentence – promote the development of productive forces and serve the basic interests of the state – with everything

[18] The SPC does have the power to issue judicial interpretations that direct lower-level courts with regard to sentencing and punishment standards.

[19] In one well-known case, the Sun Zhigang incident of 2003, the State Council abolished controversial regulations concerning detention and custody after a detained individual was unlawfully killed in Shenzhen. The NPC Standing Committee did not take the initiative to abrogate these regulations, in order to avoid creating a precedent, and to avoid a visible rift between the NPC and the State Council (He 2012).

else handled by statute' (Clarke 2007: 23). Birney goes further and argues that Chinese officials aren't expected to implement and enforce all laws as much as they must prioritise specific mandates (Birney 2014), often to the detriment of legal rationality. Unsurprisingly, this has ensured considerable power is retained by officialdom, leading to endemic corruption, abuse and arbitrariness. The fact that officials can override the law for public purposes means they are often tempted to do so for private ones as well.

2.3.2 Ideology Defines the Nature of Law

In the Party's conception, law is not a protector of minimal entitlements or standards of treatment but a facilitator of progress along a preordained historical path to a utopian future. It is not created through a legislative process based on the notion of representation or consent of the governed, but it is supposed to respond to objective development circumstances and the scientifically determined *guilü* that govern specific areas. Law is thus denied autonomy of its own. Chinese Communist Party legal reformer Peng Zhen put it succinctly in 1982, at the establishment of the Law Society of China:

> Is it law that should submit to reality, or reality that should submit to the law? Who is the mother, who is the child? Reality is the mother. Reality creates law, law and legal theory are the child. Law has its own independent structure, and it has its own logic, but it must start from social reality and be tested through social practice. If law is not suited to reality and the needs of social development, it must be studied and revised.
>
> (Peng 1982)

More recently, Smith (2018) has found that the Party leadership, in its formation of the *fazhi* concept in the 2000s, does not consider rule of law to be a worthwhile aim on its own terms, merely an instrument for other purposes.

The CCP's focus on the achievement of a collective telos conflicts sharply with liberal democratic notions of the rule of law, good governance and human rights. The latter are usually based on a philosophical framework that places individual well-being and flourishing first, implicitly assumes pluralism, and is largely organised on deontological principles. This has important consequences for the notion of rights. In the pluralist, deontological context, rights can be seen as unconditional and inalienable entitlements against coercive authority and interference

(Dworkin 1977). They also simultaneously legitimise and mitigate social and political conflict by abdicating claims of absolute moral truth and authority. In contrast, China's monist assertion that, in the end, all values are reducible to a singular, intelligible and harmonious conception of the good means legitimate conflicts of values and interests are impossible. Where they arise, someone inevitably made a deliberate or unintended mistake. This has important consequences for the position of citizens in the legal order, and particularly for the conception of rights. The CCP recognises 'rights' (*quanli* 权利)[20] only insofar as their exercise does not conflict with the Party's prerogative. The Constitution tellingly not only outlines citizens' rights, but also their obligation. As I have argued elsewhere with respect to free speech (Creemers 2016), it would be more accurate to see them as conditional privileges, informed by decades of stability preservation and social management practice. He Xin (2009) argues that rights-based, constitutional claims are often recast as administrative or disciplinary rules, implemented through state departments. This implies that, even in cases where the substance of particular claims is recognised, the notion of citizens' fundamental individual entitlement against the state is rejected. Rather, they are translated into enhanced obligations for the state's agents. In other words, law is not a method of limiting the power of the state but of empowering and channelling it.

What then to make of, for instance, Xi Jinping's dictum that power must be caught in a cage of rules? In a teleological, rule-of-law-oriented view, this can easily be understood as a bid to better protect citizens from state action. However, understanding ideology points us to a more subtle reading: in Party politics, state action itself should not be encumbered by legal constraints, but discipline is crucial. Therefore, the power that Xi refers to is not necessarily the power of the state *as such* but as exercised by the *agents acting on behalf of the state*. Ample literature exists on the topic of administrative litigation (Pei 1997; O'Brien and Li 2004; Givens 2013), often starting out from a state–society juxtaposition. Yet from the state's point of view, allowing citizens to challenge administrative acts in court is not only a matter of providing justice, but also one of preventing unrest and disciplining lower-level officials. In other words, administrative litigation largely serves to manage a principle-actor problem, with access to justice for the aggrieved as a collateral benefit.

[20] There is a linguistic point here as well: the Chinese word *quanli*, which is often translated as 'right', also has connotations with cognates of 'power' and 'authority' (Wang 1980; Li 2010).

This point illustrates the difficulties that the Party needs to navigate. On the one hand, its authority must be unassailable; on the other hand, it faces continuous demands for accountability and participation. It seeks both to establish the supremacy of law in particular spheres and to maintain flexibility for Party intervention. Ideology is often the tool by which these tensions are managed, and thus does not have to be intellectually coherent in the detail. Its point is to be useful in informing and justifying political action. Therefore, ideology on the one hand was used to justify the introduction of mediation as described by Minzner (2011), a non-conflictual way to 'resolve contradictions', particularly where local government officials are involved. On the other hand, the new focus on 'putting trials at the centre', and other court reform measures (SPC 2015) that favour formal litigation and reduce local government influence over courts, mobilises another bit of ideology: the necessity of discipline within a Leninist Party structure. A nuanced understanding of ideological content is thus necessary: in the same way that the Bible preaches both compassion and harsh punishment, ideology contains a plethora of tenets and ideas that can be leveraged in pursuit of conflicting objectives. Nevertheless, it also contains a common core that informs the fundamental division of power between the state and its citizens.

2.3.3 Ideology Conditions and Constrains the Beliefs and Acts of Legal Actors

A common question concerning Party ideology is whether Party cadres themselves even believe it. To a certain degree, this is a natural and useful question. Certainly, the CCP itself spends significant resources on ideological indoctrination, and it clearly intends Party cadres and members to internalise these lessons. As Pieke (2009) has argued, the Party School system not merely serves to impart professional knowledge and skills but also to inculcate a 'Party spirit' (*dang de jingshen* 党的精神) into aspiring cadres and socialise them into its cult of power and eliteness. Yet at the same time, the true believer/non-believer juxtaposition requires some nuancing. First, as Hart discussed, internalisation and acceptance of a particular rule or commitment does not entail full embrace of its complete content. A judge does not need to believe a particular rule is morally optimal, merely that it is a rule that should be applied in a specific case (Shapiro 2006). Similarly, the specific motivation of a Chinese cadre is of subordinate importance, as long as they fulfil their required role in the system well. Second, there are different levels of belief. If ideology consists of multiple intellectual elements, agreement on the epistemological core does not necessarily translate to full consistency on every question of specific policy.

The primary tool in which ideology manifests itself is through language, and it should therefore be no surprise that 'doing things with words' is of great importance in the Chinese context (Schoenhals 1992). Political power and formal language are closely connected, and the ability to propose terms and slogans is a shibboleth for defining political correctness. It is therefore unsurprising that many political debates in China revolve around the use and meaning of particular words and expressions. In law, a well-known recent example is the 2013 controversy over the role of the Constitution in structuring public power (Creemers 2015). This centred on, amongst others, the recuperation of Sun Yat-sen's term 'constitutional governance' (*xianzheng* 宪政). Reformist voices attempted to have it re-enlisted as part of the Party's carefully manicured dictionary, but failed. While the subsequent Fourth Plenum extolled the Constitution, and even went so far as to institute an annual Constitution Day, a different phrase 'governing the country according to the Constitution' (*yixian zhiguo* 依宪治国) entered the jargon. While the superficial reader might notice little difference between these two terms, they represent a world of difference within Chinese circles, as one entails political correctness, the other dissent.

In view of the importance given to discursive meaning, central authorities have considerable power to shape and police official language. Their influence is felt from state-approved textbooks in law schools to the regular training sessions to which officials, lawmakers and judges are subjected, from the Party-dominated *nomenklatura* system to strictly controlled media. Funding for legal scholarship is shaped by ideology, is used to evaluate the ideological quality of researchers and is aimed at enhancing the Party's theoretical framework (Law Society of China 2005; National Philosophy and Social Science Planning Office 2011). That does not mean concepts and slogans remain static. New slogans arise in the wake of political needs, while others – for instance, classical socialist jargon such as 'spiritual pollution' and 'counterrevolutionary crimes' – fade from use. It does mean that political language will be framed by the meanings determined through ideology, particularly those epistemological elements that have become a commonsensical and often implicit methodological framework by which reality is understood and debated. In other words, the ubiquity and pervasiveness of Party control over political language sets the most fundamental parameters in which political, legal and societal questions are conceived, debated and addressed.

2.4 Conclusion and Implications for Scholarship

While China's current legal system finds its roots in the era of reform that started in the late 1970s, the ideological components that structure it go as far back as, or even precede, the foundation of the Party and the People's Republic. The objective of modernisation – a method that is scientific, at least in name – and the overarching importance of Party rule and Party discipline have created the framework in which Chinese legal rules are made, implemented and enforced. The general philosophical view that connects the various elements of this system is the monist notion of harmony and unity, whereby law serves as one of many tools to engineer a society in which social tensions and conflicts do not occur, or are solved by optimised, technocratic solutions. This means legal rationality is intentionally subordinate to the exercise of power by the Party-state. Legal and regulatory rules merely provide standard norms for behaviour, and can be – and often are – overridden when an individual in a position of sufficient power decides so. Law is but one of many tools at the CCP's disposal, in addition to policy decisions and directing finance, front organisations in different economic sectors and among a number of social groups, state-owned enterprises in which senior appointments are made on the basis of political interests, and, perhaps most of all, the power of the internal Party administrations charged with internal organisation, discipline and propaganda. In other words, laws are created by, not sources of, the organisational principles of the Chinese state order. Courts, in turn, are not powerful rule-making actors but subordinate administrative departments tasked with implementation of specific rules.

This ideological construct bears a heavy burden within the Party-state architecture. It needs to combine constancy with flexibility. The foundations of the Party's authority must endure unchallenged, while at the same time it is necessary to continuously adapt to new challenges and opportunities that emerge as circumstances change. Part of this flexibility is found in the experimental policymaking process, in which law very often forms the closing link in a long process of trial, error and adaptation. Another part lies in the recognition that, while pluralism may be off the table, there are different groups in Chinese society that can, and must, be treated differently. Even so, it remains difficult for Party politics to openly recognise necessary trade-offs and provide reasonable justification for decisions taken. More often, documents exhort that subordinate officials must 'appropriately handle' or 'organically integrate' the relationship between two opposed elements, without further guidance.

These points place strong constraints on the development of China's legal system and on its concept of legality. First, legal rationality is only countenanced in distinct and clearly delineated spheres, and is kept far away from highly sensitive political areas. In other words, ideology defines how far the writ of the law applies. Second, ideology influences the nature of laws and legal concepts. Put bluntly, in a teleologically oriented, monist polity, the concept of fundamental rights is literally inconceivable. Instead, the focus of state–citizen relations as expressed in law is a far more paternalistic one. Lastly, ideology conditions legal actors. It provides a register of jargon that can serve to assess compliance with the official line, rewarding loyalty with promotion and insider status.

This is not to say that law has no importance whatsoever in the real world. Citizens and corporations do turn to courts to solve disputes and defend their interests. Particularly in the area of private and commercial law, progress towards professionalisation, legal certainty and predictability has been notable. Equally, citizens are increasingly demanding the fair implementation of promises and commitments made in legal documents. The legal profession, legal scholarship and legal education have expanded and professionalised at a rapid rate. Yet, this is not inconsistent with the notion of law as one of a number of approaches to social management and the maintenance of the political order, nor with the fact that China's legal system lacks the autonomy and independence present in many other jurisdictions.

For scholarship, this means that analyses of Chinese legal phenomena must take into account their political context. This means first and foremost, bringing in the CCP. China's legislative and judicial bodies are not in charge of their own development nor of the role they play in the overall political process. The role they play in this process is constantly negotiated and contested through Party channels. Judicial doctrine is laid down in the Politburo, and the Fourth Plenum Decision was written by the Central Committee. In this process, the role of ideology is far more than the mere cynical justification of realpolitik measures. Concisely reflecting the CCP's worldview and conception of political truth, ideology is important in this process for at least three reasons. First, understanding ideology can assist in developing an internally justified account of the conception of legal structures and processes. It allows us to reconstruct the internal logic of the legal structure, as Clarke demands, and thus provides an interpretive context for assessing legal developments. In other words, understanding ideology permits us to assess whether particular theories, hypotheses and expectations make sense within the parameters of the system itself, instead of the expectations of teleological theories of legal developments. Second, to a certain degree, a better understanding of ideology assists us in looking at Chinese legal reality from an internal perspective, through the eyes of its insiders. It enables us to better map the incentive structure that surrounds legal and political actors, and, in an empirical sense, to research how and to what extent individuals respond to these incentives. Lastly, studying ideology allows us to detect doctrinal shifts over time and narrow down the scope of potential futures. While it may not be the case that one can predict what will happen on the basis of ideology, it certainly is the case that it is clear what will not.

References

Bakken, B. 2000. *The Exemplary Society: Human Improvement, Social Control, and the Dangers of Modernity in China*. Oxford: Clarendon Press.

Birney, M. 2014. Decentralisation and veiled corruption under China's 'rule of mandates'. *World Development* 53, 55–67.

Brown, A. 2010. *The Rise & Fall of Communism*. London: Vintage.

Brown, K. 2012. The communist party of China and ideology. *China: An International Journal* 10(2), 52–68.

Cai, D., ed. 2010. *China's Journey toward the Rule of Law: Legal Reform, 1978–2008*. Leiden: Brill.

Central Committee. 1945. Guanyu ruogan lishe wenti de jueyi (Resolution on certain questions in the history of our party), issued 20 April. Translation available from: www.marx2mao.com/pdfs/maosw3app.pdf.

1949. Guanyu feichu Guomindang de liu fa quanshu yu queding jiefang qu de sifa yuanze de zhishi (Instructions concerning abolishing the six codes of the Guomindang and determining judicial principles for the liberated areas), issued 28 February. Translation available from: https://chinacopyrightandmedia.wordpress.com/1949/02/28/instructions-concerning-abolishing-the-six-codes-of-the-guomindang-and-determining-judicial-principles-for-the-liberated-areas/.

1958. Guanyu zai nongcun jianli renmin gongshe de jueyi (Resolution concerning the establishment of people's communes in rural areas), issued 17 August. Available from: http://cpc.people.com.cn/GB/64184/64186/66665/4493238.html.

1980. Ruogan dangnei zhengzhi shenghuo de ruogan zhunze (Some norms concerning intra-party political life), issued 29 February. Translation available from: https://chinacopyrightandmedia.wordpress.com/1980/02/29/some-norms-concerning-intra-party-political-life/.

1981. Guanyu jianguo yilai Dang de ruogan lishi wenti de jueyi (Resolution concerning some historical questions of our party since the foundation of the nation), issued 27 June.

2004. Guanyu jinyibu fanrong fazhan zhexue shehui kexue de yijian (Opinions concerning further letting philosophy and social sciences flourish and develop), issued 20 March. Translation available from: https://chinacopyrightandmedia.wordpress.com/2004/03/20/ccp-central-committee-opinion-concerning-further-letting-philosophy-and-social-sciences-flourish-and-develop/.

2014. Guanyu quanmian tuijin yifa zhiguo ruogan zhongda wenti de jueding (Decision concerning some major questions in comprehensively moving governing the country according to the law forward), issued 28 October. Translation available from: https://chinacopyrightandmedia.wordpress.com/2014/10/28/ccp-central-committee-decision-concerning-some-major-questions-in-comprehensively-moving-governing-the-country-according-to-the-law-forward/.

Chan, W. 1956. Hu Shih and Chinese Philosophy. *Philosophy East and West* 6(1), 3–12.

Chang, G. 2001. *Coming Collapse of China*. New York: Random House.

Cheek, T. 1984. The fading of wild lilies: Wang Shiwei and Mao Zedong's yan'an talks in the first CPC rectification movement. *The Australian Journal of Chinese Affairs* 11, 25–58.

Chen, J. 2008. *Chinese Law: Context and Transformation*. Leiden: Brill.

Cherniss, J. and Hardy, H. 2013. Isaiah Berlin. *The Stanford Encyclopedia of Philosophy*. Available from: http://plato.stanford.edu/archives/win2013/entries/berlin/.

Clarke, D. 2003. Puzzling observations in Chinese law: when is a riddle just a mistake? In S. Hsu, ed., *Understanding China's Legal System: Essays in Honour of Jerome A. Cohen*. New York: New York University Press, pp. 93–121.

2007. China: creating a legal system for a market economy. *Asian Development Bank Report*. Available from: https://papers.ssrn.com/sol3/papers.cfm?abstract_id=1097587.

Creemers, R. 2015. China's constitutionalism debate: content, context and implications. *The China Journal* 74, 91–109.

2016. The privilege of speech and new media: conceptualizing China's communications law in the internet era. In J. deLisle, A. Goldstein and G. Yang, eds., *The Internet, Social Media and a Changing China*. Philadelphia: University of Pennsylvania Press, pp. 86–105.

Dai, A. 2013. The reform predicament. In J. Esherick, ed. *China: How the Empire Fell*. Abingdon: Routledge, pp. 19–35.

deLisle, J. 2017. Law in the China model 2.0: legality, developmentalism and Leninism under Xi Jinping. *Journal of Contemporary China* 26(103), 68–84.

Deng, Xiaoping. 1979. Jianchi sixiang jiben yuanze (Persist in the four cardinal principles), issued on 30 March 1979. Translation available from: https://chinacopyrightandmedia.wordpress.com/1979/03/30/persisting-in-the-four-cardinal-principles/.

Dworkin, R. 1977. *Taking Rights Seriously*. Cambridge: Harvard University Press.

Fu, F. and Zhai, X. 2018. What makes the Chinese Constitution socialist? *I•CON* 16(2), 655–63.

Fukuyama, F. 1989. The end of history? *The National Interest* 16, 3–18.

Freeden, M. 2006. Ideology and political theory. *Journal of Political Ideologies* 11(1), 3–22.

Givens, J. W. 2013. Sleeping with dragons: politically embedded lawyers suing the Chinese state. *Wisconsin International Law Journal* 31, 734–70.

Goodman, D. 2002. *Deng Xiaoping and the Chinese Revolution: A Political Biography*. Abingdon: Routledge.

Goodman, D. S. G. 2000. *Social and Political Change in Revolutionary China: The Taihang Base Area in the War of Resistance to Japan, 1937–1945*. Lanham: Rowman & Littlefield.

He, W. 2012. *In the Name of Justice: Striving for the Rule of Law in China*. Washington, DC: Brookings Institution Press.

He, X. 2009. Administrative law as a mechanism for political control in contemporary China. In S. Balme and M. Dowdle, eds., *Building Constitutionalism in China*. New York: Palgrave MacMillan, pp. 143–61.

2012. The party's leadership as a living constitution in China. *Hong Kong Law Journal* 42, 73–93.

Heilmann, S. 2008. From local experiments to national policy: the origins of China's distinctive policy process. *The China Journal* 59, 1–30.

Hoffman, S. 2017. *Programming China: The Communist Party's Autonomic Approach to Managing State Security*. Ph.D. Dissertation, University of Nottingham.

Hu, Yaobang. 1979. Lilun gongzuo wuxu hui yinyan (Introduction at the conference on theory work principles), issued 18 January. Translation available from: http://chinacopyrightandmedia.wordpress.com/1979/01/18/introduction-at-the-conference-on-theory-work-principles/.

Hua, Shiping. 2013. Shen Jiaben and the late Qing legal reform (1901–1911). *East Asia* 30(2), 121–38.

Huang, Songyu. 2001. Xianfa sifahua ji qi yiyi (Judicialisation of the constitution and its significance). *Renmin fayuabao* (People's Court Daily), 13 August.

Kellogg, T. 2009. The death of constitutional litigation in China? *China Brief* 9 (7). Available from: https://jamestown.org/program/the-death-of-constitutional-litigation-in-china/.

Kuhn, P. A. 2002. *Origins of the Modern Chinese State*. Palo Alto: Stanford University Press.

Knight, N. 2007. *Rethinking Mao: Explorations in Mao Zedong's Thought*. Lanham: Lexington Books.

Kolakowski, L. 2005. *Main Currents of Marxism: The Founders, the Golden Age, the Breakdown*. New York: W. W. Norton.

Law Society of China. 2005. Guanyu jinyibu fanrong faxue yanjiu de yijian (Opinions concerning further letting legal research flourish), issued 11 August. Translation available from: https://chinacopyrightandmedia.wordpress.com/2005/08/11/china-law-society-opinions-concerning-further-letting-legal-research-flourish/.

Li, L. 2010. Rights consciousness and rules consciousness in contemporary China. *The China Journal* 64, 47–68.

Lieberthal, K. 2010. Reflections on the evolution of the China field in political science. In A. Carlson et al., eds., *Contemporary Chinese Politics: New Sources, Methods, and Field Strategies*. Cambridge: Cambridge University Press, pp. 266–78.

Llewellyn, K. 1930. *The Bramble Bush: On Our Law and Its Study*. New York: Oceana.

Loughlin, M. 2003. *The Idea of Public Law*. Oxford: Oxford University Press.

Mao, Zedong. 1937a. *Shijian lun* (On practice). Translation available from: www.marxists.org/reference/archive/mao/selected-works/volume-1/mswv1_16.htm.

1937b. *Maodun lun* (On contradictions). Translation available from: www.marxists.org/reference/archive/mao/selected-works/volume-1/mswv1_17.htm.

1938. Zhongguo Gongchandang zai minzu zhanzheng de diwei (The role of the Chinese Communist Party in the national war). Translation available from: www.marxists.org/reference/archive/mao/selected-works/volume-2/mswv2_10.htm.

Ministry of Foreign Affairs (MFA). 2017. Wangluo kongjian guoji hezuo zhanlüe (Strategy for international cooperation in cyberspace), issued 1 March. Translation available from: https://chinacopyrightandmedia.wordpress.com/2017/03/01/international-strategy-of-cooperation-on-cyberspace/.

Miller, A. 2017. Xi Jinping and the party's 'guiding ideology'. *China Leadership Monitor* 54. Available from: www.hoover.org/sites/default/files/research/docs/clm54am.pdf.

Minzner, C. F. 2011. China's turn against law. *The American Journal of Comparative Law* 59(4), 935–84.

Nathan, A. J. 1976. *Peking Politics: 1918–1923: Factionalism and the Failure of Constitutionalism*. Berkeley: University of California Press.

2003. Authoritarian resilience. *Journal of Democracy* 14(1), 6–17.

National People's Congress (NPC). 2012. Zhonghua renmin gongheguo laonianren quanyi baozhang fa (Law to protect the rights and interests of the elderly of the People's Republic of China), issued 28 December.

National Philosophy and Social Science Planning Office. 2011. Guojia zhexue shehui kexue yanjiu 'shi'er wu' guihua (National '12th five-year plan' for philosophy and social science research), issued 3 June 2011. Translation available from: https://chinacopyrightandmedia.wordpress.com/2011/06/03/national-12th-five-year-plan-for-philosophy-and-social-science-research/.

O'Brien, K. J. and Li, L. 2004. Suing the local state: administrative litigation in rural China. *The China Journal* 51, 75–96.

Pan, Wei. 2003. Toward a consultative rule of law regime in China. *Journal of Contemporary China* 12(34), 3–43.

Patapan, H. and Wang, Y. 2017. The hidden ruler: Wang Huning and the making of contemporary China. *Journal of Contemporary China* 27(101), 47–60.

Peerenboom, R. 2002. *China's Long March toward Rule of Law.* Cambridge: Cambridge University Press.

Pei, Minxin. 1997. Citizens v. mandarins: administrative litigation in China. *The China Quarterly* 152, 832–62.

Peking Review. 1966. Long live the great proletarian cultural revolution. *Peking Review* 25(9), 7–13.

Peng, Z. 1982. Fazhan shehuizhuyi minzhu jianquan shehuizhuyi fazhi (Develop socialist democracy, complete the socialist rule of law), issued 22 July. Translation available from: http://chinacopyrightandmedia.wordpress.com/1982/07/22/develop-socialist-democracy-complete-the-socialist-rule-of-law/ [27 October 2019].

Pieke, F. N. 2009. *The Good Communist: Elite Training and State Building in Today's China.* Cambridge: Cambridge University Press.

2012. The communist party and social management in China. *China Information* 26(2), 149–65.

Platt, S. R. 2012. *Autumn in the Heavenly Kingdom: China, the West, and the Epic Story of the Taiping Civil War.* New York: Knopf.

Qin, J. Y. 2007. Trade, investment and beyond: the impact of WTO accession on China's legal system. *The China Quarterly* 191, 720–41.

Qiushi. 2013. Yike ye buneng fangsong he xiaoruo yishixingtai gongzuo – renzhen xuexi guanche quanguo xuanchuan sixiang guongzuo huiyi jingshen (We cannot slacken or weaken in ideological work even for one moment – earnestly study and implement the spirit of the national propaganda and ideology work conference). *Qiushi* 2013/17. Translation available from: https://chinacopyrightandmedia.wordpress.com/2013/09/01/we-cannot-slacken-or-weaken-in-ideological-work-even-for-one-moment-earnestly-study-and-implement-the-spirit-of-the-national-propaganda-and-ideology-work-conference/.

Qiushi. 2014. Yishixingtai gongzuo yao jinjin zhuazai shoushang (Ideology work must be grasped tightly). *Qiushi* 2014/05. Translation available from: https://chinacopyrightandmedia.wordpress.com/2014/04/05/ideology-work-must-be-grasped-tightly/.

Rankin, M. B. 1997. State and society in early republican politics, 1912–18. *The China Quarterly* 150, 260–81.

Rudden, B. 1978. Law and ideology in the Soviet Union. *Current Legal Problems* 31(1), 189–205.

Saich, T. 1995. Writing or rewriting history? the construction of the Maoist resolution on party history. In T. Saich and Hans van de Ven, eds., *New Perspectives on the Chinese Communist Revolution*. New York: M. E. Sharpe: 299–338.

Sapio, F. 2010. *Sovereign Power and the Law in China*. Leiden: Brill.

Schell, O. and Delury, J. 2013. *Wealth and Power: China's Long March to the Twenty-First Century*. New York: Random House.

Schoenhals, M. 1986. Original contradictions – on the unrevised text of Mao Zedong's 'on the correct handling of contradictions among the people'. *The Australian Journal of Chinese Affairs* 16, 99–112.

1991. The 1978 truth criterion controversy. *The China Quarterly* 126, 243–68.

1992. *Doing Things with Words in Chinese Politics: Five Studies*. Berkeley: Institute of East Asian Studies.

Shambaugh, D. 2008a. Training China's political elite: the party school system. *The China Quarterly* 196, 827–44.

2008b. *China's Communist Party: Atrophy and Adaptation*. Berkeley: University of California Press.

2015. The coming Chinese crackup. *Wall Street Journal*, 6 March. Available from: www.wsj.com/articles/the-coming-chinese-crack-up-1425659198.

Shapiro, S. J. 2006. What is the internal point of view? *Fordham Law Review* 75, 1157–70.

Sharman, L. 1968. *Sun Yat-sen: His Life and Its Meaning, a Critical Biography*. Palo Alto: Stanford University Press.

Shue, V. 1990. *The Reach of the State: Sketches of the Chinese Body Politic*. Palo Alto: Stanford University Press.

Smith, E. 2018. The rule of law doctrine of the politburo. *The China Journal* 79(1), 40–61.

Standing Committee. 2011. Shiyi jie quanguo renda si ci huiyi shang zuo de changweihui gongzuo baogao (Standing committee work report at the 4th session of the 11th national people's congress), issued 11 March. Available from: www.npc.gov.cn/npc/xinwen/syxw/2011-03/11/content_1641626.htm.

Sun, Yan. 1995. *The Chinese Reassessment of Socialism, 1976–1992*. Princeton: Princeton University Press.

Sun, Y. 1999. John Dewey in China: yesterday and today. *Transactions of the Charles S. Peirce Society* 35(1), 69–88.

Sun, Yat-sen. 1924. Jianguo dagang (Fundamentals of national reconstruction). Speech at the first national congress of the Chinese nationalist party, issued 21 January. Translation available from: https://chinacopyrightandmedia.wordpress.com/1924/04/12/fundamentals-of-national-reconstruction/.

Supreme People's Court (SPC). 2015. Guanyu quanmin shenhua renmin fayuan gaige de yijian (Opinions concerning comprehensively deepening people's court reforms), issued 4 February.

Svensson, M. 2002. *Debating Human Rights in China: A Conceptual and Political History*. Lanham: Rowman & Littlefield.

Swain, T. 2017. *Confucianism in China: An Introduction*. London: Bloomsbury.

Ter Haar, B. J. 2009. Het hemels mandaat: de geschiedenis van het Chinese keizerrijk. Amsterdam: Amsterdam University Press.

Tsai, W.-H., and Dean, N. 2013. The CCP's learning system: thought unification and regime adaptation. *The China Journal* 69, 87–107.

Turner, K. G., J. V. Feinerman and R. K. Guy, eds. 2015. *The Limits of the Rule of Law in China*. Seattle: University of Washington Press.

Von Senger, H. 2000. Ideology and law-making. *Law-Making in the People's Republic of China*. Den Haag: Kluwer, pp. 41–54.

Wang, G. 1980. Power, rights and duties in Chinese history. *The Australian Journal of Chinese Affairs* 3, 1–26.

WTO. 2009. DS362: China – measures affecting the protection and enforcement of intellectual property rights'. Report of the panel, issued 26 January. Available from: www.wto.org/english/tratop_e/dispu_e/362r_e.pdf.

Xi, Jinping. 2012. Zai 'fuxing zhi lu' zhanlan de jianghua (Speech at the exhibition '*road to rejuvenation*'). Issued 29 November. Translation available from: https://chinacopyrightandmedia.wordpress.com/2012/11/29/speech-at-the-road-to-rejuvenation/.

2017. Zai zhongguo gongchandang di shijiu ci quanguo daibiao dahui shang de baogao (Report at the 19th national representative congress of the Chinese communist party), issued 18 October. Available from: http://cpc.people.com.cn/n1/2017/1028/c64094-29613660.html.

Xinhua. 2008. Zuigao Renmin Fayuan: jianchi 'sange zhishang' tuijin fayuan gongzuo kexue fazhan (Supreme People's Court: persist in the 'three supremes' to move forward the scientific development of court work). *Xinhuawang* (Xinhuanet), 30 October. Available from: http://politics.people.com.cn/GB/1026/8260115.html.

2015. Xi Jinping zai zhonggong zhongyang zhengzhiju di'ershi ci jiti xuexi shi qiangdiao jianchi yunyong bianzheng weiwuzhuyi shijieguan fangfalun tigao jiejue woguo gaige fazhan jiben wenti benling (Xi Jinping stresses at 20th politburo collective study session to uphold the use of the worldview and methodology of dialectical materialism to enhance skills to resolve basic issues in our country's reform and development). *Xinhuawang* (Xinhuanet), 24 January. Available from: www.xinhuanet.com/politics/2015-01/24/c_127416715.htm.

2017. Zhou Qiang: Yao ganyu xiang xifang cuowu sichao liangjian (Zhou Qiang: we must dare to draw the sword against western erroneous thinking trends). *Zhongguo xinwen wang* (Chinese News online), 14 January. Available from: www.chinanews.com/gn/2017/01-14/8124300.shtml.

Zhang, N. 2013. On the changes in the Chinese legal system for implementing WTO laws. In S. Jichun, ed., *Renmin Chinese Law Review: Selected Papers of the Jurist, Vol. 1*. Cheltenham: Edward Elgar, pp. 72–92.

Zhang, Q. 2012. *The Constitution of China: A Contextual Analysis*. Oxford: Hart.

Zhongguo Gongchandang. 1945. Zhongguo gongchandang dangzhang (1945 ban) (Constitution of the Communist Party of China [1945 version]), issued on 11 June 1945. Available from: https://zh.wikisource.org/zh-hant/中国共产党党章_(1945年) [25 September 2019].

2017. Zhongguo gongchandang zhangcheng (2017 ban) (Charter of the Communist Party of China [2017 version]), issued on 24 October 2017. Available from: https://zh.wikisource.org/zh-hans/中国共产党章程_(2017年).

Zhonghua Minguo. 1931. Zhonghua Minguo xunzheng shiqi yuefa (Provisional constitution of the Republic of China for the period of political tutelage), issued 12 May. Translation available from: http://chinacopyrightandmedia.wordpress.com/1931/05/12/provisional-constitution-of-the-republic-of-china- ?for-the-period-of-political-tutelage/.

1946. *Zhonghua Minguo Xianfa* (Constitution of the Republic of China), issued 25 December. Translation available from: http://china.usc.edu/constitution-republic-china-1946.

Zhonghua Renmin Gongheguo. 1982. Zhonghua renmin gongheguo xianfa [Constitution of the People's Republic of China], issued 4 December. Available from: www.npc.gov.cn/wxzl/wxzl/2000-12/06/content_4421.htm.

Zou, K. 2006. *China's Legal Reform: Towards the Rule of Law*. Leiden: Brill.

3

Making Sense through Ideology

GLORIA DAVIES

3.1 Introduction

'Ideology' is a highly overdetermined concept. Much ink has been spilled, and will undoubtedly continue to be spilled, in the analysis and theorising of ideology. The term itself has attracted an expanding spectrum of connotations, with simplistic definitions of ideology at one end and refined arguments (and problematisations of these arguments) at the other. Yet, as academics, when we use the term 'ideology' to refer to the dominant ideas and values of a given society, we generally do not disclose the ideas or values that we hold dear. You may say that that's the whole point of 'scholarly detachment': that one becomes a salaried academic to study ideology 'objectively', as it were, from a value-neutral vantage point. Yet is such a vantage point even possible? Or is scholarly detachment an ideological presumption that sustains academic work, without which demonstration the ascribed authority of academic work would be undermined? Is ideology unavoidable?

In asking these questions, I want to consider the norms and protocols of refereed scholarship as a form of ideology, and I am drawing on Louis Althusser's remark that academic authors are always subjected to the 'rituals of ideological recognition' pertinent to our profession (Althusser 1971: 172). For Althusser, ideology is how we see ourselves in the world we find ourselves in: it 'represents the imaginary relationship of individuals to their real conditions of existence' (Althusser 1971:162). In other words, no one is ideology-free. Transposing Althusser into ordinary language, Martin McQuillian (2001: 85) writes:

> Ideology is not a form of mind-control imposed upon the individual by external powers, rather it is the very way in which we live our lives: religious beliefs (theist or otherwise), political views, cultural identity, family history, supporting a football team, reading a newspaper, watching television and so on. All of which creates an idea of reality, imagining the way we live out our roles as members of social classes by tying us to social functions through values, ideas and images.

To the extent that ideology is also the result of spoken and written communications, texts and images, the effectiveness of any given ideology as a dominant pattern of understanding, whether religious or secular, is contingent as much on the persuasiveness of what it promises and represents as on its institutional pervasiveness. We (whether 'we' be academics, clerics, journalists, judges and lawyers, politicians or other textual producers) make sense of things *through* ideology. In this essay, I discuss this proposition in two ways: the first considers how discursive (and disciplinary) differences affect scholarship on Chinese Communist Party (CCP or Party) ideology outside China; the second explores the CCP's discursive requirements and 'ideological strengthening' under Xi Jinping.

In these two discussions, I am also highlighting by contrast two different ways of thinking about ideology: in the first, following Althusser, I consider the discipline-based and institutional 'rules' governing academic inquiry as a form of ideology, one that is internationally practised and implicitly premised on the ideal of intellectual freedom. In the second, I discuss the explicit ideology of the CCP. I consider how ideological strengthening since Xi took power has had the effect of severely undermining academic inquiry at Chinese universities. What happens then, when the 'rules' governing academic inquiry as an implicit ideology are displaced by the explicit ideology of the CCP? I reflect on this question in relation to recent mainland Chinese legal academic discourse produced in defence of China's 'socialist rule of law'.

3.2 Ideology and Scholarship

The term 'ideology' in everyday usage stands for something like a doctrine. When media and scholarly publications about China mention the 'ideology' of China's ruling Communist Party, the term is generally treated as self-explanatory and interchangeable with the articulated beliefs and goals of the Party. Statements such as 'China's official political ideology of "socialism with Chinese characteristics" allows the Government to define its form of state-backed capitalism within the socialist mould' (Birtles 2018) or 'China's President Xi Jinping has created his own political ideology, in a step towards entrenching his position at the top of the Communist Party' (Grace 2017) make this plain. The fact that the Party uses expressions such as 'correct ideas' (*zhengque de sixiang* 正确的思想) and 'guiding thought' (*zhidao sixiang* 指导思想) to describe Party thought (*dang de sixiang* 党的思想) further reinforces this synonymy between it and ideology understood as doctrine.[1] The social sciences have no shortage of more sophisticated definitions to further qualify and refine this identification of ideology with a formally stated set of ideas. Take for instance the set of definitional criteria used in a 2017 linguistics article discussing Xi Jinping's speeches and interviews (with all authorial emphases in the original reproduced below):

> '[T]he core definition of ideology as a *coherent* and relatively *stable set* of beliefs or values has remained the same in political science over time' (my emphases in italics, Wodak and Meyer, 2001: 8). Furthermore, another two common features shared by these definitions are as follows: first, ideology is a '*set*', '*systemic body*' or '*schematically organized complexes*' of ideas, rather than one or more random collection(s) of ideas; second, ideology is not ideas believed by a particular individual, but these systematic sets of ideas are shared by 'specific *social groups* [emphasis added]' (Van Dijk, 1998: 316) and function (from a Marxist or Fairclough's point of view) to establish and maintain power, dominance or exploitations of certain social groups.
>
> (Wang 2017: 415)

The article's author, a linguistics PhD candidate, employs this science-like classification of ideology to distinguish 'systematically organized' from less or non-systematically organized features of ninety-seven texts by Xi. Accordingly, Xi Jinping's utterances are studied as purely linguistic artefacts and analysed using a methodology derived from critical discourse analysis (CDA), with the stated aim of answering the question (emphasis in original): 'How are the CCP's ideologies *systematically* represented in texts and talks that contribute to the legitimacy of its governance as China's ruling party?' Jiayu Wang finds that in Xi's communications, 'the CCP's political ideologies are framed as values that are at once stable and keep on changing, being adapted and Sinicized'. Moreover, these ideologies are also presented as authoritative moral values 'that guide both the state and the society', together with elements of traditional statecraft and 'Marxist and Chinese cultural dialectics of "change"'. In concluding that 'through these discursive and cultural strategies or mechanisms, the CCP's status as China's ruling party is substantially legitimized', Wang implies an equivalence between 'systematically organized' communications and political legitimacy. Yet, the question of how legitimacy is practically achieved is left largely

[1] See Ewan Smith's essay in Chapter 4 on the relation between ideology and doctrine within the Chinese legal context.

unexplained, with the author merely noting in passing that it also involves the 'assimilation' and 'recruiting' of citizens to 'the CCP's subject position' (Wang 2017:427).

This way of studying Party ideology isolates it from the environment in which it circulates. Detailed cataloguing and analysis of linguistic features of Xi's communications are presented with reference to neither the political context nor public perceptions of these communications. The article's style reflects the highly technical nature of linguistics as an academic discipline, and its analysis is addressed to readers acquainted with the specialism CDA. Yet, while Wang confines himself to discussing 'Xi Jinping's discourse' specifically in relation to arguments and methods in discourse analysis, his choice of topic is implicitly political. A bare trace of critical reflection on Party-state rule can be discerned in his passing reference to the CCP securing its political legitimation via the involuntary 'assimilation' of Chinese citizens.

In describing the ideology that sustains an academic discourse as implicit, I mean that it is structural: it makes the practices associated with that discourse distinctive, enabling contributors to recognize and claim the discourse as theirs. Ideology so understood is better described as an operational program than a framework of belief. To use the term 'ideology' in this way is to agree with Althusser that academics operate within an institutional structure that requires them to imagine themselves as belonging to a field of expertise. Moreover, to be capable of engaging with arguments and ideas in the specialist vocabularies pertinent to one's field is to have internalised the field's discursive norms. Althusser's reference to academic writing as involving 'rituals of ideological recognition' reminds us that the production of academic discourse is a material practice, occurring in specific institutions, times and places. Academic writing is, on the one hand, the work of individual academics. On the other hand, it is also produced by individuals who, having internalised the norms, specialisms and values of the fields to which they 'belong', function as academic subjects, precisely because their discursive behaviours are dictated to by the institutional regime in which they operate.

Althusser argued that 'ideology' operates in two ways simultaneously. There are historically developed and articulated *ideologies* that we see as 'religious, ethical, legal, political' (Althusser 1971: 134): for instance, Catholic or Protestant Christianity, a liberal-democratic polity, the 'free market', the CCP and so on and so forth. We constantly make sense *of* these ideologies and consciously defend or oppose them or subject them to analysis. Then there is '*ideology* in general', which 'has no history' and is to be discerned *through* the ways in which people conform to the institutional conditions that dictate their lives (Althusser 1971:159). It is this second, more elusive understanding on which Althusser focused his attention and which he likened to the unconscious.[2] Ideology, understood as a structure, resists ready definition yet grants the theoretical insight that all that people have access to are (ideological) versions of reality. As Mary Klages puts it, glossing Althusser,

> So the 'real world' becomes not something that is objectively out there but something that is the product of our relations to it and of the ideological representations that we make of it – the stories we tell ourselves about what is real become what is real. That's how ideology operates.
>
> (Klages 2017:100)

Althusser's bifurcated way of reading ideology productively allows us to identify ideologies yet prevents us from slipping into an implicitly ideology-free posture. Because it makes us see all discursive production as institutionally (hence ideologically) constrained, it also encourages us self-reflexively to compare the ideological effects of different varieties of institutional (as structural) subjection. The different styles of academic discourse that I discuss in this section will form the comparative basis on which I discuss the production of CCP discourse in the next section.

The article by Wang cited earlier appeared in *Discourse & Society*, a linguistics journal focused on 'explicit theory formation and analysis of the relationships between the structures of text, talk, language use, verbal interaction or communication; social, political or cultural micro- and macrostructures and cognitive social representations'.[3] Wang's article, as the work of an early career academic author, conspicuously adheres to the disciplinary norms that dictate the journal's discourse. In saying that it reflects the ideologically structured nature of academic prose, I am by no means making a negative judgement. The more freewheeling style I am using here is no less ideologically structured and a result of the liberties I have been afforded in contributing to a multidisciplinary anthology.

[2] Althusser explains: 'If eternal means, not transcendent to all (temporal) history, but omnipresent, trans-historical and therefore immutable in form throughout the extent of history, I shall adopt Freud's expression word for word, and write *ideology is eternal*, exactly like the unconscious' (emphasis in original, 1971: 161).

[3] Description provided on the official website of *Discourse & Society* at http://journals.sagepub.com/home/das.

My writing style is discursively closer to Kerry Brown's 2012 article, 'The Communist Party of China and Ideology', which similarly addresses a broader readership as it was published in a multidisciplinary journal. In his article, Brown outlines the theoretical underpinnings of his understanding of ideology as drawing on arguments presented, among others, by 'Terry Eagleton, the British cultural theorist' and 'French philosopher Michel Foucault'. He offers his own deft figuration of ideology as 'the bones within the system, giving structure, cohesiveness and functionality to social practices, justifying them to key constituencies and audiences' (Brown 2012: 53).

Brown describes ideology as a structure. However, he confines himself to discussing the dissemination of the CCP's ideology within the structural constraints of its one-party system. His analysis compares the relative cogency of CCP ideology for the better part of the twentieth century with the post-Maoist contradictions that have bedevilled it since the 1990s. He highlights the 'tension between economically and intellectually embracing a market while maintaining a privileged adjudicating role for the Party' as key to understanding the CCP's construction of its ideology in the twenty-first century (Brown 2012:55). As Brown argues, the importance for the CCP of persuading Chinese citizens that it possesses a credible ideology cannot be understated, for the one-party system has historically never been without one: 'at least for the elite, the ideology did matter – it was a basis for legitimacy and for a cohesive world view which had brought the [CCP] to power' (Brown 2012: 66).

Brown outlines three 'ideological challenges' that the Party leadership cannot avoid in this regard. The first is 'how the Party is able to redefine its role in relation to the state and government' to effectively resolve or pre-empt 'inconsistency and conflict'. The second is the Party's negotiation between its own interests and those of social groups ranging from 'highly internationalised returned students . . . to the private business people with their deepening links into the global investment system, and urban professionals with their interest in protecting their property, lifestyles, and rights, to the farmers and migrant labourers'. The third is how the Party would 'manage the increasing pressures of contention, dissent and rupture'. Would Party ideology be flexible enough to provide some space for 'contrary vocabularies' and to develop 'clear mechanisms for adaptation and innovation' (Brown 2012: 67)? Brown's article was published in August 2012, four months before Xi's installation as Party General Secretary. Since 2013, Xi's administration has answered these challenges more often by coercion than persuasion. Ideological 'strengthening' (*jiaqiang* 加强, a frequently occurring verb in Xi's speeches) has involved, among other things, bans on the discussion of 'Western values' on university campuses, mandatory study of Xi's views on Party discipline for Party members, brutal crackdowns on dissent and human rights lawyers and, most distressingly, the detention of more than one million mainly Uighurs, some Kazakhs and members of other Muslim ethnic minorities in political re-education camps in Xinjiang (Batke 2019; Brophy 2019).

In his first speech as General Secretary at the Politburo's collective study session on 17 November 2012, Xi likened the 'ideals of and faith in' the CCP to the 'spiritual calcium of Party members'. He went on to say that if Party members lacked 'sturdy ideals and faith', they would become spiritually 'calcium-deficient' and develop 'rickets' (Xi 2012). Between these expressions and Brown's figuration of ideology as 'the bones within the system', there is an unmistakable resonance. Brown figures ideology as bone to make ideology's instrumental power imaginable, so that we can picture ideology as holding together an entire complex of institutional arrangements, in the way a skeleton would support a living organism. Conversely, Xi's related figuration serves a purely didactic end. He treats Party ideology as if it were indeed just like a skeleton: one that required strengthening through the 'calcium' supplement that his administration would provide.

Brown's critical survey of Party ideology is evidently poles apart from Xi's inaugural speech at the Politburo study session. Brown's international prominence as a scholar of Chinese politics ensures that readers are primed to read his 2012 article as intellectually authoritative. However, established academic practice also allows his view to be openly challenged. Conversely, Xi's speeches circulate in China as a source of unquestioned political power. They provide, among other things, instructions for Party and state institutions, and they model expressions to be faithfully reproduced in the communications of the mainland media, employees of Party and state organizations and the Party rank and file. The discursive norms and institutional conditions under which Brown's and Xi's texts were produced, and the purposes they serve, are entirely different.

That said, the related metaphors appearing in the two texts point to the authors' shared instrumentalist understanding of ideology. To liken ideology to bone or calcium is to represent a cultural construction as a natural substance. It allows us to imagine the work of analysing ideology as if a forensic anthropologist were examining a skeleton or a medical practitioner diagnosing a medical condition. To represent ideology evocatively, as if it were a stable object that lends itself to analysis, is to obscure the ideological nature of one's analysis. An evocative metaphor can lull us into believing that we are seeing something clearly and in so doing, lead us to confuse representation with reality.

In contrast, Christian Sorace tackles head-on the representational difficulties involved in discussing Party ideology in his 2017 book *Shaken Authority: China's Communist Party and the 2008 Sichuan Earthquake.* Drawing on Althusser's concept of 'interpellation', he argues that 'framing the problem of ideology as a question of belief misses how it functions as an assemblage of practices that shape people's everyday habits of speech and dispositions' (Sorace 2017: 10–11). Interpellation is the term Althusser used to describe ideology's function of turning people into law-abiding 'subjects'. Ideology predisposes them to see the social arrangements of a given system and its relations of power as simply the way things are, and in which they play their parts as subjects. Interpellation is Althusser's way of presenting socialisation as a process of ideological subjection, and he argues that it happens even before birth, for 'it is certain in advance that [the unborn child] will bear its Father's Name' (Althusser 1971:176).

Sorace points out that because the effects of interpellation are seldom discussed in scholarship on contemporary China, the field remains captive to simplistic equations of ideology with a doctrine to be believed in or rejected. This approach, he argues, has produced 'stylised snapshots of Chinese politics' in the form of statements such as: 'People join the party to improve their career opportunities, not because they believe in Party ideology. Protestors manipulate the language of the law to advance their own interest' (Sorace 2017: 11).

> What these statements miss is that people do not *stand outside* of discourse even when they manipulate it. A peasant who strategically deploys Party discourse to advance his own material interests is still thinking in, assessing from, citing, and reproducing Party discourse. A savvy college graduate who ridicules Party ideology but nonetheless joins the Party to improve her career prospects is not somehow protected from ideology by a cloak of cynical opportunism (Sorace 2017:11).

Sorace's discussion of the interpellation of Chinese citizens appears in a section titled, 'Breathing the air of ideology'. This metaphor of air, unlike those of bone and calcium, points to the *invisible* dispersal of an articulated doctrine through a multitude of everyday communications. It highlights the pervasiveness of Party ideology and the involuntary nature of people's subjection to it, through their interactions with and participation in the institutional practices of CCP rule. Luigi Tomba makes a similar point when describing the CCP as a '"multiple" cultural hegemony', using the qualifier 'multiple' to complicate Antonio Gramsci's concept of 'cultural hegemony' (Tomba 2014: 14). He points out that the 'existing, entrenched ideas' of one-party rule as expressed in the CCP's discourse have diverse and divergent local uses, such that:

> Communist activists use the language of patriotism to justify their grievances against real estate developers; disgruntled ex-workers invoke the socialist spirit of central policies to frame their dissatisfaction with the local leaders . . . middle-class homeowners claim that harmonious communities are the cornerstone of a modern, stronger China . . . the same discourses of 'harmony', 'quality' and 'security' are equally used by the state to justify intrusive policing activities inside the neighbourhood and by real estate developers to sell prestigious properties to status-hungry families.
>
> (Tomba 2014: 15)

The four accounts of Party ideology discussed above reflect the discursive norms and disciplinary expectations that have generated the differences among them. Of the four, Wang's is the most restrictively conditioned by its field of study. The other three address broader readerships with general interests in CCP ideology and its effects. Brown's focus on CCP ideology as 'the bones' within the rigidly-defined system of Party-state rule is entirely appropriate for the issues he discusses. Similarly, Sorace's and Tomba's interest in the responses of ordinary citizens to Party ideology leads them to highlight the ways in which the Party's vocabulary pervades everyday communications.

What is important is that, despite their evidently different disciplinary interests, modes of argumentation and uses of language, these four accounts are instantly recognisable to academic readers as sharing the same hallmarks of professional approval and disciplined institutional practice. Their published status invests them with the authority of the discursive fields that they address. Accordingly, academic readers will read, comment on and cite them (as I have done here) as credible peer-reviewed sources, precisely because the authors of these publications have undergone this same process of reading, commentary and citation of other peer-reviewed writings.

3.3 Party Ideology and Authority

Ideological recognition is bound up with acceptance of authority. Institutional discourses (whether they be academic, professional or party political) derive their authority from the normative expectations and 'collective meanings' that provide the institution in question with its raison d'etre (whether of advancing knowledge and the profession, or 'serving the people'). This relationship between ideology and authority is neatly captured by Alexander Wendt with the following examples:

> If society 'forgets' what a university is, the powers and practices of professor and student cease to exist; if the United States and the Soviet Union decide that they are no longer enemies, 'the cold war is over'.
>
> (Wendt 1992: 397)

Wendt explains:

> An institution is a relatively stable set or 'structure' of identities and interests. Such structures are often codified in formal rules and norms, but these have motivational force only in virtue of actors' socialization to and participation in collective knowledge. Institutions are fundamentally cognitive entities that do not exist apart from actors' ideas about how the world works.
>
> (Wendt 1992: 399)

In short, continued collective participation in institutional practices is essential for the maintenance of rules and norms of conduct and communication, and for the ways of seeing and acting they produce to 'feel right' to the participants. For it is only when the institutional practices in question feel right that they can remain (ideologically) authoritative.

In Alexei Yurchak's study of late socialism in Russia, he uses 'authoritative discourse' to describe the 'highly normalized, fixed and citational' communications that characterised Soviet socialism from the 1950s through the 1980s. Yurchak argues that focusing on the effects of 'authoritative discourse' allows for a more productive engagement with post-Stalin late socialism that does not 'reduce the description of socialist reality to dichotomies of the official and the unofficial, the state and the people, and to moral judgements shaped within Cold War ideologies' (Yurchak 2005:9). Instead, it provides more fine-grained ways of seeing how people understood and ascribed meaning to 'their socialist lives – sometimes in line with the announced goals of the state, sometimes in spite of them, and sometimes relating to them in ways that did not fit either-or dichotomies' (Yurchak 2005:9).[4]

[4] There is a clear complementarity between Yurchak's account of late Soviet 'authoritative discourse' and Sorace's and Tomba's discussions of CCP ideology, though the three authors draw on different theoretical approaches.

'Authoritative discourse' was first used by the literary scholar Mikhail Bakhtin in the 1940s to describe the kind of vocabulary and language that people learned to hold as true or sacred through their upbringing, education and socialisation.

> The authoritative word demands that we acknowledge it, that we make it our own; it binds us, quite independent of any power it might have to persuade us internally; we encounter it with its authority already fused to it . . . It is, so to speak, the word of the fathers. Its authority was already acknowledged in the past. It is prior discourse.
>
> (Bakhtin 1981: 342)

Yurchak argues that while Stalin lived, he commanded such personal power as to be capable of dictating the discourse of Soviet ideology.[5] After his death, no successor succeeded in filling his shoes. Accordingly, in the absence of Stalin's imprimatur, the discourse that transmitted Soviet ideology in the post-Stalin decades relied increasingly on 'hyper-normalisation' to sustain its authority. 'Hypernormalisation' is Yurchak's description of the increasing adherence to precise formulations by successive post-Stalin administrations, as if to reproduce the authority that the party's discourse had commanded under Stalin. The result was that normalisation, implemented via 'fixed and cumbersome forms of language that were often neither interpreted nor easily interpretable', became its own end (Yurchak 2005: 50).[6]

Yurchak's account of the hypernormalised discourse of Soviet Russia from the 1950s to the 1980s bears a striking similarity to the proliferation of prescribed formulations or *tifa* (提法, literally, the method [*fa*] of putting a point across [*ti*]) in the discourse of China's Party-state after Mao Zedong's death. As with Stalin, while Mao lived, he directed the Party's discourse. Moreover, in the Cultural Revolution decade (1966–1976), Party discourse became virtually synonymous with Mao Zedong Thought. Mao's death, the arrest of the Gang of Four and the launch of economic reforms under Deng Xiaoping's aegis (1976–1978) brought a decisive end to Maoist politics and its doctrine of class struggle. Notwithstanding Mao's superseded revolutionary vision, however, Deng

[5] On Mao's discursive authority, see David E. Apter and Tony Saich, *Revolutionary Discourse in Mao's Republic* (Cambridge, MA: Harvard University Press, 1994).

[6] Yurchak's point is that 'authoritative discourse' not only enabled the transmission of Soviet ideology but disabled its development through excessive normalisation after the death of Stalin.

saw that the authority of Mao's language had to remain inviolable for Party-state rule to continue. As he explained in 1980:

> The banner of Mao Zedong Thought can never be discarded. To throw it away would be nothing less than to negate the glorious history of our Party ... It would be ill-advised to say too much about Comrade Mao Zedong's errors. To say too much would be to blacken Comrade Mao, and that would blacken the country itself. That would go against history. (quoted and translated in Barmé 1993: 262)[7]

In these remarks, Deng proposed a normative account of the Party's historical development, one that would highlight the Party's enduring characteristics and concomitantly understate the reversal of its Maoist policies. This would then tell a story, to use a Party *tifa*, of the CCP's 'continuous advance from victory to victory' (*buduan cong shengli zou xiang shengli* 不断从胜利走向胜利).

Despite Party ideology in China after 1978 departing radically from its Maoist precedent, the prior Maoist discourse was eclectically preserved to embody political continuity and to suggest that, though mistakes were made, the Party-state system remained true to its guiding principle of 'serving the people' (*wei renmin fuwu* 为人民服务, a foundational CCP *tifa*). However, a new vocabulary of 'reform and opening up'(*gaige kaifang* 改革开放, the CCP's guiding *tifa* since 1978) was also being rapidly established that bore the imprint of Deng's own authority and his collective-style leadership. The 1980s was characterised by Deng's stated goal of 'building socialism with Chinese characteristics', a phrase that he first used in September 1982 to describe the Party's aim of 'integrating the universal truth of Marxism with the concrete realities of China', and which has since become the foundational *tifa* of successive post-Maoist administrations (Deng 1982).

Logically speaking, the contradiction between Maoist 'class struggle' toward the 'dictatorship of the proletariat' and post-Maoist market growth politically justified as 'socialism with Chinese characteristics' is irreconcilable. Rhetorically however, hypernormalised *tifa* were used to present the policies of the Maoist and post-Maoist periods as compatible, with the latter presented as the inevitable result of the former.

[7] Deng Xiaoping, 'Opinions on the drafting of the "Resolution on Certain Questions in the History of Our Party Since the Founding of the People's Republic of China"' (25 October 1980).

Yurchak drew on J. L. Austin's famous distinction between constative and performative utterances to explain the effects of hypernormalisation (Yurchak 2005: 18–20). According to Austin, 'constative' utterances describe or report a situation. For instance, 'Mao Zedong was born in 1893' is a statement to be judged as either true or false. Conversely, 'performative' utterances do something as opposed to merely describing or reporting. Xi Jinping's declaration in December 2012, on the thirtieth anniversary of China's 1982 Constitution, 'We must firmly establish, throughout society, the authority of the Constitution and the law and allow the overwhelming masses to fully believe in the law' is primarily a performative utterance.[8] It conveys an intent and promise on the part of the then newly incumbent head of state. At the time, it had yet to be proven true or false.

Yurchak's point is that as post-Stalin party discourse in Soviet Russia became increasingly normalised, its performative value outweighed its constative value over time. It mattered less and less whether the party's discourse 'stated facts and described the world and whether these statements and descriptions were true' (Yurchak 2005: 37). Instead, the practice of not deviating from wordings that were already invested with authority became the focus of the party leadership's communications. Authority derived less from belief than habitual cumulative practice. Shortly, I will argue that Xi's administration has paid close attention to harnessing the performative force of prior discourse to project a sense of 'organic' continuity between itself and previous administrations. However, because all forms of institutional and social activity involve habitual cumulative practice, we must first distinguish between the different ideological effects of different types of institutional practice.

Let me return briefly to Althusser's distinction between articulated ideologies and 'ideology in general' or ideology understood as a structure. The four accounts of party ideology in Anglophone scholarship that I discussed earlier indicate the capacity of the university system, *as an ideological structure*, to accommodate a wide range of discipline-based arguments, as well as articulated ideologies, so long as all these adhere to the norms of institutionally approved academic practice. Indeed, if there

[8] Cited and translated by David Bandurski, 'Xi Jinping, Constitutional Reformer', *China Media Project*, 13 March 2018, available from: http://chinamediaproject.org/2018/03/13/xi-jinping-constitutional-reformer/. The original speech is available from: www.xinhuanet.com/politics/2012-12/04/c_113907206_2.htm.

is a guiding idea at work in the idea of the University, it would be 'autonomy', even if, as Pierre Bourdieu has pointed out,

> Autonomy is achieved by constructing a sort of 'ivory tower' inside of which people judge, criticise, and even fight each other, but with the appropriate weapons – properly scientific instruments, techniques and methods.
>
> (Bourdieu 1996: 61)

For instance, five decades' worth of cumulative citations of and commentary on Althusser's writings about ideology have ensured that key terms used by Althusser (such as 'interpellation') have become normalised in several genres of academic discourse. However, this university-funded investment of authority in Althusser's vocabulary and oeuvre has been accompanied by university-funded critical engagement with his ideas for their assumptions and flaws. Sorace's use of Althusser to analyse Chinese society under CCP rule and my use of Althusser in this essay to consider the ideological structure of China-focused academic discourse are beneficiaries of this institutionalised process of critical engagement. Without this process, Althusser's argument could not have been extended and renewed in both its constative (meaning producing) and performative (rhetorically effective) aspects. Continuing intellectual interrogation and debate has prevented its stagnation into a dated Marxist critique of capitalist society.

In contrast, the CCP's one-party system is structurally reliant on habitual use of hypernormalised formulations to secure its authority. Party ideology, as an articulated ideology, is designed to exclude any open discussion, let alone interrogation of the CCP system that it both legitimises and is sustained by. The driving presumption is that the 'more alike and more predictable' Party discourse appeared, the more authoritative, and stable, it would feel to everyone, officials and citizens alike (Yurchak 2005: 49). Take for example the key statement in the Party's amended Constitution of 2013, which reads: 'The Communist Party of China takes Marxism-Leninism, Mao Zedong Thought, Deng Xiaoping Theory, the important thought of Three Represents and the Scientific Outlook on Development as its guide to action' (Xinhua 2013). If we agree with Yurchak that it is the performative dimension of hypernormalised discourse that we should attend to more, then what a given Party formulation means – its constative value – is of less consequence than the fact that it has to be frequently invoked as 'correct' and 'true' and its word-order is strictly followed.

This does not mean that the CCP's key formulations lack constative value. Party propagandists and theorists lend expository weight to them through their abundant publications on Party policies and slogans in Party- and state-run outlets. Nonetheless, the authority of these formulations is contingent less on what they mean than on what they 'do': the performative effects of their constant reiteration in the communications of large numbers of people working in Party and state institutions, in education and the media. In this regard, we should note that the addition of 'Xi Jinping Thought for the New Era of Socialism with Chinese Characteristics' (hereafter 'Xi Thought') to the Party's Constitution in October 2017 broke with the 'pattern of ideological amalgamation' (to use William Joseph's apt phrase) set by Xi's predecessors Jiang Zemin and Hu Jintao. Deng's 'Theory', Jiang's 'Three Represents' and Hu's 'Scientific Outlook' had each been written into the Party's Constitution at the end of their tenures. The *tifa* formulations that were used to name the guiding thought of each leader were thus

> promoted to constitutional status, genetically linked to the ideological contributions of earlier leadership generations, while being touted as having blazed new theoretical ground in advancing the cause of building socialism and the march towards communism.
>
> (Joseph 2014: 184)

The naming and induction of Xi Thought into the Party Constitution after Xi's first five years in office marked a striking departure from previous practice (Jiang and Hu had served thirteen and ten years, respectively, before their ideas acquired constitutional status). As the first Party leader after Mao to have his ideas institutionally acknowledged as an entire body of thought (*sixiang* 思想), the inauguration of Xi Thought was staged for maximum performative effect. Of the more than seventy rounds of applause that greeted Xi's 200-minute report to the 19th Party Congress, the Chinese media company Tencent extracted an eighteen-second snippet to produce a 'Clap for Xi jinping' app the same day. Within twenty-four hours of its release, the app had reportedly generated well over a billion claps for Xi (Vanderklippe 2017).

The reference in Xi Thought to a 'New Era' uses the phrase *xin shidai* (新时代) and not *xin shiqi* (新时期), which the Party had used in 1978 to hail the launch of China's economic reforms as a 'New Era' ushering in Reform and Opening Up. Party theorists were careful to distinguish between these two terms. Deng's *xin shiqi* marked the end of the Maoist command economy and 'class struggle', while Xi's *xin shidai* refers to a further development out of this Deng-led 'New Era'. A Chinese-language article published on 1 December 2017 on the *People's Daily* website explained things this way:

> *Xin shidai* has three facets of significance that together present a highly important determination of Socialism with Chinese Characteristics as it proceeds into a new period. First, *xin shidai* refers to the mighty leap taken by the long-suffering Chinese nation in its progress from standing up through growing wealthy to becoming powerful. Second, *xin shidai* refers to the powerful vitality of a glowing scientific socialism in twenty-first century China and third, *xin shidai* indicates the contributions of Chinese insights and Chinese approaches toward solving the problems of humanity. The time from the *xin shiqi* of the past to the present-day *xin shidai* is an important period of innovation.
>
> (Fan 2017)

One performative effect of Party discourse is its minimisation of the authorial voice. The author of the excerpt above is immaterial, as their function is purely instrumental: to channel the discourse and its correct formulas. A highly normalised academic discourse also has the ideological effect of minimising the author's voice. In academic discourse, however, the aim is to convey professional 'objectivity' by reducing the appearance of 'subjectivity'. Moreover, the more specialised the discourse, the narrower the scope of participation becomes. Nonetheless, narrow adherence to the discursive conventions of a discipline or subdiscipline prevents neither the production of new (and individually achieved) knowledge nor intellectual debate.

Whereas the authority of academic discourse is premised on professional expertise and reasoned inquiry, the authority of Party discourse derives from the asserted inviolability of the Party's 'correct line'. To adhere to the CCP's precise wordings is to (performatively) demonstrate one's fealty to the endorsed Party line of the moment. In this connection, the 'voices' of Party leaders, and Xi's in particular, matter not for their individuality but because they represent the Party line. (In 1980, when Deng Xiaoping criticised Mao, using the expression 'the hall of one voice', *yi tan tang* [一言堂], he warned against the dangers of allowing any one person to monopolise Party discourse.) Except for Mao and since Mao, a person who writes or speaks in the Party's 'authoritative language', whether as a leader, theorist or rank-and-file member, has been more a 'mediator of pre-existing knowledge' than a 'producer of new knowledge' (Yurchak 2005: 75). Jeffrey Wasserstrom (2018) reminds us that Mao Thought and Xi Thought are both 'the works of many authors . . . a collective creation'. However, it was Mao Thought alone, in the form of the Little Red Book, that 'was waved aloft at rallies and read aloud from in hospitals by true believers, convinced that its sacred words could make the deaf hear'. Xi Thought, conversely, in the form of 'Volume One of *The Governance of China* is a bit like working your way through a compilation of stump speeches . . . Volume Two is more like a brochure from a company's PR department, introducing and celebrating a brand'.

The authority of modern academic discourse is sustained by the trust placed in it by academics themselves, their students and the reading public. Trust is ideological to the extent that it is based not only in university-based practices but in the belief that these practices can be relied upon to provide reliable research. The standards generated out of institutionalised routines of peer review that are performed without question by university academics and administrators do more than regulate scholarship. They make scholarship believable as academic expertise, thus ensuring that society does not 'forget' what a university is. If we use Althusser's notion of 'ideology in general' to understand the structure of assumptions and expectations implicit in university work as an ideology, then we can also see that this ideology has proven sufficiently capacious to accommodate, over time, conflicting ideas and changes in institutional beliefs and practices.

The explicit, articulated ideology of the CCP is something else. It is an active construction of the social world presented as true knowledge. The CCP's assumption that it alone knows best what everyone needs puts the authority of Party discourse on a far narrower footing than that of academic discourse. CCP ideology is sustained more by compliance than trust, even though trust is writ large in Party mottos such as 'trust the Party' (*xiangxin dang* 相信党). In practice, the motto translates into the injunction to never openly challenge what the Party says.[9] Consequently, the Party's institutional practices are organised to promote the Party's message, translate it into practice and eradicate or at least minimise the threat of dissent. Party ideology is inherently paranoid, for, to quote Xi, it

[9] An example of this is the Party motto used in 2009 to warn against rumour-mongering in the aftermath of the riots in Xinjiang that year: *bu xin yao, bu chuan yao, bu gen yao, xiangxin dang* 不信谣，不传谣，不跟谣， 相信党 (Don't believe rumours, don't spread rumours, don't follow rumours, believe in the Party). See Tom Cliff, *Oil and Water: Being Han in Xinjiang* (Chicago, IL: University of Chicago Press, 2016), p. 193.

requires Party members to be always 'vigilant in defending against the destabilization and collapse of their ideals and faith' (Qiu Shi 2013a).

3.3.1 *Rule of Law: Ideal or Ideology?*

This called-for vigilance extends to the use of prescriptive Party formulations. Hypernormalised *tifa* are supposed to convey, as it were, the eternal verities of CCP rule and wisdom. However, they must also show adaptation over time, to express the Party's ability to answer new challenges. The efforts of Xi's administration to turn an existing formulation, 'to govern the nation according to the law' *yifa zhiguo* (依法治国), into a defining feature of Xi's 'New Era' illustrates how this is done.

Susan Trevaskes points out that when the phrase *yifa zhiguo* was first used in the mid-1990s under then Party Secretary Jiang Zemin, it served to highlight the Party leadership's active promotion of 'institution building for a socialist rule of law' (Trevaskes 2018: 347–8). In Xi's reiteration of this prescriptive formulation two decades on, the same words now expressed a different and more focused intent: that of 'fortifying and legitimizing the Chinese Communist Party's leadership through law over institutions' (Trevaskes 2018: 348). This was a significant shift in intent, the institutional ramifications of which were evident to mainland Chinese and international legal scholars. However, critical scholarship such as Trevaskes's that analyse the political intricacies behind 'to govern according to the law' can only be published outside China. Within China, explanations of the formulation's institutional and political importance – its constative value – are monopolised by the Party-state. Moreover, state censorship ensures that no public discussion and scrutiny of the CCP's performance in relation to governing 'according to the law' can occur.

In this regard, what matters most in the formulation's circulation in mainland public culture is its performative value: Xi's frequent mentions of it, in combination with other carefully chosen words, which are then reproduced and cited in countless Party and state publications. What matters is that Xi's words give the impression that 'socialist rule of law' has developed continuously from the 1990s to the 2010s: that, by means of authoritarian control, the story that Xi tells about what is real gets imposed, unchallenged, as what is real.

A higher law is generally implicit in invocations of authority, whether secular or religious, political or cultural. As Hannah Arendt puts it, the idea of 'the law of the land or the constitution' is 'supposed to incarnate the "higher law" from which all laws ultimately derive their authority'

(Arendt 2006:176). Similarly, implicit in the idea of the rule of law is an ideal law, to quote Richard Flathman, 'a law of laws, a law that authorises, sanctifies, makes binding each of the particular laws that gather under the "genre" that the law of laws regulates or constitutes': in short, the very idea of the rule of law projects an ideal, what we might call a hypostatised Rule of Law (Flathman 1994: 312). The problem, however, is that any attempt to articulate this higher law invariably fails, for any such wording is unavoidably contingent on the discursive conventions of its time. The conceit of the 'higher' fails because, as Flathman points out, 'there is no such thing as an ahistorical concept or idea – of law or anything else' (1994: 312).

As with the comparisons drawn earlier between academic discourse and Party discourse, I want to contrast here the rule of law, as a topic of scholarly inquiry outside China, and 'socialist rule of law' as defined and theorised in China. Anglophone scholarship has produced different and often conflicting ways of thinking about the rule of law that are not reducible to the one 'correct' account. As critical surveys of the concept (such as Stewart 2004; Sypnowich 2014; Waldron 2016) demonstrate, there are varieties of liberal and radical arguments, positivist, constructivist and post-structuralist perspectives, that disagree on such basic issues as the extent to which the rule of law is generalisable, the extent to which it is shaped by social and political factors and, indeed, whether it should be regarded (as Marxist, feminist and Critical Legal Studies scholars have argued) as ideological.

These divergent understandings of the rule of law point to an implicit distinction drawn between the rule of law as an ideal and existing laws. Intellectual debate keeps this distinction always in view. Describing the ideal as 'the highest pretensions of that law of laws that is the rule of law' and contrasting it with actual legal systems, Flathman explains the importance of such debate:

> [W]e liberal theorists should expose the historicity and contingency of the rule of law and thereby contest the claim that fidelity to it will banish arbitrariness and indeterminacy from the law . . . [W]e cannot do without standards by which to identify and assess laws, and in much of our thinking and acting, we do and must accept them 'blindly'. But if we recognise, at least in our more self-critical moments, that they inevitably 'disappoint' us, we may loosen their hold on our thinking, may prepare ourselves to think and act against as well as with the law and its messengers/interrupters.
>
> (Flathman 1994: 314)

Cameron Stewart makes a similar point when he writes: 'The rule of law is a fundamental ideological principle of modern Western democracies, and, as such, we are often asked to believe in it with unquestioning acceptance, even though Western states often honour the principle in the breach' (Stewart 2004).

In contrast, 'socialist rule of law' as promulgated by the CCP and elaborated on under its supervision is intolerant of debate, leaving no room for critical perspectives of the kind that Flathman and Stewart recommend. In China, one can neither publicly interrogate the standards used by the Party to identify and assess the laws nor express disappointment in them. This is because, unlike the rule of law, which theorists outside China debate as both an ideal and a set of legal norms and principles, 'socialist rule of law' and 'to govern according to the rule of law' are prescribed *tifa* whose purpose (as CCP publications featuring these terms have shown) is to justify the Party's comprehensive leadership.[10] As Trevaskes suggests in the title of her 2018 article (discussed earlier) on the institutional and policy implications of 'to govern according to the rule of law', the higher law implicit in 'socialist rule of law' is none other than the Party leadership acting as 'A Law unto Itself'.

The promotion of 'socialist rule of law' first gained momentum in October 2014, in a speech that Xi gave to the Party's top leadership, excerpts of which were published in January 2015. The published speech was titled 'Accelerating the establishment of a socialist-rule-of-law nation', with 'socialist rule of law' presented throughout as if it already existed and had become a defining attribute of CCP rule. The essay's first sentence is a subheading that reinforces this idea. Instead of invoking 'socialist rule of law' as an ideal, Xi prescribes an ideal attitude that Party members must adopt toward it: 'With unswerving commitment, take the path of the socialist rule of law with Chinese characteristics' (Xi 2015).[11]

Xi outlined five key aspects of 'socialist rule of law' that must be 'upheld' (*jianchi* [坚持], a favoured verb in Party discourse): the leadership of the CCP; the dominant position of the people; the principle that everyone is equal before the law; the integration of the rule of law and

[10] Ewen Smith's essay in Chapter 4 provides a nuanced account of how the 'rule of law' in post-Maoist China operated first as 'one form of social control among many' and then developed, under Xi, into a doctrine '*subordinate* to Party leadership'.

[11] My translation of Xi's essay differs from the official English translation, 'Accelerating the establishment of socialist rule of law in China', *Qiushi*, 16 March 2015. Available from: http://english.qstheory.cn/2015-03/16/c_1114459319.htm.

rule by virtue; and proceeding from China's unique situation. The formulations he used in 2014 to describe these five aspects were not new: all have served, in previous Party publications, as authoritative post-Maoist *tifa*. What was new was their combination in Xi's speech as an essential posture for achieving the 'acceleration' he called for.

Of these five aspects, Trevaskes observes that 'the integration of the rule of law and rule by virtue' was given a significant institutional boost when the establishment of the National Supervision Commission (NSC) was announced at the 19th quinquennial CCP Congress in October 2017 (Trevaskes 2018: 363–6). The NSC was formed to merge the operations of existing party and state anti-corruption agencies. It authorizes Xi's administration to set the standards of virtue by which to define and implement 'socialist rule of law'. Viewed practically, the NSC represents 'the culmination of Xi's efforts to rebuild party credibility in the wake of the anti-corruption campaign' (Trevaskes 2018: 364). The justification for this new institution (Trevaskes calls it a 'mega-structure mechanism') is couched in terms of achieving the 'organic unification' (*youji tongyi* 有机统 – of 'intra-party law') (as implemented by the CCP's existing disciplinary inspection agencies) with 'state government supervision' (as carried out by anti-corruption government agencies and state prosecution offices) (Trevaskes 2018: 364).

To merge existing Party and state agencies is to initiate an enormous change in the everyday operations of the one-party system, and it is no accident that 'organic unity', a key concept in Marxism-Leninism, was used to justify the change. Marxist-Leninist dialectical materialism involves understanding human social development as progressing through different historical stages to culminate in 'Scientific Socialism' as the highest expression of human society as an 'organic unity'. 'Organic unity' thus offers big-picture (or 'mega-structure') reasoning of the kind required to justify the massive institutional changes announced at the 19th Party Congress in October 2017.[12] One commentator has noted that

[12] The dialectical materialist understanding of history presents nature, society and human consciousness as 'qualitatively different yet organically related' dimensions of reality. Accordingly, human existence develops 'organically', with each stage of social development having 'its own kind of material organisation and special laws of development' and progressing by stages toward the organic unity of 'Scientific Socialism'. My summary here draws on George Novack (writing as William F. Warde), 'Elements of Dialectical Materialism', first published in *Fourth International*, Vol. I, No. 4 (August 1940). Available from: www.marxists.org/archive/novack/works/1940/aug/x01.htm. Antonio Gramsci's reading of historical materialism as a philosophy in which 'the general

'organic unification' was used eight times to describe the Party's key objectives in the 200-minute report that Xi presented on that occasion. Of these eight mentions, four were repetitions of a formulation Xi had used in his October 2014 speech on accelerating 'socialist rule of law' in China: namely, '[we must] organically unify the leadership of the party, the position of the people as masters of the country, and the rule of law' (Li 2017).

This *tifa* invokes Marxist-Leninist 'organic unity' as the higher law (the law of dialectical materialism) authorising the Party to lead and thereby to determine both how the people should become (and see themselves as) the nation's masters and what the rule of law means. In Xi's 2014 speech, he spells out what 'organic unification' entails:

> It is only when governing the nation according to the law is done under the Party's leadership that the rule of law can be strictly enforced and [the ideal of] the people becoming masters of the country can be fully realised. It is only by this means that the rule of law can be systematically advanced throughout the nation and into the life of society.
>
> (Xi 2015)

Repeated citations of this and other statements by Xi in Party and state publications from 2014 onwards have made them familiar to the mainland public. *Tifa* such as 'socialist rule of law' and 'governing the nation according to the law' have acquired a reality-effect through constant reference in the communications of Party and government institutions. (For comparison, consider the reality-effect of such terms as 'key performance indicators' and 'performance targets' that have directed academic governance and practice since the 1990s). By the time that amendments to the Party's Constitution were announced in October 2017, the cumulative weight of repetition had normalised the idea of increased Party control of state institutions. Characteristic of Party discourse, the new statements that had been inserted into the CCP Constitution, such as 'The party exercises overall leadership covering all areas of endeavour in every part of the country', were announced as if they simply ratified what had already become 'reality' (Xinhua 2017).

concepts of history, politics and economics are tied together in an organic unity' has been influential in Anglophone Marxian scholarship and has also gained ground in China since the 2000s. See Antonoio Gramsci, *Prison Notebooks Volume 2*, ed. and trans. Joseph A Buttigieg (New York: Columbia University Press, 1996), 188.

To read the amended 2017 Party Constitution and the creation of the NSC as ostensibly confirming that China is 'accelerating' toward becoming a 'socialist-rule-of-law nation' as Xi had urged three years earlier (to regard what Xi said in 2014 as having become 'true' by 2017) is to make sense through Party ideology. Within China, it has become increasingly difficult for university teachers and students to do otherwise. Since 2013, Xi's administration has imposed bans on the discussion and publication of topics that it perceives as presenting a threat to its own ideology. These include universal values, freedom of the press, civil society, civil rights, judicial independence (or what the Party calls 'Western values') as well as studies of modern China and the CCP, together with social and political commentary that differs from official Party-endorsed accounts. This censorship has been accompanied by a concomitant intensification of Party propaganda, outlined in documents such as the 'Sixteen Suggestions of the Chinese Communist Party on Strengthening Ideological and Political Work among Young Teachers in Higher Education' (CCP 2013) and 'Opinions on Strengthening and Improving Propaganda and Ideological Work in Higher Education under New Circumstances' (CCP Central General Office and State Council of the PRC 2015). Consequently, on mainland university campuses, teaching and research in the humanities have been subjected to tighter control, while the Party's discourse has also become more widely used. Xi has often held up the former Soviet Union as a cautionary example of the failure to strengthen Party ideology. As he put it in a speech to local Party cadres in Henan in 2013:

> The disintegration of a regime often starts in the ideological realm. Once the ideological line of defence is breached, other lines become difficult to defend. Why did the Soviet Union disintegrate? Why did the Communist Party of the Soviet Union collapse? One important reason is that they wavered in their ideals and convictions. Gorbachev said in private that Communist thinking had become obsolete to him. When the spirit of conviction no longer exists, where is the core of a Party and a country? Because of this, wavering ideals and convictions are the most dangerous wavering, a slide of ideals and convictions is the most dangerous slide.
>
> (cited in Qiu Shi 2013b)

Yurchak's study of Soviet discourse in Russia in the 1980s is helpful for understanding increased Party control and ideological education under Xi. Yurchak observed of post-Stalin Soviet discourse that 'the paradox of late socialism stemmed from the fact that the more the immutable forms of the system's authoritative discourse were reproduced everywhere, the more the system was experiencing a profound internal displacement'. By the time that *perestroika* got underway, 'authoritative discourse was imploding and with it the system itself, and the process was irreversible' (2005:283). Xi and his administration are anxious to prevent China's one-party system from experiencing any such internal displacement or implosion. (They have thus dealt swiftly with threats of displacement posed by corruption and dissent.) Party discourse under Xi combines 'immutable forms' or long-standing *tifa* (such as 'organic unification') with newer policy formulations (such as 'to govern according to the law' and 'socialist rule of law'). It features traditional sayings (Xi is fond of quoting from classical Chinese texts) and promotes the Party's message in both colloquial and formal language, adopting a friendly tone in the Party's 'external discourse' and a typically austere diction in 'internal' Party communications (Davies 2017:116–17).[13]

On this point, I want to highlight a growing problem in mainland scholarship of the commingling of CCP propaganda and academic argumentation, and of the challenges that this development poses to academic inquiry in general. Chinese legal scholarship of the 1980s and since has developed along two trajectories: on the one hand, there has been a concerted effort to examine and explicate different aspects of law aimed at strengthening law and the justice system in China under Party-state rule.[14] On the other hand, however, there has also been critical scholarship in defence of constitutionalism aimed at strengthening the rule of law in China, best illustrated by the work of Peking University-based professor of law He Weifang.[15] In recent years, while this latter trajectory has become perilously uncertain, the former trajectory has also narrowed to increasingly converge with Party ideology. Let's take the arguments advanced by two legal academics in China in favour of the implementation of 'socialist rule of law' in China. In defending 'socialist rule of law' as a necessary corrective to flawed understandings of 'the rule of law' in

[13] On Xi's quotations from premodern Chinese texts, see Benjamin Penny, 'Classic Xi Jinping: On Acquiring Moral Character', Geremie R Barmé, Linda Jaivin, and Jeremy Goldkorn, eds. *Shared Destiny: China Story Yearbook 2014* (Canberra: ANU Press, 2015). Available online at: http://press-files.anu.edu.au/downloads/press/p328871/pdf/introduction_forum_penny.pdf.

[14] See, for instance, the accounts of Chinese legal scholarship and practice discussed in Yun Zhao and Michael Ng, eds. *Chinese Legal Reform and the Global Legal Order: Adoption and Adaptation* (Cambridge: Cambridge University Press, 2017).

[15] See He Weifang, *In the Name of Justice: Striving for the Rule of Law in China* (Washington, DC: Brookings Institute, 2012).

China, Jiang Shigong, an influential professor and He's colleague at Peking University Law School, writes:

> Some people argued that strengthening the rule of law meant strengthening the absolute authority of the state system in constitutional and legal terms, and hence advocated the so-called 'realisation of the People's Congress as the highest power', bringing out 'judicial independence' and the judicialisation of the Constitution. They further proposed a debate on the so-called question of 'Party domination' versus 'legal domination', implicitly calling into question the Party's leadership of the state. In addition, the development of the rule of law led to calls for the protection of human rights, and some movements with political demands used the formal development of 'human rights' and 'rule of law' and the notion that the 'rule of law' would lead to 'democracy' to put forth a new strategy leading to 'political democratisation'.
>
> (Jiang 2018)

According to Jiang, it became imperative for the Party leadership to provide its own definition of the rule of law because of these contentions that developed when the concept became widely discussed in China from the 1980s onward. He argues that it was because the construction of China's rule of law had 'gradually [fallen] into the erroneous zone of Western concepts in the process of [people] studying the Western rule of law' that Xi needed to establish a 'Leadership Small Group on Governing the Country According to the Rule of Law'. This leadership approach enabled the Party to select only 'beneficial elements of the Western legal tradition' to incorporate into Chinese law and legal practices, thereby ensuring that the establishment of 'a new Chinese legal system' would occur 'on the basis of the Chinese legal system' (Jiang 2018). Jiang had earlier emphasised (in a much-cited 2009 article, translated and published in English in 2010), that it was important to see the CCP's political legitimacy and the political sovereignty of the Chinese state as resting as much on China's 'unwritten constitution' (comprised of 'the party's constitution, constitutional conventions, constitutional doctrine and constitutional statutes', not to mention selective classical allusions from China's dynastic past) as on the People's Republic of China's (PRC's or China's) written constitution (first enacted in 1954, then revised in 1975, 1978 and 1982). In essence, Jiang claims that CCP-state rule is uniquely suited for China because of

> The special cooperative relationship between the written constitution and the unwritten constitution, between the system of multiparty cooperation under the CCP's leadership and the people's congress system, between

> 'the people' formed on the basis of political ideology and class interests and 'the people' formed on the basis of individual rights, and between the political representatives of the people and the legal representatives of the people. In short, at the heart of China's constitutional regime lies a unique interactive connection between the party and the state.
>
> (Jiang 2010:24)

Ding Xiaodong, an associate professor of law at Renmin University, has contended that Jiang's defence of China as a 'single-party constitutionalist state' is flawed, albeit correctly oriented towards understanding 'the internal logic of the Chinese party-state regime'. Ding notes that by presenting China as having 'an English-like unwritten constitution, which constrains the power of the party and makes China a constitutionalist state', Jiang assumes that law consists of 'positive norms that exist independently of politics and independently of the process by which the norms are identified'. Ding argues that this is an erroneous understanding shared by Western liberal conceptions of the rule of law, in which law is held to be based in 'positive and objective norms' (Ding 2017:323). In Ding's view, norm-based perspectives are fundamentally incommensurate with the CCP's view of law as 'a reflection of the Party's and the people's will' and as 'a form of the Party's and the people's self-discipline'. This is because the CCP sees law as inherently political: something that 'must be constantly affirmed and overseen by the party and the people' (Ding 2017: 324). Accordingly, because 'the party views law as a form of the party's and the people's self-discipline', socialist rule of law should be regarded as a 'project' consisting of 'the party's and the people's effort to discipline themselves' (Ding 2017: 324). Consequently, the only test that the Party must meet (as a 'political leading party, rather than just an elite party or a competitive party like those in a parliamentary system') is whether it 'can continue to provide political momentum to lead the people and represent them in the future' (Ding 2017: 324).

To all intents and purposes, these publications share the qualities of academic writings everywhere. Jiang's argument and Ding's critique of it are reasoned and eloquent, and both authors offer scholarly evidence for their claims. Moreover, Jiang's 2010 article and Ding's 2017 article both appeared in *Modern China*, the same journal that published Trevaskes's article (cited earlier). Outside China, we can certainly read Jiang and Ding as providing academic endorsements of CCP rule that, by virtue of their publication in *Modern China*, have demonstrably satisfied the criteria of peer review. The fact that they treat the CCP as a source of absolute authority does not pose a problem outside China, for we are afforded the intellectual freedom, as Jiang's and Ding's academic peers, to contest their arguments. We may point to the restrictions imposed on academic and judicial autonomy in China or to overwhelming prioritisation of state funding (such as the funding provided by China's largest grant agency, the National Social Sciences Foundation, which is supervised by the CCP's Central Propaganda Department) for 'major research projects' on 'Socialism with Chinese Characteristics' and, more recently, Xi Thought, as a necessary context for reading articles such as Jiang's and Ding's.

Within China, however, there is an increasing number of publications that profess 'trust in the Party' as the purpose of salaried academic work. However, state and self-censorship ensures that this integration of propaganda in academic discourse is never publicly contested. Moreover, when publications that endorse and explain what Xi and his administration mean by 'socialist rule of law' enjoy international peer-reviewed stature, they increase their instructive value within China. They provide academics and graduate students not only with a model as to how to present CCP rule as inherently, or constitutively, correct; they also serve as citational precedents in international academic discourse. This glaring asymmetry between academic work in democratic countries and academic work in China should give us pause.[16]

As academics, the 'authoritative word' (to recall Bakhtin's term) that binds us ideologically is autonomy, which grants the academic freedom we regard as essential to our work. We expect, indeed require, that the arguments we present and those arguments we encounter in the writings of others can and must be thoroughly inspected, dissected and openly interrogated and debated to the most rigorous degree. Autonomy or academic freedom remains for us 'the key legitimising concept of the whole [university] enterprise', no matter how much the ideal continues to be problematic in practice (Menand 1996:4). That this ideal is flawed

[16] Although it is beyond the scope of this book to consider the ramifications of this asymmetry, we should at least ask these questions: How would we measure the quality of pro-Party publications in the audit culture of universities in Australia and the UK? How would we measure the quality of what mainland refereed journals and academic publishers produce, given the growing range of topics that these outlets have deemed 'unsafe'? While reliance on narrow criteria and functional metrics might allow us to avoid facing the difficulties raised by these questions, the difficulties remain and there are no easy answers to these questions, precisely because there is no calculus to determine the degrees of divergence or convergence between universities in and outside China with regard to academic freedom.

in practice presents no impediment to our ideology, for we do not know how to even begin to see academic work as serving a higher goal of state unity, as Jiang and Ding do. Rather, we (outside China) have been trained to approach inquiry as always already intellectually independent and quite removed from any obligation to bow to the state's *Diktat* or serve its interests. Indeed, the 'rituals of ideological recognition' that sustain academic practice would lose their entire motivational force without this foundational presumption of autonomy.

Under Xi Jinping however, the eradication of any such foundational presumption of autonomy in mainland Chinese universities is an essential aspect of ideological strengthening: epistemology or 'theory' takes second place, if it takes any place at all. To defend ideological strengthening, Jiang argues that critical reflection about one-party rule is detrimental to the nation's well-being. In his words,

> As a principled political Party, if the CCP loses the philosophical analytical tools and methods provided by Marxism and Mao Zedong Thought, it will lose the theoretical magic weapon [*lilun fabao* 理论法宝] pointing out the future direction of development and will necessarily lose the values supporting confidence in ideals and the theoretical weapon to consolidate the people's hearts, thus opening the door to a politics of convenience. Once this happens, the market economy's principles of profit and exchange will penetrate the inner realms of the Party, and various forces will 'stalk' government officials and form interest groups to seek political power. They will even attempt to seize the highest power of the Party and state and change the nature of the Party. China will face the danger of repeating the collapse of the former Soviet Union.
>
> (Jiang 2018)

The prospect of Chinese universities functioning as instruments of Party ideology is implicit in Jiang's argument. The fact that Peking University, where Jiang is based, is ranked thirtieth out of 1,000 universities in the 2019 QS World University Rankings, coupled with the growing importance of these rankings in the management and strategic direction of universities internationally, presents us with a serious problem if we are keen to defend autonomy as integral to the very idea of the university. I appreciate that Jiang's defence of Xi Jinping Thought as a 'theoretical magic weapon' is, to some extent, analogous to my description of academic autonomy as a commanding 'authoritative word'. However, the difference is that whereas Jiang exalts Party ideology as a 'theoretical magic weapon' I am urging us to do the opposite: to acknowledge the impact of an 'authoritative word' on us, so that we may afford ourselves some critical distance, however momentary, from the language that binds us, ideologically, to a way of seeing and thinking. In Paul de Man's succinct formulation: 'What we call ideology is precisely the confusion of linguistic with natural reality, of reference with phenomenalism' (de Man 1986:11). J. Hillis Miller's gloss on de Man's wording is worth quoting here:

> 'Phenomenalism' is a word de Man chooses carefully to indicate that he is not talking about 'reality' as it is in itself, but as it appears to our limited senses. Ideology is a confusion of linguistic with natural reality as the latter appears to our eyes, ears, taste and touch.
>
> (Miller 2016: 141–2)

The extent to which Chinese citizens see the world through Party *tifa* remains an open question. Nonetheless, the increasing dominance of Party *tifa* in mainland academic discourse is evident. In China, to claim that 'socialist rule of law' is inexorably right for China and ('Western') rule of law is unavoidably wrong is to enjoy the Party's approval. The triumph of 'socialist rule of law' as a commanding *tifa* in mainland academic and public discourse is as good an indication as any that the Party's 'ideological strengthening' has borne rhetorical fruit and proven effective.

However, suppression of debate and critical reflection on 'socialist rule of law' in China ensures that this derivative concept is incapable of eliciting and inspiring the range of arguments that the originary concept of the rule of law has and continues to enjoy outside China. These arguments that draw our attention to 'the historicity and contingency of the rule of law' have also had the effect of renewing 'the rule of law' as an ideal (Flathman 1994: 314). Whereas the authority of 'socialist rule of law' rests on the Party's hypernormalised discourse under Xi, the authority of the rule of law is inextricable from the ongoing debate it has engendered, for it is productive disagreement that has ensured that this ideal, or 'authoritative word', is never confused with the existing laws of a given time and place. Hence it is not as if 'rule of law' and 'socialist rule of law' can be productively compared, as if the latter were an alternate mode of the former. For reasons of autonomy, they are ultimately incompatible.

References

Althusser, L. 1971. Ideology and ideological state apparatuses: notes towards an investigation. In Ben Brewster, trans., *L. Althusser, Lenin and Philosophy and*

Other Essays. New York: Monthly Review Press, 127–86. Available from: www.marxists.org/reference/archive/althusser/1970/ideology.htm.

Arendt, H. 2006. *On Revolution*. London: Penguin.

Bakhtin, M. 1981. *The Dialogic Imagination: Four Essays by M. M. Bakhtin*, Caryl Emerson and Michael Holquist, trans., Austin and London: University of Texas Press.

Barmé, G. R. 2015. History for the masses. In Jonathan Unger, ed., *Using the Past to Serve the Present: Historiography and Politics in Contemporary China*, London and New York: East Gate Book, Routledge, pp. 260–86.

Batke, J. 2019. Where did the one million figure for detentions in Xinjiang's camps come from? *China File*, 8 January. Available from: www.chinafile.com/reporting-opinion/features/where-did-one-million-figure-detentions-xinjiangs-camps-come.

Birtles, B. 2018. China's president Xi Jinping is pushing a marxist revival – but how communist is it really? *ABC News*, 4 May. Available from: www.abc.net.au/news/2018-05-04/china-xi-jinping-is-pushing-a-marxist-revival/9724720.

Bourdieu, P. 1996. *On Television*, P. P. Ferguson, trans., New York: The New Press.

Brophy, D. 2019. China's uyghur repression. *Jacobin*, 31 May. Available from: www.jacobinmag.com/2018/05/xinjiang-uyghur-china-repression-surveillance-islamophobia.

Brown, K. 2012. The communist party of China and ideology. *China: An International Journal* 10(2), 52–68.

CCP Central Organisation Department, CCP Central Publicity Department, CCP Committee of the Ministry of Education. 2013. Zhonggong 16 tiao yijian jiaqiang gaoxiao qingnian jiaoshi sixiang zhengzhi gongzuo (Sixteen suggestions of the Chinese communist party on strengthening ideological and political work among young teachers in higher education). *People.cn*, 28 May. Available from: http://edu.people.com.cn/n/2013/0528/c1053–21643996.html.

CCP Central Committee General Office and Administrative Office of the State Council, PRC. 2015. Opinions on strengthening and improving propaganda and ideological work in higher education under new circumstances. English translation at *China Copyright and Media*, 19 January, updated 15 February. Available from: https://chinacopyrightandmedia.wordpress.com/2015/01/19/opinions-concerning-further-strengthening-and-improving-propaganda-and-ideology-work-in-higher-education-under-new-circumstances/. (The original text, Guanyu jinyinbu jiaqiang he gaijin xin xingshi xia gaoxiao xuanchuan sixiang gongzuo de yijian, published on *Xinhuanet*, 19 January 2015, is no longer available).

Davies, G. 2017. The language of discipline. In J. Golley, L. Jaivin, and L. Tomba, eds., *China Story Yearbook 2016: Control*. Canberra: ANU Press, pp. 110–29.

de Man, P. 1986. *The Resistance to Theory*. Minneapolis: University of Minnesota Press.

Deng, X. 1982. Opening speech at the twelfth national congress of the communist party of China, 1 September. Available from: http://en.people.cn/dengxp/vol3/text/c1010.html.

Ding, X. 2017. Law according to the Chinese communist party: constitutionalism and socialist rule of law. *Modern China*, 43(2), 321–52.

Fan Wen. 2017. Xi Jinping xishiqi Zhongguo tese shehuizhuyi sixiang de lilun chuangxin (The theoretical innovativeness of xi jinping thought for the new era of socialism with Chinese characteristics). *Renmin wang*, 1 December. Available from: http://theory.people.com.cn/n1/2017/1201/c40531-29680097.html.

Flathman, R. 1994. Liberalism and the suspect enterprise of political institutionalization: the case of the rule of law. *Nomos* 36, 297–327.

Grace, C. 2017. China's Xi Jinping consolidates power with new ideology, BBC News, 20 October. Available from: http://www.bbc.com/news/world-asia-china-41677062.

Jiang, S. 2010. Written and unwritten constitutions: a new approach to the study of constitutional government in China. *Modern China* 36(1), 12–46.

2018. Philosophy and history: interpreting the 'Xi Jinping era' through xi's report to the nineteenth national congress of the CCP. David Ownby, trans. *The China Story*, 11 May. Available from: www.thechinastory.org/cot/jiang-shigong-on-philosophy-and-history-interpreting-the-xi-jinping-era-through-xis-report-to-the-nineteenth-national-congress-of-the-ccp/.

Joseph, W. A. 2014. Ideology and China's political development. In W. A. Joseph, ed., *Politics in China: An Introduction*. Oxford and New York: Oxford University Press, pp. 149–191.

Klages, M. 2017. *Literary Theory: The Complete Guide*. London and New York: Bloomsbury.

Li, Zhao. 2017. Xi Jinping de 'youji tongyi': ni bu dongde bianzheng zhexue (Xi Jinping's 'organic unification': a dialectical materialist philosophy that you don't know about). *Duowei xinwen*, (DW News), 22 October. Available from: http://news.dwnews.com/china/news/2017-10-22/60018878_all.html.

McQuillian, M. 2001. *Paul de Man*. London: Routledge.

Menand, L. 1996. The limits of academic freedom. In Louis Menand, ed. *The Future of Academic Freedom*. Chicago: University of Chicago Press, pp. 3–20.

Miller, J. H. 2016. Reading Paul de Man while falling into cyberspace in the twilight of the anthropocene idols. In T. Cohen, C. Colebrook and J. Hillis Miller, eds., *Twilight of the Anthropocene Idols*. London: Open Humanities Press, pp. 176–194.

Qiu Shi. 2013a. Geming lixiang gao yu tian – xuexi Xi Jinping tongzhi guanyu jianding lixiang xinnian de zhongyao lunshu (Our Revolutionary ideals are higher than heaven: study comrade Xi Jinping's important discussion of the need for making our ideals and faith sturdy). *Qiushi* (Seeking Truth), No. 21, 1 November. Available from: www.qstheory.cn/zxdk/2013/201321/201310/t20131030_284176.htm.

2013b. Geming lixiang gao yu tian (Our revolutionary ideals are higher than heaven). *Qiushi* (Seeking Truth), No. 21, 1 November. Available from: www.qstheory.cn/zxdk/2013/201321/201310/t20131030_284176.htm.

Sorace, C. 2017. *Shaken Authority: China's Communist Party and the 2008 Sichuan Earthquake*. Ithaca and London: Cornell University Press.

Stewart, C. 2004. The rule of law and the tinkerbell effect: theoretical considerations, criticisms and justifications for the rule of law. *Macquarie Law Journal* 4, 135–64. Available from: www.austlii.edu.au/au/journals/MqLawJl/2004/7.html.

Sypnowich, C. 2014. Law and ideology. *Stanford Encyclopedia of Philosophy*, 24 October. Available from: https://plato.stanford.edu/entries/law-ideology/.

Tomba, L. 2014. *The Government Next Door: Neighborhood Politics in Urban China*. Ithaca, NY, and London: Cornell University Press.

Trevaskes, S. 2018. A law unto itself: Chinese communist party leadership and *yifa zhiguo* in the Xi era. *Modern China* 44(4), 347–73.

Vanderklippe, N. 2017. With a new app, China claps until their fingertips ache for president Xi Jinping. *The Globe and Mail*, 19 October. Available from: www.theglobeandmail.com/news/world/with-a-new-app-china-claps-until-their-fingertips-ache-for-president-xi-jin-ping/article36662036/.

Waldron, J. 2016. The rule of law. *Stanford Encyclopedia of Philosophy*, 22 June. Available from: https://plato.stanford.edu/entries/rule-of-law/.

Wang, Jiayu. 2017. Representations of the Chinese communist party's political ideologies in president Xi Jinping's discourse. *Discourse & Society* 28(4), 413–35.

Wasserstrom, J. 2018. From the little red book to the big white one. *The Times Literary Supplement*, 15 May. Available from: www.the-tls.co.uk/articles/public/little-red-book-big-white-one/.

Wendt, A. 1992. Anarchy is what states make of it: the social construction of power politics. *International Organization* 46(2), 391–425.

Xi, Jinping. 2012. Jinjin weirao jianchi he fazhan Zhongguo tese shehuizhuyi, xuexi xuanchuan guanche dang de shiba da jingshen (Firmly surround, uphold and develop socialism with Chinese characteristics: study and propagate the all-encompassing spirit of the eighteenth party congress). *Xinhua she* (Xinhua News Agency), 17 November. Available from: www.gov.cn/ldhd/2012-11/19/content_2269332.htm.

2015. Jiakuai jianshe shehuizhuyi fazhi guojia (Accelerating the establishment of a socialist-rule-of-law nation). *Qiushi* (Seeking Truth), 5 January. Available from: http://theory.people.com.cn/n/2015/0105/c83846–26323829.html.

Xinhua. 2013. Full text of constitution of communist party of China. *News of the Communist Party of China*, 29 March. Available from: http://english.cpc.people.com.cn/206972/206981/8188065.html.

2017. Full text of resolution on amendment to CPC constitution. *Xinhua News*, 24 October. Available from: www.xinhuanet.com/english/2017-10/24/c_136702726.htm.

Yurchak, A. 2005. *Everything Was Forever, until It Was No More: The Last Soviet Generation*. Princeton: Princeton University Press.

4

The Conception of Legality under Xi Jinping

EWAN SMITH*

4.1 Introduction

Since 2013, the Communist Party has underlined Xi Jinping's commitment to legality. Xi began his tenure with a speech to commemorate the Constitution. A few weeks later, he pledged to uphold the Constitution and promote rule of law. Nine months later he convened the first Plenary Session of the Central Committee devoted to rule of law. That meeting ushered in important institutional developments. Since then, Xi has established a new Leading Small Group, the better to govern the country according to law. Party propaganda has amplified these developments. Among other gestures, the Party has designated rule of law a Socialist Core Value and a part of its tetrarchy of 'comprehensive' political priorities.

These might seem like the words and actions of a party committed to upholding rule of law. But rule of law bears a singular meaning for the Party. In a previous study titled 'The Rule of Law Doctrine of the Politburo' (Smith 2018), I asked what the Party means when it says it is 'governing the country according to law' (*yifa zhiguo* 依法治国). That study expanded on the meaning of *yifa zhiguo* – a concept conceived at the Party centre and deployed to indoctrinate Party members – in the period between the 16th Party Congress in 2002 and the Decision of the Fourth Plenum in 2014. This chapter takes a second look at the Party's conception of legality, with a focus on what has happened since then.[1]

* I would like to thank Jesus College, Oxford, the Shaw Foundation and Oxford University's Programme for the Foundations of Law and Constitutional Government, which supported my research. I would also like to thank Samuli Seppänen, Ryan Manuel and the editors of this volume for their helpful comments on this new draft. Finally, I would like to thank the editors of the *China Journal* for permitting these ideas to be reframed in this volume. I restate the credits and disclaimer set out there.

[1] This chapter updates and expands on the argument set out in Smith (2018). That article gives a more fully reasoned and exemplified account of the ideas developed in the Hu period than is set out here.

The Rule of Law Doctrine of the Politburo identifies three important features of the Party's conception of legality and traces them back to the 16th Party Congress through a doctrine developed in collective study sessions under Hu Jintao. First, the article explored the ephemeral and instrumental nature of the rule of law, and how this was connected to a literature on rule by law that we will address presently. Second, the article showed how the Politburo has sought to reconcile *yifa zhiguo* rule of law discourse and the idea of 'Party leadership'. The Politburo had initially considered the possibility that it might have to change its leadership style to accommodate the rule of law. But by 2014, the meaning that the CCP gave to *yifa zhiguo* had changed to accommodate the primacy of Party leadership. Third, it highlighted a shift in rule of law emphasis from governing institutions to governing and disciplining individuals. *Yifa zhiguo* came to be recast as a theory of individual obedience to the Party-state, rather than a theory of how Party power could be rectified through institutions, standards and procedures (Fewsmith 2003). The article concluded that these changes lead us away from the sort of polity that embodies a liberal, rational theory of the rule of law.

This present chapter shifts the frame of reference towards Xi Jinping's theory of the rule of law and sets out three important changes in Party doctrine since 2013. Under Xi, 'Party leadership' comes to enjoy an explicit supremacy, and the demand for obedience extends to non-legal (Party) rules as well as legal ones. In this new doctrine, the rule of law is not merely an ephemeral concept but a superstructural concept, one that yields to China's development needs. Finally, governing the country according to law comes to be relativised, as 'Socialist Rule of Law with Chinese Characteristics': characteristics that render close comparison with foreign ideas nugatory.

This chapter first explains the key moves in the iteration of the Politburo's rule of law doctrine under Hu Jintao. It then turns to the development of those ideas during the tenure of the 18th Central Committee from late 2012 to late 2017, introducing and evaluating new material from study sessions since the 2014 Decision of the Fourth Plenum. It connects Xi's evolving theory of the rule of law with practical developments, including the expansion of China's system of social credit and supervision. Finally, it considers what this development might mean for politics and law in China. In this administration, the emphasis in *zhengfa* falls firmly on the *zheng*.[2]

[2] The word *zhengfa* (政法) connects politics (*zheng* 政) and law (*fa* 法).

4.2 Rule of Law, *Yifa zhiguo* and Doctrine

Section 4.2 restates and expands the account of doctrine set out in the 'Rule of Law Doctrine of the Politburo' (Smith 2018). It briefly describes the idea of rule of law in the Deng era and *yifa zhiguo* rule of law doctrine as it emerged under Jiang Zemin. It then looks at what I refer to as 'doctrine' and how it is possible to trace changes in doctrine over time.

4.2.1 Yifa zhiguo *and Rule of Law*

The rule of law refers to a legal system 'in legally good shape' (Finnis 2011: 270). It describes conditions that enable law to make 'the differences it purports to make' (Barber 2018: 85). It underpins a state in which 'all acts of public power are manifested in such a way that they are capable of being regulated by law' (Dyzenhaus 2012: 247).

The rule of law, in this orthodox sense, should not be confused with mere legality, which obtains in any constitutional order where law is an important instrument of social control. The state *may* choose to clothe public power in law, but law is not the supreme means of social control, and it does not restrain arbitrary government.[3] We often refer to this limited sense of legality as rule by law.

There are various Chinese terms that refer to these ideas, and to similar ones. None can adequately be translated as rule of law without some qualification. They include fazhi (法制 – the legal system), fazhi (法治 – legal governance), yifa zhiguo – (依法治国 – governing the country according to law) and fazhi guojia (法治国家 – the Rechtstaat or State-under-rule-of-law). For present purposes, I am content to use rule of law to translate these ideas, not because this connotes the exact meaning in Chinese but because it is less jarring (and no less accurate) than the available alternatives.

In doing so, I remain mindful of the fact that CCP doctrine does not endorse an orthodox account of rule of law, and there is no suggestion that China enjoys rule of law in this sense. 'Document Number Nine' for example, draws a sharp distinction between a rule of law that reflects the 'concepts, model of governance and systemic designs of a bourgeois state'. It explicitly rejects concepts that 'purport to set the leadership of the Party in opposition to the Constitution and the implementation of the law',

[3] Rule by law takes on a separate meaning in Chinese legalist philosophy, where the point of contrast is not rule of law but rule by man.

including such hallmarks of the rule of law as judicial independence (Central Committee General Office 2014).

Elsewhere (Smith 2019), I describe how the terminology of *yifa zhiguo* emerges in Chinese discourse. In brief, China was more cautious in its inspection of legality than other socialist states. In the 1980s, the glasnost that should have accompanied opening-up and reform was chastened by the fear of 'bourgeois liberalisation'. In many respects, the Communique of the Third Plenum of the 11th Central Committee in 1978 proposed a renewed role for legality in China and said 'there must be laws to follow, these laws must be observed, they must be strictly enforced and law-breakers must be dealt with'.[4] This is certainly a vision of rule by law, but, as Pittman Potter notes, law in this tradition 'is not a limit on the party-state, but rather is a mechanism by which political power is exercised and protected' (Potter 1999: 674). In 1988, Mikhail Gorbachev told the Central Committee that the Soviet Union had to 'move along the path of the creation of a socialist state under the rule of law' (Quigley 1990: fn 1), but it was almost ten years before Jiang Zemin included comparable language in his Work Report to the 15th Party Congress. By western standards, Jiang's 'basic strategy' of governing the country according to law was a heterodox one. We will address it in detail in due course.

The point of this section is to sound a note of caution regarding the meaning and translation of rule of law. In a careful study of the semiotics of these words, Deborah Cao concludes that *fazhi* (and *yifa zhiguo*) 'are used as the semantic equivalent of the English "rule of law" back translated into *fazhi*' (Cao 2001: 236). In turn, '*Fazhi* may signify differently to the Chinese as the rule of law to a Western audience' (Cao 2001: 232). However, the key question for this chapter is not what people think *fazhi*, or *yifa zhiguo*, means but the meaning as construed in Party doctrine and as projected in Party indoctrination. We turn to that question in the next section.

4.2.2 The Doctrine of the Politburo

Ideology is a map of the ideas that we create, project, receive and reproduce when we describe the world around us. To describe an ideology is to describe the locations on the map and the waypoints between

[4] The Chinese terminology for these phrases in the Communique are *youfa keyi, youfabiyi, zhifabiyan, weifabijiu* (有法可依，有法必依，执法必严，违法必究).

them. It is to suggest meanings for the component concepts of a complex of ideas and to suggest how these ideas may relate to one another.

Writing about Soviet law, Bernard Rudden says 'ideology first describes things as they are; this leads to rules; and the latter include a duty to believe the description. Once this is done the system is sewn up' (1978: 189, 204). The problem that Rudden encapsulates – that we see the world in light of the law, but that the law is not a scientific reflection of the world – is not a uniquely Soviet problem. To say that the Soviet Union had 'ideology' whereas Britain, or the United States, does not is to misunderstand what ideology is. But perhaps this is not the 'ideology' that Rudden is referring to. Soviet ideology did not merely refer to thought practice. It also referred to a distinctive political institution. It referred to formal, doctrinal rules – to articles of faith that Marxists were expected to accept.

Doctrine is teaching about belief. It proposes an authoritative account of an ideology. It is anchored in an authoritative discourse about that ideology. Lawyers, communists, Methodists and homeopaths, respectively, share doctrines that bind them into a community of belief. Churches, for example, have laws that establish what constitutes doctrine, who can develop it and what counts as fidelity to doctrine.

The exposition of doctrine is a bounded problem, whereas the exposition of ideology is not. The process of identifying and reproducing legal doctrine, for example, is supposed to be guided by tolerably clear rules that tell lawyers where to find law. When superior courts discuss the rule of law or legislative supremacy, they are not merely suggesting ideas that inferior courts may find appealing. They propose authoritative meanings for concepts and authoritative accounts of the way those concepts relate to one another. We might therefore describe a doctrine – legal, religious, medical or political – as a *practical, working type* of an ideology.

The elaboration of doctrine is not necessarily a philosophical enterprise. There is a difference between an *authoritative* account of an idea and a *justified* account.[5] Doctrine may aspire to avoid contradiction, fallacy, vacuity and other errors, but it does not have to. In fact, so far as it seeks to reconcile conflicting ideas, doctrine is often dissonant. Hence, we should underline the fact that the doctrine set out here makes no attempt to supply a justified account of the rule of law. One important feature of the CCP's account of the rule of law considered below is that it

[5] For an example of the pitfalls of taking a philosophical approach to doctrinal claims, see Fuller (1949).

is idiosyncratically socialist and idiosyncratically Chinese, such that it forbids comparison to larger accounts of the rule of law. Hence we should not mistake doctrine for theory. Andrew Nathan pithily responded to John Bell's claim that Marxism was dead as a motivating ideology in China by saying, 'Marxism is not dead because it lacks conceptual elegance or moral commitment, but precisely because it came to be used as an official "motivating ideology"' (Nathan 2015: 73).

While doctrines share common features, they are also subject to important and subtle differences. Communist Party documents seem harder to parse than, say, US Supreme Court opinions. The doctrine of the US Supreme Court, for example, tends to reify the Court as an actor. This does not prevent us assigning agency to individuals. Aspects of these decisions are written by clerks, but they are attributed to Justices. They are authored in this sense. We speak meaningfully and separately of 'the Warren Court' and 'the Roberts Court' and, in doing so, we highlight the differences between these separate groups,[6] not least because the procedures of the Supreme Court lay plain divisions between dissenting authors (compare Lasser 2004). Some people argue that law is a prediction of what judges do in fact. But if that is what we want to predict, then there are less elliptical ways to do so. The elaboration of doctrine is not lexicography but neither is it biography.

Some statements by the Party Centre are authored in a similar way. As Michael Schoenhals notes, 'speechwriting was where the philosophical, ideological, and political tensions of the leadership got worked out' (1992: 55). Schoenhals intimately describes the work of the personal ghost-writing team of Hu Yaobang, among other ad hoc writing teams. More recently, scholars such as Tsai Wen-Hsuan and Kao Peng-Hsiang have updated this scholarship, drawing on the work of the writing teams at the *People's Daily* (Tsai and Kao 2013).

However, we might question whether it is correct to think of the Politburo – a politically diverse group of officials whose opinions are not authored in this way – as if it were an individual who speaks. Indeed, when we read collectively authored documents, from Decisions of Party plenums to international treaties, the wording may hint at points of conflict. When the wording is clear and unambiguous, it suggests unity. Where issues are presented vaguely or glossed over altogether, it suggests uncertainty. But problems of authorship and attribution are common to

[6] I am grateful to Mary Gallagher for this insight.

many sorts of doctrine, from legal doctrine to papal encyclicals. Doctrines potentially raise philosophical problems of joint and collective intention (Bratman 1999). To read the statements of a group as a doctrine may involve imputing a unity to the group that is not really present. However, we can head off some of these arguments, and defend the method used here, without exploring these interesting objections in full.

A member of the Communist Party who sincerely believes that the views of the Party Centre on constitutional and legal development are profoundly misguided, and who knows that there are others at the Centre who share her views, can nevertheless recite the Party line. Provided one accepts the doctrine for certain public purposes, one can adopt a degree of private, critical distance from these rules. It is possible for Party members to recapitulate the spirit of a Party Congress without assuming that all the delegates agreed about everything. Indeed, a key methodological claim in 'The Rule of Law Doctrine of the Politburo' is that Politburo study sessions are digested in this manner. Members of a group can propagate ideas that teach members of that group what they ought to believe. The authors of those ideas need not share them unanimously, still less uncritically. The indoctrinated can speak meaningfully of 'the opinion of the court' or 'the Party line' without assuming that this opinion is unanimous or even harmonious.

We might therefore adopt a working hypothesis that the way that the Party Centre projects its doctrine is an imperfect, but nevertheless broadly reliable, guide to the political position of the authors of that doctrine and, ultimately, of the senior leadership. It should certainly come as no surprise that the doctrinal changes described here are reflected in wider political, policy and institutional changes described elsewhere in this volume (among others, see Chapters 5 [Lin and Trevaskes], 7 [Li] and 8 [Seppänen]). There is no pretence that this should be read as a guide to the particular beliefs of any member of the senior leadership.

As noted above, the 2018 'Rule of Law Doctrine of the Politburo' paper was an exercise in describing and analysing discourse. It focused not on the way doctrine is disseminated or policed but on the way it is elaborated, and on the way it ought to be construed. We should underline the fact that this is a limited account of doctrine. It was focused on Politburo group study sessions,[7] a type of Politburo meeting that has been reported in the *People's Daily* since the early 2000s (Miller 2004a, 2004b, 2006, 2015).

[7] Renmin Ribao (*People's Daily*) keeps a record of Group Study Sessions at http://politics.people.com.cn/n/2014/1105/c1001-25978576.html.

As such, the method used in the description in Section 4.3 seeks to shed light on how the Party teaches its members about their common beliefs. Changes in the formulation of that discourse are signals to party members, among others, about the scope for acceptable debate about doctrine. As we will see, we can observe changes in positioning over time, and these shifts track some of the broader developments in politics and law addressed in this volume.

4.3 The Politburo Doctrine on the Rule of Law between the 16th and 18th Party Congresses

This section explains the key steps that lead to the conception of the rule of law set out in the introduction. As we noted above, Jiang Zemin's work report to the 15th Party Congress labelled the rule of law as 'the basic strategy employed by the Party in leading the people in running the country' (Jiang 1997). One consequence was that advocates of rule of law could no longer captiously be labelled as right-deviationists or bourgeois liberals, provided they remained within the boundaries established by Party doctrine.[8] In 1999, an amendment put the slogan 'governing the country according to law' and 'building a socialist country under rule of law' into the Constitution.[9]

Designating the rule of law as a 'basic strategy' provided cover for advocates of greater rule of law. However, although the terms sound similar, labelling it a basic strategy did not make rule of law a Cardinal Principle. Jiang's Work Report to the 16th Party Congress, delivered five years later on the eve of Hu Jintao's assumption of power in 2002, co-located the rule of law with the Cardinal Principle of Party leadership (*gongchandang de lingddao* 共产党的领导) and the principle that the people are masters of their own domain (*dang jia zuo zhu* 当家做主).[10] In his address to the 16th Party Congress in 2002, Jiang emphasises the need for Party members to 'know how to integrate the adherence to Party

[8] In the post opening-up and reform era, this point of view is most forcefully expressed in the Resolution of the Sixth Plenum of the Twelfth Central Committee on the 'Guiding Principles for Building a Socialist Society with an Advanced Culture and Ideology' of September 28, 1986.

[9] The amendment added new language to Article 5 of the Constitution: 'The People's Republic of China governs the country according to law and makes it a socialist country under rule of law'.

[10] This is a pseudo democratic principle, which connects the people to the government through the People's Congress System. See Xu (2014).

leadership and the people being the masters of the country with ruling the country by law' (Jiang 2002).

Jiang also said the Party ought to 'combine the rule of law with the rule of virtue'. As we will see, this refrain has been reprised under Xi. For now, it should suffice to note that it was present in Party rule of law doctrine from the beginning. As Delia Lin and Susan Trevaskes note in Chapter 5, the elision of law and virtue is 'a way of asserting that there indeed exist both laws and Party rules [that constrain] individuals' power'. However, 'the Party recognises that this move alone cannot motivate the kind of propriety and discipline required to rule over everything across the nation'. Randall Peerenboom put the point in a different way. He argued that, in the Jiang era, the rule of virtue:

> was subsumed under the Party's general attempt to deal with principal-agent problems and in particular corruption by emphasizing clean and virtuous officials . . . Rule of virtue however was sometimes interpreted as a quasi-Confucian aspirational idea that all legal systems involve both *ren zhi* (rule of man) and *fa zhi* (rule of law).
>
> (Peerenboom 2015: 60)

These themes were iterated in doctrine over the years that followed. Indeed, Hu Jintao's early speeches in collective study sessions adopt an explicitly constitutional view of the power of the Politburo, but one based on the Party Charter rather than the state Constitution (Xinhua 2002). Formally speaking, the Politburo is elected by the Party Congress and is appointed to realise goals established by the Congress, and by the Central Committee.[11] The goals established by that Congress set the general line. For example, establishing a moderately prosperous society was one of these goals. If the establishment of a modern system of law was a necessary step towards that goal, then the Politburo needed to establish a modern legal system.

The Rule of Law Doctrine of the Politburo drew three conclusions about these study sessions conducted from 2002 to 2014. First, *yifa zhiguo* was presented in explicitly instrumental terms. For example, in the twelfth study session the rule of law is described as a 'powerful, legal, systemic guarantee for the ongoing extension of socialism with Chinese characteristics' (Renmin Ribao 2004). However, this was a temporary

[11] Constitution of the Communist Party Article 15. Only the Central Committee of the Party has the power to make decisions on major policies of a nationwide character.

guarantee – a guarantee limited to China's immediate needs under prevailing historical conditions.

The tension between *yifa zhiguo* and other constitutional political principles – a tension to which Jiang Zemin alludes in his Work Report to the 16th Party Congress – is a second important theme. The Rule of Law Doctrine of the Politburo characterised the early study sessions as attempts to reconcile competing values. These new requirements of the rule of law would necessarily affect China's constitutional order, especially the principles of Party leadership and the principle that the people are masters of their own affairs. Both of these are highlighted in the quotation from Jiang's Work Report to the 16th Party Congress, above.

In particular, the Politburo expressed caution about the potential threat that rule of law posed to Party leadership These ideas were presented, initially, as ideas that the Politburo ought to unite and, later, as existing aspects of an 'organic unity'.[12] The first few study sessions suggest that the Party leadership and socialist democracy are both vouchsafed by *yifa zhiguo* – that it is the basis for the other two parts of the trinity. By this account, the institutional reforms that *yifa zhiguo* demands buttress Party leadership and the principle that the people are masters of their own domain. The interesting and important thing is that, in this period, *yifa zhiguo* is not subordinated to Party leadership (or at least not explicitly).

The final theme developed under Hu Jintao was a shift of emphasis, from a vision of *yifa zhiguo* that demands institutional reform to a vision that demands individual compliance. This connects to the language of Rule of Virtue set out at the beginning of this section and to what Randall Peerenboom describes above as the 'principal-agent problem.' First, there is a shift in focus away from institutional development and towards personal moral and spiritual development. Second, there is a shift in focus away from the Party's leadership style and towards the nexus between the Party Centre – the principal – and leading cadres – its agents. Starting in the first Collective Study Session of the 17th Politburo in 2007, Hu Jintao takes aim at cadres who do not follow the law. His speech changes the focus of *yifa zhiguo* from something that rectifies institutions to something that rectifies people.

[12] The most important exposition of this concept in the Chinese Marxist Canon is Mao Zedong's 'On Contradiction', which, alongside 'On Practice', explains how history develops through unities of opposites. These are glossed in Žižek (2007).

The idea of rectifying individuals is an integral part of traditional Chinese political philosophy. Confucians believed a morally righteous state is an edifice built from morally righteous components, including the village and the family, and that the morally righteous man is the atom from which these components are assembled (Legge 1971; Xiao 1979). Marxists believed that the legal order is one dimension of a broader moral landscape. Law does not merely regulate the relationship between the state and the individual, it 'engineer[s] the transformation of the present, imperfect Soviet *Homo juridicus* into a new, ideal man, *Homo Sovieticus* (Osakwe 1985: 4).[13] Chris Osakwe describes this idea:

> The code that perhaps best reflects the theological principles of modem Soviet law is the Moral Code of the Builder of Communism . . . This is not a code of law strictly speaking, but rather a code of moral conduct. It is the highest form of codification of those rules of personal conduct to which the ideal Homo Sovieticus must conform . . . The Moral Code is the nucleus from which the entire system of rules of socialist communal life radiates. It binds all Soviet citizens at all times; it governs both public and private conduct.
>
> (Osakwe 1985: 24–5, 30)

We might note that institutions are comprised of individuals. Even if the CCP is less concerned with building autonomous institutions and more focused on subordinating individuals, the two tasks are connected. *Yifa zhiguo*, by most accounts, requires law to be enforced without favour. However, as Andrew Nathan notes in respect of an earlier period, the doctrine developed under Hu, and now Xi, can lead 'in quite a different direction from constitutionalism – it can lead to the authoritarianism that says that rules and regulations are powerless to enforce good government in the absence of indoctrination or 'thought reform' and such that indoctrination makes constitutions superfluous' (Nathan 1976: 22). We will return to this theme when we consider the development of rule of law under Xi.

This leaves us with three points of focus as we turn in Section 4.4 to the Doctrine of the Politburo under Xi. The first is the characterisation of the rule of law as one form of social control among many, as rule by law rather than rule of law. The second, is the shift in focus from institutions, systems, norms and procedures,[14] and towards the problem of

[13] See also Zinoviev (1986).

[14] This formula is drawn from the Spirit of the 16th Party Congress. See Fewsmith (2003).

compliance, and the impact of the rule of law on cadres rather than individuals. Third is the relationship between rule of law and other ideas in China's constitutional pantheon. Before the 18th Party Congress, the doctrine did not state that rule of law was doctrinally *subordinate* to Party leadership.

4.4 Politburo Doctrine on Rule of Law after the 18th Party Congress

In the period between the 16th Party Congress and the significant constitutional amendments heralded by the 19th Party Congress, the Politburo met about 120 times for a study session, and it has continued to meet since. Fifteen of these sessions address rule of law or a topic closely connected to it. Though the numbers are small, we cannot say that the rule of law has been considered less frequently since Xi Jinping took office. What we can say is that it is less prominent and that it is more likely to be considered together with other, potentially dissonant, ideas. The first topic on the agenda following both the 16th and 17th Party Congresses was the rule of law. Under Xi Jinping, first billing was given to the spirit of the preceding Party Congress.

There have been two other significant changes. The year following the 18th Party Congress in 2012 saw a revision in the Politburo's procedure for collective study. The new procedure replaced academic experts with apparatchiks, at least in sessions that considered politically sensitive topics, including legality and supervision.[15] Xi's first study session on rule of law saw the Politburo briefed by ministerial-level officials from the Legal Affairs Committee of the National People's Congress, the State Council Legislative Affairs Office and government organs of Politics and Law, and since then this pattern has continued.[16]

The change in procedure poses questions of its own. The Politburo did not lose faith in study – the sessions continued – but it appeared to lose

[15] For example, the 14th Study Session of the 18th Politburo – on National Security and Social Stability – was addressed by Wang Yongqing, of the Commission for Political Science and Law.

[16] Subsequent sessions have been addressed by, e.g., Xiao Pei, a ministerially ranked official from the Propaganda Department of the Central Commission for Discipline Inspection (18th PB 24th Session); Ma Senshu, director of the Legal Department of the Central Commission for Discipline Inspection (19th PB 11th Session); and Yu Zhigang, a member of the National People's Congress (NPC) Standing Committee, and its Constitution and Law Committee (19th PB 17th Session).

faith in teaching. Gone was the cautious inspection of ideas from outside that we saw under Hu Jintao. The experts who had previously briefed the Politburo under Hu were not all soft-collar liberals. They were drawn from institutions such as the Central Party School (Smith 2018: fn. 37). It seems unlikely that the change was a simple matter of ensuring political reliability. Hence, we might ask how the Party Centre came to view its evolving relationship with the academy and what it gained by changing the nature of study sessions.

Third, since the 18th Party Congress, the Politburo has tended to consider rule of law under other rubrics, especially those of discipline and intraparty regulation. In a very broad sense, all of these study sessions are concerned with political reform of some sort. But when the Politburo met to consider reform of the government,[17] law cast a shadow over the discussion. For example, the two sessions of the 16th Politburo that consider these themes – the 8th and 27th Sessions – are entitled 'Supporting a Government Culture of Socialist Rule of Law' and 'Administrative Reform and the Economic Legal System'. Indeed, the sole exception we can find in this period was the 17th Session of the 17th Politburo in 2009, which considered the theme 'Building a Service Oriented Government.' As we noted above, under Hu Jintao the themes of institutionalisation, standardisation and proceduralisation were generally framed using the rule of law.

Although earlier rule of law study sessions did evoke disciplinary themes, not one study session under Hu Jintao and Wen Jiabao was framed using supervision, discipline or corruption. This is remarkable, in light of what has happened since the 18th Party Congress. In the 5th Study Session, that Politburo discussed clean government in a session scheduled immediately after the rule of law. Since then, corruption and supervision have been considered about as often as law has. As we will see, the two topics have even been addressed in counterpoint – in sessions that consider anti-corruption laws and regulations, and the rule of law and the rule of virtue. Over the last seven years, Politburo study sessions have been more discipline focused: legality has been addressed alongside, and even in the context of, discipline. On this evidence, we can conclude that legality is a less important frame for political reform than it was under Hu Jintao. Its importance has been diluted by supervision.

[17] Separate concerns apply to Party-building, which usually accounts for three study sessions.

In this section we will also consider how the three themes identified earlier developed under Xi Jinping. Study sessions under Xi have explicitly subordinated *yifa zhiguo* to Party leadership. They have also reinforced the voluntarist approach to rule of law evident after the 17th Party Congress, introducing new language on the connection between law and virtue, and relativising 'socialist' rule of law. The seeds of these developments are evident prior to the Fourth Plenum Decision, but they take root in the doctrine published afterwards.

In the 21st Study Session of the 18th Politburo, Xi Jinping said, 'since the 18th National Congress of the Communist Party of China, the Party Central Committee has . . . maintained a keen focus on building a socialist rule of law system with Chinese characteristics [and on] building a socialist country ruled by law' (Xinhua 2015). There is substance to his claim. The Fourth Plenum of the 18th Central Committee in 2014 was the first plenary meeting to be devoted solely to rule of law, and its Decision is the most authoritative account of the rule of law in the Party canon (CCP Central Committee 2014). However, the ideas in the Decision can also be characterised as a retrenchment of ideas developed under Hu and Jiang.

First, Xi's first speech on the rule of law in 2013 explicitly subordinated *yifa zhiguo* to Party leadership (Renmin Ribao 2013). He said 'we must persist with the organic unity of governing the country according to law, Party leadership and making the people masters of their own affairs, *in order to carry through the program of Party leadership according to law*' (emphasis added). This theme is taken up by the Decision, which inverts the relationship between *yifa zhiguo*, Party leadership and the principle that the people are masters of their own affairs. By that account, Party leadership must 'penetrate into the entire process and all aspects of governing the country according to law'. It is now 'the most fundamental guarantee for socialist rule of law'.

Second, from the outset, Xi's signature initiative was a crackdown on official corruption. He explicitly connects the rule of law to the need for personal rectification. He stressed the need to 'resolutely eliminate illegal interference in the enforcement of the law, resolutely guard against and overcome local and ministerial protectionism, [and] resolutely punish the phenomenon of corruption'. The connection between law and morals served as an important framing device. Xi said 'China should continue to be run both according to law and according to morals. We need to combine the construction of our legal and ethical [systems], to combine autonomy and dependency, and to develop them mutually, so as to create an inseparable connection between rule of law and rule by morals'.

The Decision also echoes the frank language of the first session of the 17th Politburo in 2007, by which the rule of law is concerned not with institutions but with individual obedience to the Party Centre. It recalls the language of the 16th Party Congress – 'institutionalisation, standardisation and proceduralisation' – which is repeated under Hu Jintao.[18] But in this new idiom, it is not the Party that is being institutionalised, standardised and proceduralised, but its membership. The aim is to create 'effective mechanisms so no-one dares to be corrupt, can be corrupt, and wants to be corrupt'.[19] This connects the rule of law and rule by virtue, a connection developed in study sessions under Xi Jinping. Indeed, the Decision explicitly says as much – we must persist 'in integrating governing the country according to law and governing the country according to virtue'.

The Decision also Sinifies Party doctrine on the rule of law. The early study sessions under Hu Jintao might be read as a cautious inspection, a testing of unfamiliar concepts against the relatively solid wall of Party leadership. Hu Jintao's account of the rule of law was forged in a period in which China became more economically and politically embedded in the world, especially post World Trade Organization (WTO) accession (Smith 2018: 47). This partly explains the spirit of cautious inspection evident there. But the Decision establishes a distinctively and explicitly Chinese account of rule of law. Xi repeatedly refers to 'Socialist Rule of Law with Chinese Characteristics'. Like socialism with Chinese characteristics, the effect of the formula is, of course, to deter comparison with accounts of the rule of law that *lack* Chinese characteristics. While some of the indigenous meanings given to rule of law in China are clear, there is no single authoritative and comprehensive account of these Chinese characteristics. Advocates of the rule of law who fail to give due regard to the difference between Chinese and foreign ideas step outside the political boundary established by Party doctrine.

In this way, Xi's nativist vision of 'Socialist Rule of Law with Chinese Characteristics' unpicks a progressive reform under Jiang Zemin, which made it possible to advocate the rule of law without inviting captious

[18] Joseph Fewsmith describes a 'more institutionalized, more formalized, and more procedure-based system' as a key aim of the 16th Party Congress. However, he concludes that this would nevertheless result in 'anything but institutionalization and the development of "inner-Party democracy"' (Fewsmith 2003).

[19] This language originates in Xi (2013). It is reflected in the broader commentary to the Decision.

allegations of bourgeois liberalisation. This nativist turn is carefully formulated in the Decision. Officials are invited to 'learn from beneficial experiences in rule of law abroad', but they 'can absolutely not indiscriminately copy foreign rule of law concepts and models'.

Between the 2014 Decision and the 19th Party Congress in 2017, the Politburo met twice more to discuss rule of law, and it has met three times since. These sessions expand on the themes set out above, and the focus of this final section will be three key extensions: legality is now formally subordinate to Party leadership, discipline is now a foil for legality, and legality is both local and ephemeral.

First, study sessions under Xi Jinping confirm the order of priority for Party leadership and the rule of law memorialised in the Decision. The 21st Session of the 18th Politburo in 2015 considered reform of the judicial system. Party leadership was the 'fundamental guarantee of socialist rule of law' and upholding Party leadership 'is a fundamental feature of China's socialist judicial system and an important political advantage to that system'. In the 17th Session of the 19th Politburo – the most recent prior to publication – Xi lists three important features of China's national system: party leadership, the people as masters of their own domain, and (finally) the rule of law (Xinhua 2019).

Second, they collocate legality and discipline. Indeed, Xi convened a study session that directly addresses the connection between the rule of law and the rule of virtue. In the 37th Session of the 18th Politburo addressing the rule of law and rule by virtue (Renmin Ribao 2016), Xi Jinping notes that the rule of law and the rule of virtue 'supplement each other, complement each other and bring out the best in each other'. This amalgamation of rule of law with wider non-legal standards is explicitly cited as a 'characteristic' that makes China's indigenous theory of the rule of law different to its Western counterpart: 'The path that we follow is the road to socialist rule of law with Chinese characteristics. A distinctive feature of this road is the way in which it combines ruling the country according to law with ruling the country according to virtue'.

In that session Xi enjoins 'the legislature, executive and judiciary' to 'embody the requirements of socialist morality' and stresses that 'we need to allow socialist core values to permeate legislation, application and enforcement of law'. The effect of the elision of law and virtue is to erode the distinction between lawful and unlawful behaviour. In the 24th Session of the 18th Politburo Xi says the 'cage of anti-corruption laws and regulations is closely welded. It is connected fore and aft, left and right, above and below. It is an integrated system' (Xinhua 2015: 2).

So too, in the 37th Session the question was not whether morality permeates law but whether it can transcend law, or supplant law:

> We must clarify disciplinary measures for immoral behaviour ... [and] strengthen the way we rectify immoral behaviour that attracts public opprobrium ... We must improve the reward mechanisms for law-abiding and honesty and disciplinary mechanisms for law-breaking and bad faith, so that people do not dare to act in bad faith and cannot act in bad faith. For those who forsake principle for profit, and who engage in illegal behaviour to propagate falsehood, we step up law enforcement and let those who break law or morals be punished and pay the price.
>
> (Renmin Ribao 2016)

This is not empty theology. Xi has a specific non-legal form of social control already in mind. He identifies 'untrustworthy' behaviour as the main problem and says, 'we must establish a social credit system covering all of society with all deliberate speed'. There is, however, a wider agenda in play here. It is interesting that Xi refers almost interchangeably to legal and non-legal standards in this passage. This reflects a shift away from legality – from the use of law as a pre-eminent tool of social control – and towards a model in which law exists alongside other techniques of social control, especially discipline (Potter 2003). That shift includes social credit, but it also includes other forms of supervisory justice. Whether you behave unlawfully, or just badly, the state will take action against you.

We do also see supervision discussed in terms of rule of law. In the 11th Session of the 19th Politburo Xi Jinping emphasised:

> that the initial intention for deepening reform of the state supervision system was to extend oversight over holders of public office and public power ... The intention was to subject the operation of public power to the rule of law, eliminate gaps in oversight, and cabin arbitrary power ... It is necessary to ensure that departments, organisations and individuals charged with public power ... operate strictly within the scope of the constitution and the law and never to allow any organisation or individual to exercise extra-legal prerogatives.
>
> (Xinhua 2018)

In the 21st Study Session of the 18th Politburo Xi stressed that we must 'take the bull by the horns', which means holding judges responsible for their decisions. Xi proposes to cabin judicial power 'under the supervision of the law, society and public opinion'. We might be inclined to view this elision of legality and discipline as a step towards greater rule of law (albeit a nominal one). However, this is an eccentric conception of legality, a legality where law is often superfluous.

One of the distinctive features of socialist legality is its relative indifference to the form in which state power is exercised. Chris Osakwe said even though both socialist legality and rule of law subscribe to the idea of the supremacy of law, 'they hold different views of what is law' (Osakwe 1987: 1265),[20] meaning a much wider view of what might count as law. A. Y. Vyshinsky, the most prominent legal ideologue of the Stalinist era, described law not only as the totality of 'the rules of conduct ... established in legal order' but also 'of customs and rules of community life sanctioned by state authority – their application being guaranteed by the compulsive force of the state' (Vyshinsky 1948: 50).[21] The elision of the law and virtue arguably extends the concept of the rule of law to include rules and standards that would not universally be described as legal.

Finally, Xi presents rule of law as something that is both instrumental and ephemeral. In his Explanation of the Decision, Xi underlines why the *yifa zhiguo* is important:

> the 16th Party Congress put forward that we ... must organically integrate persisting in the leadership of the Party, the people mastering their own affairs, and governing the country in accordance with law. The 17th Party Congress pointed out that governing the country according to law is a fundamental requirement of socialist democratic politics ... The 18th Party Congress put forward that the rule of law is a basic method to govern the country.

Yifa zhiguo, by this account, is a necessary step towards non-negotiable objectives established by several Party Congresses. Xi noted in the Explanation, it is a 'fundamental requirement' for 'safeguarding social harmony and stability', 'guaranteeing the long-term peace and order of the Party and the country' and promoting 'the sustained and healthy development of our country's economy and society'. But the mission is more concrete than this. The Party must implement rule of law 'to realise the series of strategic deployments made at the 18th Party Congress and the Third Plenum of the 18th Party Congress' and 'to

[20] The claim is attributed to L. Garlicki: 'Constitutional and Administrative Courts as Custodians of the State Constitutions – The Experience of East European Countries', cited in Osakwe (1987).

[21] Not all prominent Soviet jurists of the revolutionary generation thought about law in this way. See especially Tay and Kamenka (1970).

comprehensively construct a moderately well-off society' (*quanmian jiancheng xiaokang shehui* 全面建成小康社会).

However, Xi also presents *yifa zhiguo* as ephemeral in a new way. He says, 'as superstructure, the Constitution must adapt to changes in the economic base'. This echoes language in the 21st Study Session of the 18th Politburo in 2015, which describes the judicial system as 'an important part of the superstructure'. In Marxist doctrine, law, along with all other forms of ideology, ultimately reflects the material basis for economic relations. Legal ideas – including the constitution itself – evolve as these underlying relations evolve. In this session, Xi expands on this idea. The Constitution 'must follow the ceaseless drive for development – a development practice in which the Party leads the People in building socialism with Chinese characteristics'.

These sessions repeat the nativist and relativistic tone of the Decision. In the most recent study session prior to publication – the 17th – Xi describes this trinity of political values as 'rooted in profound historical and cultural traditions accumulated by the Chinese nation over the course of more than 5,000 years of civilisation'. He underlines that this qualified sort of legality is a hallmark of China's national system. In the 21st Session of the 18th Politburo Xi said China's judicial system is adapted to China's national situation, and any reform must take place in accordance with that national situation. When referring to the "national situation" he uses the same turn of phrase Hu Jintao uses in the 40th Session of the 16th Politburo (*guoqing* 国情). Xi adds that reform must be compatible with 'China's fundamental political system'.

In this discourse, the Constitution is not merely subordinated to Party leadership but to economic development. The language recalls constitutional scholar Xi Zhong's theory of benign violations. Twenty years ago, Xi suggested that the CCP might depart from the Constitution under two circumstances: to further the needs of economic development and to further the fundamental interests of the people (Xi Zhong 1998). A violation of the Constitution in furtherance of the 'ceaseless drive for development' would be a 'benign violation'. Xi Zhong's theory has been criticised as a sublimation of the rules in the Constitution to threadbare priorities, priorities that are determined with conclusive authority by the CCP (Clarke 2003).

A key argument set out in Smith (2018) is that the Decision of the Fourth Plenum can be viewed as essentially continuous with Party doctrine on rule of law under Hu Jintao. I expand on this view in a subsequent paper (Smith 2019), taking in a broader waterfront of Party documents and critical commentary. This section below serves to highlight what has changed under Xi. The changes are subtle, but they are important. *Yifa zhiguo* has been explicitly subordinated to Party leadership. The voluntarist turn that begins under Hu Jintao, a turn that shifts the lens onto leading cadres, rather than Party institutions, connects with an earlier discourse of rule of virtue. In Xi's account, set out above, legal and disciplinary sanctions can be used interchangeably to 'punish' people who attract 'public opprobrium'. Finally, while law has always been discussed instrumentally in Party doctrine, in Xi's account, law is superstructure. It reflects basic economic relations and it yields to the demands of economic development. Those demands are essentially political.

4.5 Conclusion

'The Rule of Law Doctrine of the Politburo' considered three ways in which the conclusions of the Fourth Plenum were underpinned by study session discussions ten years prior to that Decision. First, 'governing the country according to law', or *yifa zhiguo*, was not presented as something valuable for its own sake but for the sake of other things. Second, that vision of *yifa zhiguo* presented in Politburo meetings for discussion began as an idea that regulates institutions, then evolved over the decade into an idea that regulates people. Third, *yifa zhiguo* began as a concept which potentially challenged the contemporary doctrine of Party leadership. Over time, it became a concept that was subjected to Party leadership.

These trends in Party doctrine have been recapitulated and entrenched under Xi Jinping. First, the Party has created a doctrinal hierarchy which subordinates *yifa zhiguo* to Party leadership. According to the Decision, Party leadership 'is ... the most fundamental guarantee for socialist rule of law', and it must 'penetrate into the entire process and all aspects of ruling the country according to law'. Second, there has been a shift in emphasis from institutional reform to individual obedience, with a newfound focus on the connection between law and virtue. It is not just that the rule of law is presented as a demand for compliance; it is not even presented as a demand for compliance *with law*. The rule of law, in this aspect, rectifies both unlawful and immoral behaviour. It demands that those who break law or morals be punished and pay the price.

These sessions also leave the impression that the 'basic strategy' of governing the country according to law might be more tactical than strategic. Xi restates the classical Marxist view that the judicial system – and, indeed, the constitution – are merely superstructure that reflects basic economic changes. Under Xi, *yifa zhiguo* is explicitly an instrument by which China's leadership can pursue its ends. Not only this, the rule of law 'must yield' to these more immediate requirements, including the demands of development. Finally, Xi reformulates governing the country according to law as a component of Socialist Rule of Law with Chinese Characteristics. He emphasises the need for rule of law to cleave to China's 'national situation' and to reflect China's 'fundamental political system'. This native vision of rule of law bends to superior fundamental principles, as it did before it was labelled a basic strategy.

The identity of the CCP makes and is made by the language used to construct, maintain and direct its ideology. Whereas the post-2002 *yifa zhiguo* doctrine began as a cautious move towards a developing international order, it also moved the Party away from positions it held in the past, indeed from what it was in the past. The shifts in Xi-era doctrine set out here prefigure the larger shifts in policy considered elsewhere in this volume, notably the advent of the Supervision Commission and social credit. These changes in doctrine, and perhaps in ideology also, reconnect the Xi-era with an earlier Mao-era tradition, a tradition in which both law and rule-of-law are cabined by Party leadership.

References

Barber, N. 2018. *The Principles of the Constitution*. Oxford: Oxford University Press.

Bratman, M. 1999. *Faces of Intention*. Cambridge: Cambridge University Press.

Cao, D. 2001. 'Fazhi vs/and/or rule of law?' *International Journal for the Semiotics of Law* 14, 223–47.

CCP 2013. CCP central committee general office communiqué on the current state of the ideological sphere. 22 April. Available from: www.chinafile.com/document-9-chinafile-translation.

2014. CCP central committee decision concerning some major questions in comprehensively moving ruling the country according to law forward. 28 October 2014. Available from: https://chinacopyrightandmedia.wordpress.com/2014/10/28/ccp-central-committee-decision-concerning-some-major-questions-in-comprehensively-moving-governing-the-country-according-to- ?the-law-forward/.

Clarke, D. 2003. 'Puzzling observations on Chinese law – when is a riddle just a mistake?' In C. S. Hsu, ed., *Understanding China's Legal System: Essays in Honor of Jerome A. Cohen*. New York: New York University, pp. 93–121.

Dyzenhaus, D. 2012. Constitutionalism in an old key: legality and constituent power. *Global Constitutionalism* 229–60.

2015. The concept of the rule-of-law state in Carl Schmitt's verfassungslehre. In J. Meierhenrich and O. Simons, eds., *The Oxford Handbook of Carl Schmitt*. Oxford: Oxford University Press.

Fewsmith, J. 2003. The sixteenth national party congress: the succession that didn't happen. *The China Quarterly* 173 (1), 1–16.

Finnis, J. 2011. *Natural Law and Natural Rights*. Oxford: Oxford University Press.

Humanae Vitae, Encyclical Letter of Paul VI of 25 July, 1968, Part II – 'Doctrinal Principles'.

Jiang, Zemin. 1997. Work report to the 15th national congress of the communist party of China, issued 12 September. Available from: www.bjreview.com.cn/document/txt/2011-03/25/content_363499.htm.

2002. Work report to the 16th national congress of the communist party of China, issued 18 November. Available from: www.fmprc.gov.cn/mfa_eng/topics_665678/3698_665962/t18872.shtml.

Lasser, M. 2004. *Judicial Deliberations – A Comparative Analysis of Judicial Transparency and Legitimacy*. Oxford: Oxford University Press.

Legge, J. 1971. *Confucian Analects, The Great Learning, and The Doctrine of the Mean*. London: Dover Publications.

Li, Buyun. 2003. *Guanyu Fazhi yu Fazhi de Qubie, Cong Fazhi dao Fazhi Ershinian Gai Yizi*. Fali Tansuo (Jurisprudential Explorations). Changsha: Hunan Publishing Company.

Fuller, L. 1949. Pashukanis and Vyshinsky: a study in the development of Marxian legal theory. *Michigan Law Review* 47, 1157–66.

Lubman, S. 1999. *Bird in a Cage: Legal Reform in China after Mao*. Stanford: Stanford University Press.

Miller, H. L. 2004. Hu Jintao and the party politburo. *China Leadership Monitor* 9. Available from: http://media.hoover.org/sites/default/files/documents/clm9_lm.pdf.

Miller, A. 2004. Party Politburo processes under Hu Jintao. *China Leadership Monitor* 11. Available from: www.hoover.org/research/party-politburo-processes-under-hu-jintao.

2015. Politburo processes under Xi. *China Leadership Monitor* 47. Available from: www.hoover.org/research/politburo-processes-under-xi-jinping.

Miller, A. L. 2006. More already on Politburo procedures under Hu Jintao. *China Leadership Monitor* 17. Available from: www.hoover.org/research/more-already-politburo-procedures-under-hu-jintao.

Nathan, A. 1976. *Peking Politics, 1918–1923: Factionalism and the Failure of Constitutionalism*. Berkeley and Los Angeles: University of California Press.

2015. Beijing bull, the bogus China model. *The National Interest*, 22 October. Available from: https://nationalinterest.org/feature/beijing-bull-the-bogus-china-model-14107.

Osakwe, C. 1985. The four images of soviet law: a philosophical analysis of the soviet legal system. *Texas International Law Journal* 21, 1–37.
1987. The greening of socialist law as an academic discipline, *Tulane Law Review* 61(6), 1257–78.
Peerenboom, R. 2002. *China's Long March toward Rule of Law* Cambridge: Cambridge University Press.
2015. Fly high the banner of socialist rule of law with Chinese characteristics! *Hague Journal on the Rule of Law* 7, 49–74.
Potter, P. 1999. The Chinese legal system: continuing commitment to the primacy of state power. *The China Quarterly* 159, 673–83.
2003. *From Leninist Discipline to Socialist Legalism: Peng Zhen on Law and Political Authority in the PRC.* Stanford: Stanford University Press.
Quigley, J., The Soviet Union as a state under the rule of law: an overview. *Cornell International Law Journal* 23, 205.
Renmin Ribao. 2004. Hu Jintao zai zhonggong zhongyang dishierci jiti xuexi shi qiangdiao: yifa zhiguo, yifa zhizheng (At the 12th politburo study session, Hu Jintao emphasises: govern the country and the executive according to law). *Renmin ribao* (People's Daily), 28 April.
2013. Xi Jingping zhuchi zhonggong zhongyang zhengzhiju disici jiti xuexi (Xi Jinping chairs the fourth politburo collective study session). *Renmin ribao* (People's Daily), 25 February.
2016. Jianchi yifa zhiguo he yide zhiguo xiang jihe, tuijin guojia zhili tixi he zhili nengli xiandaihua (Xi Jinping: persist in combining governing the country according to law, and according to morals, push forward the modernisation of the system of national governance, and of our national governing capacity). *Renmin ribao* (People's Daily), 11 December.
Rudden, B. 1978. Law and ideology in the Soviet Union. *Current Legal Problems* 31(1), 189–205.
Schoenhals, M. 1992. *Doing Things with Words in Chinese Politics: Five Studies.* London and Los Angeles: University of California Press.
Schurmann, F. 1986. *Ideology and Organization in Communist China.* London and Los Angeles: University of California Press.
SEC Compliance & Disclosure Interpretations of 4 April 2018, Question 102.09.
Smith, E. 2018. The rule of law doctrine of the politburo. *The China Journal* 79, 40–61.
2019. The rule of law in party documents. *China Law and Society Review* 4, 41–69.
Stalnaker, R. 2014. In A. Perry, ed., The internal aspect of social rules. *35 OJLS* 283 at note 14.
Tay, A. and Kamenka, E. 1970. The life and afterlife of a bolshevik jurist. *Problems of Communism* 19, 72–9.
Tsai, W.-H. and Kao, P.-H. 2013. Secret codes of political propaganda: the unknown system of writing teams. *The China Quarterly* 214, 394–410.

Unger, R. 1976. *Law in Modern Society*. New York: Macmillan.
Vyshinsky, A. 1948. *The Law of the Soviet State*. New York: Macmillan.
Xi, Jinping. 2013. Address to the second plenary meeting of the central discipline and inspection commission of the eighteenth central committee. Xinhua, 22 January.
Xi, Zhong. 1998. Dui liangxing weixian de fansi (Reflections on benign violations of the constitution. Pinyin (*Legal Science Review*) 6, 26–33.
Xiao, K.-C. 1979. *A History of Chinese Political Thought*. Princeton: Princeton University Press.
Xinhua. 2002, Jiaqiang lingdao ganbu xuexi. Tigao zhizheng xingguo benling (Strengthen study among leading cadres, enhance our capacity for governance and national revival), 26 December.
2011. Wu Bangguo 'Qi queli' yu 'wu bu' gao miaoshu zhongguo tese zhengzhi wenming (Wu Bangguo: The 'seven establishes' and 'five nos' describe a political culture with Chinese characteristics), 11 March.
2015. Xi Jinping: yi tigao sifa gongxinli wei genben chidu. jianding buyi shenhua sifa tizhi gaige (Xi Jinping: We must resolutely engage in profound reform of the judicial system, making higher public confidence in the judiciary the yardstick), 25 March.
2015. Xi Jinping: jiaqiang fubai changlian fagui zhidu jianshe, rang fagui zhidu de liliang chongfen shifang (Xi Jinping: strengthen the system of anti-corruption laws and regulations, fully release the power of law and regulation), 27 June.
2017. Zui fao fa Zhou Qiang: Yao ganyu xiang xifang 'sifaduli' deng cuowu sichao liangjian (SPC's Zhou Qiang: We must dare to draw out weapon against erroneous western ideas like judicial independence), 14 January.
2018. Xi Jinping zai zhonggong zhongyang zhengzhiju di shiyici jiti xuexi shi qiangdiao: Chixu shenhua guojia jiancha tizhi gaige tuijin fanfubai gongzuo fazhihua guifanhua (At the eleventh politburo study session Xi Jinping emphasises: persist in profound reform of the supervision system, push forward the subjection of anti-corruption work to law and to norms), 14 December.
2019. Xi Jinping zai zhongyang zhengzhiju di shiqici jiti xuexi shi qiangdiao jixu yanzhe dang he renmin kaipi de zhengque daolv qianjin, buduan tuijin guojia zhili tixi he zhili nengli xiandaihua (At the 17th politburo collective study session, Xi Jinping emphasizes: carry on along the road of the party and the people, push forward the modernisation of our governance system and governing capacity), 24 September.
Xu, Xianming. 2014. Jianchi he fazhan dang jia zuo zhu de hao zhidu (Uphold and develop a good system: the people as masters of their own affairs). *Qiushi* (Seeking Truth) 19.
Zinoviev, A. 1986. *Homo Sovieticus*. London: Paladin.
Žižek, S. 2007. *On Practice and Contradiction*. London: Verso.

5

Law–Morality Ideology in the Xi Jinping Era

DELIA LIN AND SUSAN TREVASKES

5.1 Introduction

In October 2017 the Chinese Communist Party (CCP or Party) amended the Party Constitution to add the claim that 'the Party leads over everything' (Gan 2017). In line with this claim, it amended the state Constitution's Article 1, adding the assertion that: 'The leadership of the Chinese Communist Party is the defining feature of socialism with Chinese characteristics.' This chapter examines the Party's attempts to create discursive coherence around the claim of its leadership over everything in the Xi Jinping era. In doing so, it looks at the elevated political importance that the Xi leadership has bestowed on the concept of 'governing the country by moral virtue' (*yide zhiguo* 以德治国). We are particularly interested in how *yide zhiguo* is linked to two other strategic narratives: the newly espoused Socialist Core Values and the Party's longstanding rule of law governance strategy of 'governing the nation according to law' (*yifa zhiguo* 依法治国). *Yifa zhiguo* rule of law discourse has been central to the ideological discourse of governance in China since the mid-1990s. But since 2014, the Xi Jinping administration's strategic vision for sustained Party leadership over all state affairs means that *yifa zhiguo* has taken on a new ideological life. Under Xi, *yifa zhiguo* is no longer merely about promoting law-based governance. It is about law-based governance that requires Party primacy over the law (Trevaskes 2018).

The realm over which the Party explicitly says it leads – that is, everything, including all aspects of law and governance – opens up questions of constraint on this ubiquitous power. What constrains individual Party-state members from abusing their power if the law does not and cannot exist outside of CCP powers? The CCP's solution is to call for 'iron self-discipline' (*tie de jilü* 铁的纪律) to enable 'the Party to constrain the Party itself' (*dang yao guan dang* 党要管党) (Seeking Truth 2017). Since the law is not above the Party, it alone is insufficient to create a control mechanism for individuals. Another entity, that is, moral rules, must act, with law, to ensure conformity and self-discipline. Party theorists now attach a heightened significance to an individual's ability to draw on their moral values to constrain their behaviour. We see this style of governance at work in the newly created social credit system (Knight Chapter 9). This system amounts to a form of morality-building technology that punishes undisciplined behaviour by state officials and ordinary citizens (State Council 2019) and encourages individuals to 'regulate' themselves – more self-consciously check and discipline themselves by monitoring and correcting their own moral compass settings. This and other developments to build a comprehensively 'transparent' society in China through AI surveillance technology have created a greater urgency for the Party to explain to their members, and to society at large, the dynamic relationship between law and morality as dual power constrainers. An investigation of Party rule of law discourse in recent years reveals the pivotal role that morality is expected to play in disciplining individual behaviour and constraining power.

In this chapter we argue that moral values and the law–morality amalgam embedded in the Confucian and Legalist traditions have an integral part to play in the ideological makeup of *yifa zhiguo* in this era of unequivocal commitment to the absolute supremacy of Party leadership. Xi Jinping stresses that '[T]here is profound wisdom and resources embedded in the Chinese ancient rule by law system. The Chinese legal family [*zhonghua faxi* 中华法系] is unique and independent among the major legal families of the world', including civil law and common law systems (Xi 2015). Through the ideological cementing of the traditional law–morality amalgam, Xi Jinping's Chinese Socialist Rule of Law for the New Era endeavours to revive the traditional political idea of the state 'as an intrinsically moral institution that is capable of delivering justice in perfect harmony with unitary collective interests' (Rosenzweig 2017: 27).

In this chapter, we focus on how the elevated supremacy of Party leadership goes hand in glove with an increasing emphasis on governing the country by moral virtue in shaping the architecture of the Chinese socialist rule of law for the new era. We do so from three perspectives. First, we examine the shift in the Party's 'language of the law' towards a pronounced supremacy of Party leadership in the Xi Jinping era and the idea that the law contains intrinsic moral qualities. Second, we examine the shifting discourses of governing the country by moral virtue and Socialist Core Values in the context of strengthening centralised Party leadership. Third and finally, we address the use of Confucian and

Legalist legacies of morality politics and centralised power, which provides further discursive lucidity to the 'Party leads over everything' claim in Xi Jinping's New Era.

5.2 The Discourse of Party Supremacy and the Intrinsic Moral Quality of Law

That morality is now on centre stage of the Party's politico-legal discourse is in no doubt. On 7 May 2018 the CCP Central Committee announced a plan to 'fully incorporate Socialist Core Values into all legislation' in the next five to ten years, claiming the integration of *yifa zhiguo* and *yide zhiguo* to be the most distinct feature of the China-style socialist rule of law (Xinhua News Agency 2018a). A document titled 'The Central Committee of the Communist Party of China Plan to Integrate Socialist Core Values into Rule of Law Construction and Legislation and Revision of the Law' was announced in the *People's Daily* the next day, which proclaimed that:

> Integrating socialist core values into the legislative system ensures a clear value orientation at the top source of power. We will comprehensively advance the reform of the judicial system with justice system accountability as the core, improve the judicial management system and functional mechanisms of judicial power and strive to enable the people to feel a sense of fairness and justice in every judicial case.
>
> (People's Daily 2018)

The Party leadership is today communicating to its citizens a model of best-practice governance that offers a clear alternative to the Western–liberal model of governmental accountability. Rather than continue to play a reactive or defensive propaganda game with the West on the issue of values and human rights, the Party has changed its strategy by much more confidently asserting its alternative vision of good governance. This alternative version entails an assumption that in China effective governance does not need dispersed power arrangements and independent checks and balances. Rather, it requires strong and virtuous Party supervision and leadership over all aspects of decision-making across the state. To begin our discussion of how Party discourse-builders have created discursive coherence around the role of its claimed virtuous leadership, we need to first outline a number of new claims about the Party's relationship to the law. These claims are discursive building blocks that, when assembled, fit together to make rhetorical sense of the claim that

Xi's 'Party rules over everything' governance-style is what is best for China and its quest for national rejuvenation.

5.2.1 *Yifa zhiguo* and Party Leadership

In his speech on 4 March 2018 to the minor Party representatives attending the 13th Chinese People's Political Consultative Conference, Xi Jinping coined a term to refer to the Party-state system, calling it a 'new-style political Party system' (*xinxing zhengdang zhidu* 新型政党制度). This new system features the Party's leadership itself as the core mechanism of accountability and supervision of state power. He described the Party-state led by the CCP as an entity that grows out of 'the Chinese soil', is capable of 'truly, widely and sustainably representing and realising the fundamental interests of the broad masses of the people' and hence is able to deliver 'wider and more effective democracy' than the 'old-style' multi-party system in the West (Xinhua Net 2018). Core to the new-style political Party system is a comprehensive integration of Party and state 'through all processes of the law', the ideological underpinnings of which have their origins in the Decision of the Fourth Plenum of the 18th Party Congress in October 2014 (hereinafter the 2014 Decision).

The 2014 Decision is the first in the history of the People's Republic of China (PRC or China) to focus exclusively on *yifa zhiguo*. The Decision is also a watershed moment in the history of Party theorising concerning the rule of law in China. It is the touchstone document that has opened the doors to reimagining the concept of rule of law in terms of Party leadership and not merely in terms of state power. Three statements in the Fourth Plenum document are particularly instructive in this regard. The first relates to the newly espoused idea of incorporating intraparty regulations as part of the empire of what is imagined as 'rule of law' in China. The 2014 Decision states:

> Intra-party regulations are an important basis for managing and governing the Party as well as a powerful guarantee for building a socialist rule of law state. The Party must . . . pay attention to linking and coordinating intra-Party regulations with state laws.
>
> (China Law Translation 2014)

A second statement in the Decision reimagines the Party's conception of the function of *yifa zhiguo*. It states: 'Party leadership must be implemented *across the entire process* of governing the country according to law' (*ba dang de lingdao guanche dao yifa zhiguo quanguocheng* 把党的领导贯彻到依法治国全过程) (China Law Translation 2014). This is the definitive statement used by the Party to claim that not merely 'law' but *yifa zhiguo* in its ideological entirety has become the actual conduit through which the Party leads in all aspects of state governance (Trevaskes 2018).

Bringing together the logic of these two statements above – one on intraparty rule of law and the other on the process by which the Party exercises its leadership over all Party and state power – is a third statement that rationalises the relationship between the Party and the law. It is the assertion that 'the Party's leadership and socialist rule of law are compatible' (*dang de lingdao he shehui zhuyi fazhi shi yizhi de* 党的领导和社会主义法治是一致的) (China Law Translation 2014). Since 2014 legal scholars in China have been increasingly talking up the link between rule of law and Party leadership. For instance, Zhang Xiaojun explains that rule of law and intraparty disciplinary rules 'work in harmony and are mutually reinforcing, integrating the leadership of the CPC and the rule of law into the modern socialist legal practice' (2019:10).

Making the claim that 'the Party leads over everything', including the law, requires ideological justification to explain how key power relations in society – namely the law, the Party and the people it represents – are configured. As we explain below, a key discursive building block in creating a conceptual link between these three entities is the term 'benevolent laws' (*liangfa* 良法). In Section 5.2.2 we examine how this concept has been discursively united with the idea of Party leadership to support the claim that the Party must necessarily lead throughout the entire legislative and judicial processes, since it reflects the scientific truth that the law is a realisation of the will and the interests of the people.

5.2.2 'Organically Unifying' Party Leadership, the Will of the People and Benevolent Laws

To communicate this new China model of power described above, the CCP has been promoting not merely its leadership but the virtuous nature of its leadership and creating a new rule of law discourse system that gives morality central billing. Central to this new rule of law discourse system is the rationalisation of a claim that the Central Party apparatus in Beijing needs to act as the core supervisor and overseer of governmental and legal decision-making. This accentuated role given to the Party's leadership has entailed creative reimagining of how the moral authority of the Party to rule fits with its claim that the Party's laws are intrinsically a reflection of the will of the people.

As we noted above, a claim that the Party 'leads over everything' has been added to the Party Constitution. But if the Party leads over everything, then the law cannot. Yet Xi Jinping continues to urge all Party members to perform their duties 'within the cage of the [legal] system' (*fang jin zhidu de longzili* 放进制度的笼子里). Placing intraparty regulations within the gamut of what is considered to be under the Party's definition of rule of law is a way of asserting that there indeed exist both laws and Party rules to constrain individuals' power. But the Party recognises that this move alone cannot motivate the kind of propriety and discipline required to rule over everything across the nation. This is where the crucial role of morality or, more specifically, the concept of 'governing the nation by moral virtue' plays a vital role in this new ideological vision of rule of law in China. The underlying ethos behind this new type of Party governance system is that concentrated power, which is virtuous in nature, is a more effective accountability mechanism than separation-of-power type arrangements. This has been justified through a series of ideological assertions, starting with the idea that the CCP holds this concentrated power because it is the purist representation of the people (Ding 2017). It leads over governance in China because its leaders possess, in classic Leninist parlance, an advanced nature, capable of representing the will of the people.[1]

In order to put to greater ideological use the standpoint that the Party represents the will of the people, the Xi Jinping administration has sought to reinterpret the configuration of power relations among the law, the Party and the people it represents. Here Party theorists employ the idea of 'unifying' (*jiehe* 结合) concepts, a method of shifting the discourse to fit changes in ideological priorities that has its modernist origins in dialectical materialism. This is a well-worn method of 'organically unifying' concepts that might otherwise be seen as incongruous. Broadly in line with the Jiang Zemin and Hu Jintao eras, the 2014 Decision stresses adherence to the organic unity of 'the leadership of the Party, the people mastering their own affairs, and ruling the country according to the law'.[2]

[1] For a discussion on promoting the advanced nature of the CCP, see Fewsmith (2005).

[2] The idea of integrating the trio values of 'the leadership of the Party', 'the people mastering their own affairs' and 'ruling the country according to law' as the key to the political path taken by the CCP was first introduced in the 1997 government report given by Jiang

However, there is a difference in the relationship between the three parties in this organic unity which marks a shift in the post 2014 era. Instead of viewing *yifa zhiguo* merely as a means of realising the people as masters of the nation managing their own affairs under the leadership of the Party, the 2014 Decision stresses that 'only by ruling the country according to the law and rigorously enforcing the law under the leadership of the Party, will it be possible to fully realise that the people are masters of their own affairs, and will it be possible to move the legalisation of the life of the country and the society forward in an orderly manner' (China Law Translation 2014).

The reason why the Party leading over and strictly enforcing the socialist rule of law is now asserted as the *precondition* for realising the socialist ideal of the people being the masters of the nation is precisely due to the accentuated claim that the Party, and only the Party, represents the will and the interests of the people. Indeed, Xi Jinping has repeatedly emphasised the paramount status of Party leadership in this organic unity, warning that one must not waver over or deny the leadership of the Party by using the excuse of people mastering their own affairs and that to do so is 'ideologically wrong and politically dangerous' (cpcnews.cn 2015).

Placing 'the Party's leadership' at the centre of rule of law discourse is based in large part on this ideological claim that the Party embodies the common will of the people. But importantly, another element that has emerged to prominence in recent years which further connects the three entities – Party's leadership, the people and the law – is the idea of that law contains intrinsic moral qualities that embody those of the people. The Party has communicated this by asserting a concept of 'benevolent laws and good governance' (*liangfa shanzhi* 良法善治). This concept, introduced into official Party discourse in the 2014 Decision, is now increasingly being employed as a catchcry in the China-style socialist rule of law discourse system. And, as we will see, it is now a linchpin in the ideological amalgam between law and morality governance in the Xi era.

Party propagandist and legal scholar Li Lin first proposed the concept of 'benevolent laws and good governance' in his book *Legislative Theory*

Zemin at the 15th National Party Congress. In his speech addressing Party leaders at the Central Party School on 31 May 2002, known as the 5.31 Speech, Jiang Zemin explicitly started the 'unity' of the three. The phrase 'organic unity' was first used by Hu Jintao in his speech at the 90th anniversary of the CCP in 2011.

and System in 2005 (Li 2005). In the book Li proposes that formulating 'benevolent laws' is the precondition for good governance, making a distinction between these laws and those that might be regarded as 'malicious laws', that is, ones that are unable to reflect the will of the people, are not sustainable and are prone to dictatorial practice of law. Li refers to 'benevolent laws' as those comprising the legal system and legal institutions which reflect the common values held by the people, and, in modern times, include values such as justice, fairness, democracy, freedom, human rights, order, harmony and safety (Li 2007). It was only after 2012 that discussion of 'benevolent laws and good governance' began gaining popularity in academic and official discourse, and the use of the term has grown exponentially since 2014, after promulgation of the 2014 Decision.

One way of tracing the rise in political importance of new concepts is to track their appearances in scholarly journal articles and newspaper reports. According to a China Core Newspapers Full-text Database (CCND) search, *liangfa shanzhi* first appeared as a subject in 2007. As of 11 July 2018, there are 213 newspaper articles with *liangfa shanzhi* as a subject on CCND. Of the 213 articles only 8 (3.8 per cent) were published between 2007 and 2011, and 205 (96.2 per cent) were published after 2012; 48 (22.5 per cent) were published in 2014 alone, and 52 (24.4 per cent) in 2015. According to the China Journal Articles Full-text Database (CJFD) search, *liangfa shanzhi* first appeared as a subject in 2005. As of 11 July 2018, there are 241 scholarly articles with *liangfa shanzhi* as a subject on the CJFD database. Of the 241 articles only 18 (7.5 per cent) were published between 2005 and 2011, and 223 (92.5 per cent) were published after 2012; 26 (10.8 per cent) were published in 2014 alone, and 64 (26.6 per cent) in 2015. Both the newspaper and scholarly articles published after 2014 share a common conceptual thread: the claim that 'benevolent laws and good governance' is the sine qua non of the 'ethos' (*jiazhi yaoyi* 价值要义) of socialist rule of law and that laws which are moral in nature are those reflecting the will of the people, translated into Socialist Core Values (e.g., Zhang 2016).

In the 2014 Decision, officially stated to be the 'precondition for good governance', 'benevolent laws' is defined around Socialist Core Values:

> Laws are important tools for governing the country, and benevolent laws are the precondition for good governance . . . We must scrupulously abide by the ideas of putting people first and legislating for the sake of the people, implement Socialist Core Values, ensure that every piece of legislation conforms to the spirit of the Constitution, reflects the will of the people and is endorsed by the people. We must let the principles of

> fairness, justice and transparency penetrate into the entire process of legislation, perfect legislative systems and mechanisms, persist in simultaneously carrying out legislation, revision, abolition and interpretation, strengthen the timeliness, systemic nature, focus and effectiveness of laws and regulations.
>
> (China Law Translate 2014)

Here the concept of 'benevolent laws' is intrinsically tied to Socialist Core Values and Party leadership. 'Implementing Socialist Core Values is an important characteristic of benevolent laws today', an article in *Guangming Daily* states (Wang et al. 2018). It further stresses that the China-style socialist rule of law system is fundamentally different from the rule of law system in Western countries. It uses the value of 'democracy' as an example, stating that one should not confuse socialist democracy with the Western concept of democracy. Whereas the Western concept of democracy is an 'abstract', 'confusing' and 'hypocritical' conflation of democracy, freedom and human rights, the essential requirement for Chinese socialist democracy is to adhere to the people being the masters of the nation, to protect the fundamental interests of the people and to ensure that the people have the freedom to manage state and civil affairs under the leadership of the Party, the article posits (Wang et al. 2018).

To make the enhanced role of Party leadership in all state affairs more ideologically sound in this new China-style socialist rule of law system, the Party has now deemed it essential that the language of the law, throughout the entire legislative and judicial processes, be couched in a way that embodies the idea that the law is a realisation of the will and the interests of the people, thus being benevolent and hence able to guarantee good governance. As legal theorist Jiang Shigong states, under the China-style socialist rule of law, the authority of the Party does not derive from state violence, nor the law or rule of law itself, but from the political ideals, the pursuit of faith, and the pursuit of ethical and moral goals represented by the Party (Jiang 2015). These ideals and values play an important ideological role in constructing the new socialist rule of law system with Chinese characteristics, as we will see. Understanding of the ideological configuration of the ideals and values that underpin the authority of Party leadership is important to our discussion in Section 5.3 of the rule by moral virtue and Socialist Core Values.

5.3 Ruling by Moral Virtue and Socialist Core Values

Thus far we have described a number of important movements in politico-legal discourse that have enabled the Xi administration to make claims about the paramount importance of Party leadership to all governance processes. In so doing, the Party has reimagined the CCP concept of the rule of law, making its leadership the pivotal axis upon which state power and the law operate. It has done so in part by claiming that its leadership is the conduit through which *yifa zhiguo* is implemented. 'The Party leads over everything' is a bold statement that raises the question of constraint on power. The realm over which the Party leads – that is, everything, including all aspects of law and governance – opens up the discourse to questions of constraint on this ubiquitous power. What constrains individual Party members from abuse of their power if the law does not and cannot lead *over* this power?

This question leads us to consider an important reason why the Party has introduced morality into the equation. The Party has long held the power to lead over all aspects of state governance through what scholar Ling Li (2015; Chapter 7) describes as a dual normative system of governance. One side of the governance coin is the Party's own complex system of disciplinary rules and organisations that provides a grid-like chain of command up through the Party system (Li 2015; Chapter 7). On the other side of the governance coin, a second grid-like structure glues the Party to the state through the presence of Party officials who hold dual Party and state offices in state organisations, along with the presence of Party committees within state organs that function to lead in the production of policy and in the coordination of Party-state relations (Li 2015). Li, in Chapter 7, describes the features of what she calls 'party-state-ness' as a dual Party-state structure that comprises two self-contained substructures: 'one of the state and one of the CCP' and the other, the Party structure, 'which is paired to the state structure in parallel', linking the Party to the state in a way that does not supplant the state. Another key feature of party-state-ness is that 'the primacy of the Party's power is accomplished through organisational arrangements rather than the law' (Li Chapter 7, p. 189).

Laws (both state law and intraparty regulations) are the conduit through which the Party governs in the dual normative systems that Li describes. What has occurred in recent times is a ramping up of the adhesive process, further gluing Party to state, to the extent that by 2014, the Fourth Plenum Decision was able to comfortably claim, as noted in the Introduction of this chapter, that the 'Party leadership must be implemented *across the entire process* of 'governing the country according to law' (*yifa zhiguo*). Before Xi Jinping came to power in late 2012, the Party made no explicit attempt to publicly promote the idea that *yifa zhiguo* was subordinate to its leadership. But, by 2014, Party descriptions of what elements comprise *yifa zhiguo* had shifted to accommodate the primacy of Party leadership, highlighting a move in focus from institutions to individuals (Smith 2018 and Chapter 4). By 2014, the rule of law 'came to be recast as a theory of individual obedience to the Party-state, rather than a theory of how Party power could be rectified through institutions, standards and procedure' (Smith Chapter 4, p. 98).

Since 2014, Xi Jinping has repeatedly called a (supposedly) frequently asked question, 'What has more power, the Party or the Law?' (*dangda haishi fada* 党大还是法大) a 'pseudo-proposition' and a 'political trap', instructing that one must not avoid this question nor be ambivalent about its answer (cpcnews.cn 2015). Xi's response is that the absolute power of the Party as the ruling Party is unequivocal but that when it comes to Party leaders and organisations the true question should be 'What has more power, their [individual] authority or the law?' This question is posed by Xi in concern for the potential of Party individuals to abuse their power. Although the law itself is not above the Party, Party members and organisations which they lead must nevertheless exercise their authority according to the law, under conditions newly described in the Party Constitution: that is, with the understanding that the Party (as a collective whole) leads over everything. Certainly, Party members must act 'within the cage of the [legal] system' and are expected to exercise their authority according to the law. But what *constrains* individual Party members from abuse of their power if the law should merely be observed but cannot 'lead over' or sit 'above' collective Party power? We address this question in Section 5.3.1.

We preface that discussion by pointing out that we do not downplay the importance that the Xi leadership attaches to state laws and Party rules. As we noted previously, intraparty regulations are now assumed to be included in the pantheon of laws that go to make up the CCP's rule of law.[3] As Samuli Seppänen explains in Chapter 8, intraparty regulations can be thought of as the 'partially concealed plumbing' (p. 221) of the Chinese state and indeed have the potential to constrain individual power to a certain degree. But intraparty regulations and the establishment of the National Supervision Commission (NSC) (described by Ling Li and

[3] The 2014 Decision has listed five systems within the gamut of socialist rule of law with Chinese characteristics: a comprehensive system of legal regulations, an efficient system of law enforcement, a strict supervisory system for the rule of law, a strong system to safeguard the rule of law, and a perfect intraparty regulatory system.

Samuli Seppänen in Chapters 7 and 8, respectively) are only a partial response to the issue of constraint. They certainly can help to constrain power to some extent by deterring abuse of power, but they alone cannot motivate and drive the kind of propriety and self-discipline that is required to rule in a country where law cannot 'lead over everything'. When law cannot sit outside the Party-state dual normative system to act as the ultimate constraint of an individual's or an institution's power, then another vital ingredient is needed to supplement it. Hence, according to the political logic at play here, Party-state functionaries' behaviours must be controlled and contained through means including but not limited to state law and intraparty rules. This is where the concept of 'governing the nation by moral virtue' enters the discursive fray. As Wang Qishan, the then Secretary of the Central Commission for Discipline Inspection (CCDI), remarked at the Fourth Plenary Session of the CCDI in 2014, 'No matter how robust the laws and regulations are and how perfect the system is, eventually they must be executed by an individual. As soon as the leaders and cadres begin to have problems with their moral virtues, discipline becomes slack, and laws and rules unenforceable' (2014).

5.3.1 *The Shift in Rule by Moral Virtue Discourse in the Xi Era*

'Governing the nation by moral virtue', or *yide zhiguo*, means that the government assumes the obligation to construct morality as a means of governing the nation. According to the Party Documents Research Office, *yide zhiguo* as a concept of governance was first espoused by Jiang Zemin in 2001 (Li 2009). Below is Jiang Zemin's much quoted first statement on *yide zhiguo:*

> During our process in building socialism with Chinese characteristics and developing socialist market economy we must unremittingly build socialist rule of law, ruling the country in accordance with law. At the same time, we must also unremittingly strengthen socialist moral construction, ruling the country by moral virtue. For the governance of a nation, rule of law and rule by moral virtue have always been complementing and supporting one another. One does not exist without the other and neither should be favoured over the other.
>
> (Li 2009)

Jiang Zemin's strong emphasis on the concept of ruling by moral virtue in 2001 was not at all a surprising move. Influenced by the Confucian political philosophy that assumes supremacy of moral forces (which we will discuss in the next section), morality campaigns have long been part of the Party's moves to install a civilising process aimed at building up the nation's 'spiritual civilisation' (*jingshen wenming* 精神文明). Post-Mao, the Party has variously inscribed its ideological agenda to install moral codes and guidelines in various campaigns such as the 'four haves' (1980), 'five emphases and four beautifications' (1981), 'five emphases, four beautifications and three loves' (1983), and 'eight honours and eight shames' (2006).[4] However, as we examine Jiang Zemin's quote more closely we find a significant shift in the rule by moral virtue discourse in the Xi Jinping era. In the Jiang Zemin and through to the Hu Jintao administration, rule by moral virtue was not an integral part of the Chinese socialist rule of law. In other words, back then, the rule of law essentially meant a strategy for law-based governance, that is, 'ruling the nation according to law'. 'Ruling by moral virtue' was a parallel moral construction process not discretely tied to rule of law.[5] For instance, in the 2011 White Paper on the Socialist Legal System with Chinese Characteristics, there was no mention of 'ruling by moral virtue'. Arguably, this means that prior to 2013, there remained at least some conceptual space, albeit limited, for discussing and critiquing the role of morality in law within the rule of law/legal system debate within China.[6]

[4] 'Four haves' (*siyou* 四有) refers to having lofty ideals, moral integrity, education and discipline. 'Five emphases and four beautifications' (*wujiang simei* 五讲四美) refers to emphasising civilities, good manners, hygiene, orderly conduct and morality, and beautifying soul, language, behaviour and the environment. Since 1983, 'Three loves' (*san re'ai* 三热爱) – loving the PRC, loving socialism, loving the CCP – were added to the 'five emphases and four beautifications'. The 'eight honours and eight shames' (*barong bachi* 八荣八耻) are to: regard loving the country as honourable and harming the country as shameful; regard serving the people as honourable and betraying people as shameful; regard following science as honourable and superstition as shameful; regard diligence as honourable and indolence as shameful; regard being united and helping each other as honourable and gains at others' expense as shameful; regard honesty and trustworthiness as honourable and sacrificing ethics for profit as shameful; regard being disciplined and law-abiding as honourable, and chaos and lawlessness as shameful; and regard frugality and working hard as honourable, and indulging in extravagance and debauchery as shameful. For a detailed account of these civilising projects, see Lin (2017a).

[5] We note that it was first Jiang Zemin who called for the integration of *yifa zhiguo* and *yide zhiguo*, but this integration was never developed theoretically within the single framework of socialist rule of law until the Xi era.

[6] Some of the key texts by Chinese legal scholars critiquing the dual emphasis on law and morality include Liu (1998), Sun (2002), and Ji (2014). For a review of these works, see Lin and Trevaskes (2019).

After 2013, in line with the ideological upgrade given to the rule of law by including intraparty rules, 'ruling by moral virtue' has become an integral part of the China-style socialist rule of law project. Whereas the Jiang-era version of 'rule by moral virtue' focused on the educational function of morality campaigns aimed at normalising the moral landscape of the society and transforming citizens for nation building,[7] the current ideological push for 'rule by moral virtue' has discursively elevated its status to the same level as 'ruling the nation in accordance with the law', acclaiming the integration of the two as 'the most distinct feature of the China-style socialist rule of law' (Xinhua News Agency 2018a). Not only has *yide zhiguo* been reasserted in the Xi era as a key governance principle but the Party has also promoted it as an ideological component of the China-style socialist rule of law system with Chinese characteristics, accompanying 'governing the nation according to law'.

Essentially, we find below that this ideological push is to cover the ground that state law – by dint of its inferior status to Party leadership – cannot. In the absence of law as the ultimate constrainer of all power in China, upstanding moral behaviour and self-discipline fills the gap.

5.3.2 *Creating Discursive Coherence through Socialist Core Values*

Central to this ideological push is that for the first time, the Party has required a set of prescribed values, known as the Socialist Core Values, to be integrated into the entire gamut of legal and judicial processes. We argue that this discursive and paradigm shift in regard to *yide zhiguo* is a necessary move to create ideological coherence for the newly established China-style socialist rule of law system characterised by the unmitigated power of the CCP Central Committee with Xi as its core. The logic is this: as the Socialist Core Values incorporate the 'highest common denominator' (*zuida gongyueshu* 最大公约数) of the values of the people of all ethnicities within the nation' (Xinhua News Agency 2018a), every piece of legislation and judicial activity must therefore demonstrate the Socialist Core Values to show that the law, which is benevolent (*liangfa*), reflects the will of the people. And because the Party represents the will and interests of the people, the Party's very authority and leadership lie in its capacity to ensure that every functionary, every custom, every piece of legislation and every judicial activity demonstrates the Socialist Core

[7] For the transformational purpose of morality campaigns in post-Mao China and its Confucian roots, see Lin (2017a).

Values. This is what *yide zhiguo* is all about in the new era. Below we unpack this logic by reviewing the evolution of the discourse of the Socialist Core Values, with special reference to the key issues and concepts we have discussed in Section 5.3.1.

The Socialist Core Values are comprised of twelve designated moral virtues, each promoted as a concept without detailed theoretical explanation. They are the national values of prosperity, democracy, civility and harmony; the social values of freedom, equality, justice and rule of law; and the individual values of patriotism, dedication, credibility and friendship. The first government directive that focused specifically on the Socialist Core Values was issued by the CCP Central Committee in 2013. Entitled 'Opinions on Cultivating and Practising Socialist Core Values', this document acclaims the Socialist Core Values as the inner core of the socialist value system, requiring these Values to be integrated across the full range of administrative processes, such as civil education, economic development, social governance, and media and propaganda, and also across various types of social activities and all levels of administrative and other leadership (People's News Online 2013). The document also specifies the relationship between the law and the Socialist Core Values. Under the subheading of social governance, the Socialist Core Values statement features a paragraph stipulating that these ideals are to be implemented into the country's administrative and governance practices in accordance with law, by 'using the authority of law to cultivate and practise the self-consciousness of Socialist Core Values' and 'by paying attention to elevating relevant requirements of Socialist Core Values into specific laws and regulation' (People's News Online 2013).

The historic 2014 Decision explicitly requires dual emphasis be placed upon *yifa zhiguo* and *yide zhiguo*, thus setting the ideological groundwork for subsequent declarations relating to the law–morality dialectic (China Law Translation 2014). In this document, Socialist Core Values are mentioned three times, each supporting the key concepts in configuring the new China-style socialist rule of law system.

The first mention is in the very paragraph devoted to the integration of *yifa zhiguo* and *yide zhiguo*, in which the Socialist Core Values are used to elaborate on the meaning of *yide zhiguo*, which is to 'forcefully carry forward the Socialist Core Values, carry forward China's traditional virtues, foster social morals, professional ethics, household virtues and personal character' (China Law Translation 2014). The paragraph goes on to say that dual emphasis must be placed upon 'the role of the law in standardising behaviour' and 'the role of morality in educating and transforming the people' (China Law Translation 2014). Subsequent official documents and speeches further develop and clarify the expansion of the regulatory system to the moral realm and the disciplinary function of both law and moral virtue. For example, Chinese legal scholar Xu Xianming published an article in a Party-based human rights online journal explaining the unique relationship between *yifa zhiguo* and *yide zhiguo*, in which he quoted Xi Jinping's conflated notion of law and morality, that is, 'law is moral virtue put down in words, and moral virtue is law borne in people's hearts' (*falu shi chengwen de daode, daode shi neixin de falu* 法律是成文的道德，道德是内心的法律) (Xu 2017a). Law and morality are, therefore, two sides of the same coin, reinforcing each other in disciplining and regulating behaviour. Hence, Party-state functionaries' behaviours must be controlled and contained through means including but not limited to National People's Congress (NPC)-legislated law and intraparty law. Rule by moral virtue fills in the cracks left in a system where law cannot be the ultimate constrainer of power: it provides a means of justifying the idea that a Party-state functionary's self-discipline (which creates morally virtuous behaviour), and not merely the law, guarantees virtuous governance. Xu Xianming further explains this law–morality relationship, quoting Xi Jinping:

> General Secretary Xi Jinping has profoundly pointed out, it is not enough to govern a nation by the rule of law alone; effective implementation of the law depends on moral support, and moral practice is inseparable from the law. Morality can play a role in realms of control that are difficult for law to reach, and law can be used to discipline and punish behaviours that cannot be contained by morals.
>
> (Xu 2017a).

The second mention of the Socialist Core Values in the 2014 Decision is within the definition of 'benevolent laws and good governance' (*liangfa shanzhi* 良法善治), quoted in Section 5.3.1. The total alignment of legal and judicial processes with the Socialist Core Values becomes part of the broad program of institution-building for the purpose of establishing 'benevolent laws' (*liangfa* 良法) to demonstrate the total alignment of the Party's will and the will of the people as a 'precondition for good governance'. The third mention is the part of the 2014 Decision relating to training high quality rule of law functionaries, under which Socialist Core Values are treated as part of the ideological and political construction for future leaders.

The 2014 Decision set up the ideological significance of Socialist Core Values, and their importance has been reinforced through subsequent documents. In October 2015, the Supreme People's Court (SPC) responded to the 2014 Decision by issuing 'Opinions on Cultivating and Practising Socialist Core Values at People's Courts'. Repeating the Decision's statements on Party leadership, the SPC Opinions further state that 'all judges and other court personnel must ensure a high degree of uniformity in thought and action with the CCP Central Committee and Xi Jinping as the General Secretary' (Court.gov.cn 2015). In December 2016, the CCP Central Committee and State Council followed this up by issuing 'Guiding Opinions on Further Integrating Socialist Core Values into the Construction of Rule of Law' (Guiding Opinions), which called for Party-state functionaries to turn 'soft' moral principles into 'solid, binding legal rules' (Xinhua Net 2016).

The Guiding Opinions details the modelling of the Socialist Core Values in the legal realm in five respects. First, it instructs functionaries to incorporate the spirit of Socialist Core Values into the law. The Guiding Opinions states that 'the requirements of the Socialist Core Values must be reflected in the Constitution, laws, rules and regulations and public policies' (Xinhua Net 2016). It adds that emphasis must be placed on converting basic moral norms and effective policies into laws and regulations to promote the legislation of civilised behaviour (*wenming xingwei* 文明行为), honesty and credibility (*shehui chengxin* 社会诚信), good Samaritan behaviour (*jianyi yongwei* 见义勇为), reverence for heroes (*zunchong yingxiong* 尊重英雄), volunteer services (*zhiyuan fuwu* 志愿服务), hard work and frugality (*qinlao jiejian* 勤劳节俭), and respect for parents and the elderly (*xiaoqin jinglao* 孝亲敬老). There is also a call to improve the capacity of making specific laws in cities containing district governments (Xinhua Net 2016). Second, this document requires functionaries to reinforce the value orientation of socialist governance by advocating and encouraging behaviour that is in conformity with the Socialist Core Values and restraining and punishing behaviour that contravenes the Socialist Core Values. In order to do this, administrative leaders are called upon to integrate public emotions, common understandings and stipulations of law (*fa, li, qing* 法、理、情) in legal and judicial processes (Xinhua Net 2016). Third, the document asks functionaries to use 'judicial justice'[8] to guide social justice by allowing the people to feel that fairness and justice have been applied in each and every judicial case. One means of achieving this is by publishing

[8] For a discussion on the meaning of judicial justice, see Nesossi and Trevaskes (2018).

exemplar court cases that cultivate and promote the Socialist Core Values as models to ensure the standard application of the law (Xinhua Net 2016).

Fourth, the Guiding Opinions requires functionaries to promote and nourish the spirit of socialist rule of law by harnessing the moral foundation of the rule of law and integrating moral teaching into law dissemination and education. Furthermore, it directs cadres to deepen education in areas such as public social morals, professional ethics, family virtues and individual character, and to promote patriotism, collectivism and Socialist thought (Xinhua Net 2016). Fifth and finally, the document asks functionaries to strengthen organisational leadership by reinforcing the ideological and political qualities (*suzhi* 素质) and the professional expertise and ethical standards of legal personnel as a means of ensuring that they are loyal to the Party, to the nation, to the people and to the law (Xinhua Net 2016).

Following the issuing of the 2016 Guiding Opinions, both the SPC and the Supreme People's Procuratorate (SPP) published statements detailing the way in which functionaries in these organisations would work to integrate law and morality into everyday case-loads.[9] In April, 2017, SPC Deputy President and Vice Party Secretary, Shen Deyong, published an article reiterating the key points of the 2016 Guiding Opinions and the importance of integrating rule by moral virtues with the socialist rule law (Shen 2017). He called for unification of thought in order to fully understand the significance of integrating the Socialist Core Values into the construction of the rule of law (Shen 2017). Judicial functions, he noted, should be used to promote Socialist Core Values. For example, fair trials must be carried out to resolutely combat behaviour that distorts the history of the Party and that denies the fine tradition of the Party and the People's Army (Shen 2017). Here the law is portrayed as contributing to the armoury against behaviour that would challenge Party credibility. In April 2017, the SPP issued a notice demanding that, as the soul of the socialist rule of law, Socialist Core Values must be integrated into the entire judicial process (Xu 2017b). Given the movements in the language of law and morality described above, it comes as no surprise that on 7 May 2018 the Central Committee of the CCP issued an action plan to

[9] In April 2017 the SPP of the PRC issued a notice demanding procuratorates at all levels in the nation integrate the Socialist Core Values into all judicial and case-handling procedures (Xu 2017b).

fully integrate Socialist Core Values into the construction of the rule of law system and into the legislation and revision of the law.

5.4 Putting History to Work: Xi's Ideology Growing Out of the 'Chinese Soil'

The CCP leadership has repeatedly referred to this amalgamation of law and morality in governing (*defa hezhi* 德法合治) as China's treasured heritage (e.g., Wang 2014; Xu 2017b). Xi Jinping is known to be an ardent advocate for constructing the China-style mode of governance, or the China model, based upon China's traditional culture. It has been reported that Xi Jinping often quotes the ancient Confucian principle of 'governing through a combination of propriety and law' (*lifa hezhi* 礼法合治) and 'granting moral rules primacy over penal codes' (*dezhu xingfu* 德主刑辅) at CCP Central Committee Politburo study sessions, urging his colleagues to study Chinese history and traditional culture in order to deliver good governance to China today (Xinhua News Agency 2014). In the 37th collective study session of the politburo on rule by law and rule by morals in Chinese history, participants describe the morality–law amalgam as a means of standardising social behaviour, regulating social relationships and maintaining social order, hence making law and morality equally important to state governance (People's News Online 2016). In his speech at the National Organisation Conference in July 2018, Xi Jinping directly quoted the Chinese traditional Legalist doctrine of power 'concentrated in one single authority' (*dingyu yizun* 定于一尊) to stress the paramount authority the Party Central Committee must hold:

> The strength of the Party derives from its organisation. The realisation of the comprehensive leadership of the Party and all the Party work rely on Party's resilient organisational system. The Central Committee is the brain and the pivot. It must have the power concentrated in one single authority and the power of having the final say.
>
> (Xinhua News Agency 2018b)

Confucianism and Legalism are the two most influential political philosophies that shaped statecraft throughout the two millennia of the imperial era. The political legacy of this historical trajectory, argues sociologist Zhao Dingxin, is the resilient and persistent Confucian–Legalist state, characterised by an amalgam of political and ideological power with the meritocratic selection of officials who administer the country using a combination of Confucian moral ethics and Legalist regulations and techniques (Zhao 2015).

Both Confucianism and Legalism focus on order and discipline. Confucianism is a political philosophy and social ethic in one. Based on an assertion of the power of morality and custom in governing the people, Confucianism is built upon the disciplinary and transformational forces of prescribed moral codes through observing *li* (礼), decorum and ritual proprieties (Lin 2017a). Legalism, on the other hand, regards morality as a set of natural sentiments coming from within and therefore mistrusts any imposition of moral principles. It dismisses the use or relevance of moral principles altogether and instead stresses absolute power of the ruler and strict, impartial enforcement of the law as prudent officials are prone to corruption and cannot be trusted. In the Confucian ideal, the ruler is constructed as a saintly moral figure who, by virtue of his very position as ruler, becomes the nation's moral teacher (*junshi heyi* 君师合一). This logic has established the Chinese political cultural norm that a mandate to rule relies on the moral authority of a regime (Lin and Trevaskes 2019). In other words, political legitimacy and moral authority are two sides of the same coin. Delia Lin has argued that Confucianism and Legalism have become particularly important for the Xi Jinping regime for two reasons (Lin 2018). Firstly, these traditional philosophies are capable of offering a shared fund of political ideas and principles, justifying not only the Party's centralised rule but also Xi's dual rhetoric of 'rule by moral virtue' and 'governing the nation according to law'. Secondly, by tapping into these cultural and philosophical roots, the CCP is not only able to legitimise its leadership and governing principles but also to claim 'cultural self-confidence' in formulating ideologies that are separate from the kind of political liberalism that has dominated Western society (Lin 2018). Lin and Trevaskes (2019) further argue that the Party's calls for a law–morality amalgam through all processes of governing the nation according to law, drawing from the traditional repertoire of political ideas related to the law–morality dialectic, can be understood as a form of pan-moralism, that is, an exaggeration of the claim of the moral standpoint. This self-proclaimed moral authority, they argue, defines the Party's own political legitimacy and allows the Party to declare unity with its people at a time in history when the Party is looking to merge completely with the state, yet at the same time it limits individuals' ability to act as autonomous moral agents (Lin and Trevaskes 2019).

Here we want to make three further points based on our discussion in the previous sections to highlight the major shifts in the law–morality amalgam in the Xi Jinping regime in order to understand the nature of the China-style socialist rule of law system for the new era. The first relates to the emerging discourse of 'benevolent laws and good governance'. We want to highlight that this in effect gives an unequivocal moral value to law. According to the Party's logic, since it is possible to make 'benevolent laws' – defined as those aligned to the Socialist Core Values, which are preconditions for good governance – then submission to law and the Party must not only be absolute but must also be a moral imperative; disobedience to law is not only illegal but also immoral. Indeed 'rule of law' (*fazhi* 法治) itself is listed as one of the Socialist Core Values. This leaves no room for any positivist critique of the role of morality in law, critique that was not uncommon in the Jiang Zemin and Hu Jintao eras.

The second point relates to the claimed alignment between the Party's will and the will of the people. The Socialist Core Values, eulogised to be the 'highest common denominator' of the values held by all the people of all ethnicities within the nation, become an ensemble of the highest values of the nation. The Party – owner and author of this ensemble of the highest values – while representing the will of the people, holds the highest moral authority that legitimises its absolute political authority. What can be concluded is that Socialist Core Values is a socialist manifestation of what was long ago embedded in the Confucian imagination: an assumption that all the dispersed knowledge and diverse moral values individuals hold can be extracted and refined by a single central authority as Core Values, and that once these Core Values are imposed upon individuals, be it through coercive or educational means, these individuals will be transformed into virtuous beings capable of delivering perfect justice and fairness, through which all social problems, including corruption, will be resolved once and for all.

The third point relates to the very nature of law and society governed by the age-old principle of the law–morality amalgam. Rule by morals was essential to law enforcement in imperial China, as it was through the moral code that hierarchical social order was maintained. Tung-Tsu Ch'ü observes that through a prescribed moral code the Confucian School strives to maintain a clearly differentiated social order relying on differentiated modes of behaviour (*li*) (Ch'ü 2011). Ch'ü (2011) aptly terms law and society in imperial China the Confucianisation of law, defined by Bodde and Morris (1967: 29) as 'the incorporation of the spirit and sometimes of the actual provisions of Confucian *li* into the legal codes'. Characteristic of such a legislative and judicial system is differentiation in treatment of cases by motivation, the social or familial status of the suspect and victim, and the particular circumstances under which an alleged crime is committed (Bodde and Morris 1967). When a prescribed moral code such as Socialist Core Values becomes integral to law enforcement, differentiation in treatment of people according to moral judgement is justified and inevitable, as a graded society requires a graded law (Lin 2017b).[10] The Central Government calls upon law enforcement and judicial authorities to ensure that behaviour in conformity with Socialist Core Values be promoted and encouraged, and behaviour contravening Socialist Core Values be restrained and punished (Xinhua Net 2016). This gives the prescribed moral code – Socialist Core Values – primacy over the law in guiding decision-making in legal and judicial processes.

In light of the discussion in this section, the statement about embedding Socialist Core Values into all legislation quoted from the *People's Daily* in May 2018 in Section 5.2 of this chapter now becomes clearer: the new Xi era socialist rule of law system with Chinese characteristics is one that must ensure that the Socialist Core Values are embedded throughout the entire legal, judicial and intraparty regulatory processes and that all functionaries act within the constraints of the law – which in turn reflects and protects Socialist Core Values – when exercising their authority.

To sum up the argument, the elevated law–morality amalgam discussed in Sections 5.2 through 5.4 of this chapter no doubt resonates with a Confucian governing tradition, but its Confucian overtones are not merely for the purpose of nostalgia or as a callout to Chinese nationalism. We find that it is foremost a solution to a theoretical need to explain why, according to the 2014 Decision, Party leadership must be implemented through the conduit of *yifa zhiguo*. Based on the rationalisation that the Party represents the will of the people, the diverse moral values held by autonomous individuals can and must be grasped and used by a few who, by dint of their claim to represent the many, can therefore also claim absolute moral authority to rule and absolute political authority to do so. Seen in this light, defining what the people's values are and then incorporating them into the laws that the Party rules through cuts off the possibility for alternative visions of governance and their accompanying values to challenge this power. The new Chinese rule of law discourse system is therefore as much about staving off challenges to alternative

[10] The terms 'a graded society' and 'a graded law' are taken from Bodde and Morris (1967: 50).

visions of rule of law and political power as it is about enhancing the ideological rationale of Party supremacy.

5.5 Conclusion

In this chapter, we have examined the elevated supremacy granted to rule by moral virtue and Socialist Core Values in relation to another major shift in the discourse of socialist rule of law: the unequivocal supremacy of the Party over the law. The Party's collective authority now unequivocally stands above the Constitution and therefore above all law, while individual Party members (the vast majority of whom are state functionaries) must act according to law.

We find that, in building this expanded vision of a Party-led rule of law, it has become necessary, according to Party logic, to assert that the moral value of law be injected into the discourse of 'governing the country according to law' through the concept of 'benevolent laws and good governance' –'benevolent' here being defined as those laws reflecting Socialist Core Values and the will of the people. The rule by moral virtue discourse in the Xi Jinping era therefore differs from previous administrations' use of the term in the sense that its objectives are now defined through Socialist Core Values. Rule by moral virtue is no longer a separate moral campaign slogan but an integral part of socialist rule of law building, to the extent that values must now be explicitly integrated into the entire legal and judicial decision-making processes.

One important consequence of this new post-2014 China-style socialist rule of law push is that the Party's new rule of law claims to operate proactively and systematically to reject a liberal rule of law, which contains a foundational premise that is dangerous to the Party. The dangerous idea underpinning Western–liberal rule of law is that pluralistic societies whose constitutions (at least in theory) allow the law to 'lead over everything' can cohere and remain relatively socially stable despite competing values and interests (Rosenzweig 2017: 29). In this model of rule of law, the actions of state actors can be constrained by laws that sit above the institutions in which they exercise power. Since such a system is open to resolving pluralities of interests and values by mediating them through agreed-upon level-playing-field procedures, through dispersed power arrangements and through independent checks and balances, society can remain relatively stable. But this stability requires that the authority of the law – and not the Party that happens to be in power – sits above the institutions that administer power. In stark contrast, Xi Jinping's vision of socialist rule of law relies on undivided and – in the case of the 'Party leadership' – constitutionally unconstrained collective power. The Party leadership asserts that the Party is not only capable of 'disciplining itself' but that it must necessarily be the entity that constrains its own power: since the Party leads over everything, the law cannot perform a role as the ultimate mechanism for constraining overall Party power.

This type of governing principle is certainly at odds with the growing consciousness of individual liberty that has developed in many pockets of China over the past four decades in this increasingly complex society. Throughout the last half of the Hu Jintao era from 2008 to 2012, citizen dissent was a constant fixture of political life in China. Many citizens' doubts over the self-proclaimed moral authority of the Party were increasingly voiced as was their unwillingness to submit their individual liberty to the collective will defined by the Party. The Party's response since 2013 has been not only to crack down on dissent but also to assert 'cultural confidence' in developing a new vision of rule of law. It has progressively doubled-down on its claim that this new rule of law dictates that the Party must necessarily lead the state through the exercise of laws that embody socialist values. The law–morality amalgam has indeed become a potent ingredient in Xi-era 'Party rules over everything' governance.

References

Bodde, D. and Morris, C. 1967. *Law in Imperial China: Exemplified by 190 Ch'ing Dynasty Cases Translated from the Hsing-an Hui-lan with Historical, Social and Juridical Commentaries*. Philadelphia: University of Pennsylvania Press.

China Law Translate. 2014. CCP central committee decision concerning several major issues in comprehensively advancing governance according to law. Available from: www.chinalawtranslate.com/fourth-plenum-decision/?lang=en.

Ch'ü, T.-T. 2011. *Law and Society in Traditional China*. Beijing: The Commercial Press.

Court.gov.cn. 2015. Zuigao renmin fayuan guanyu zai renmin fayuan gongzuo zhong peiyang he jianxing shehui zhuyi hexin jiazhi de ruogan yijian (The SPC's Opinions on cultivating and practising Socialist Core Values at People's Courts). Available from: www.court.gov.cn/fabu-xiangqing-15791.html.

Cpcnews.cn. 2015. Xi Jinping lun fazhi: 'Dang da haishi fa da' shi wei mingti, shi zhengzhi xianjing (Xi Jinping on rule of law: 'What has more power?

the party or the law' is a pseudo-proposition and a political trap). Available from: http://cpc.people.com.cn/xuexi/n/2015/0511/c385475-26978527.html.

Ding, X. 2017. Law according to the Chinese communist party: constitutionalism and socialist rule of law. *Modern China* 43(3), 322–52.

Fewsmith, J. 2005. CCP launches campaign to maintain the advanced nature of Party members. *China Leadership Monitor* 13. Available from: http://media.hoover.org/sites/default/files/documents/clm13_jf.pdf.

Gan, N. 2017. Xi Jinping thought – the Communist Party's tighter grip on China in 16 characters. *South China Morning Post*. 25 October. Available from: www.scmp.com/news/china/policies-politics/article/2116836/xi-jinping-thought-communist-partys-tighter-grip-china.

Ji, Weidong. 2014. Zhongguo de chuantong falu siwei moshi (Patterns of Chinese traditional legal thought). *Zhongguo Falu Pinglun* (China Law Review) 1, 119–26.

Jiang, Shigong. 2015. Dangzhang yu xianfa: duoyuan yiti fazhi gongheguo de jiangou (Party constitution and the constitution: building a rule of law republic based on a unity of multiple notions of law). *Beijing Cultural Review* 4, 18–29.

Li, Lin. 2005. *Lifa Lilun yu Zhidu* (Legislative Theory and the System). Beijing: Zhongguo fazhi chubanshe.

2007. Dali hongyang 'liangfa shanzhi' de fazhi jingshen (Vigorously carrying out the rule of law spirit of 'benevolent laws and good governance'). *Fazhibao* (Legal Daily), 31 August, p. 3.

Li, Ling. 2015. 'Rule of law' in a party-state – a conceptual interpretive framework of the constitutional reality of China. *Asian Journal of Law and Society* 2(1), 93–113.

Li, Qi. 2009. Jiang Zemin 'yide zhiguo' sixiang wenxian jiedu (Interpretation of documents on Jiang Zemin's 'governing the nation by moral virtue' thought). *Renminwang* (People's Daily online). n.d. Available from: http://dangshi.people.com.cn/GB/138903/138911/8734557.html.

Lin, D. 2017a. *Civilising Citizens in Post-Mao China: Understanding the Rhetoric of Suzhi*. London and New York: Routledge.

2017b. High justice versus low justice: the legacy of Confucian and Legalist notions of justice. In F. Sapio, S. Trevaskes, S. Biddulph, and E. Nesossi, eds., *Justice: The China Experience*. Cambridge: Cambridge University Press, pp. 67–91.

2018. The CCP's exploitation of Confucianism and Legalism. In W. W. Lam, ed., *Routledge Handbook of the Chinese Communist Party*. London and New York: Routledge, pp. 47–71.

Lin, D. and Trevaskes, S. 2019. Creating a virtuous leviathan: the party, law, and socialist core values. *Asian Journal of Law and Society* 6(1), 41–66.

Liu, Zuoxiang. 1998. Falu yu daode: zhongguo fazhi Jincheng zhong de nanjie zhiti – dui falu yu daode guanxi de zai zhuiwen he zai sikao (Law and morality: China's rule of law predicament – re-questioning and re-thinking the relationship between law and morality). *Fazhi yu Shehui Fazhan* (Law-based Governance and Social Development) 1, 1–9.

Nesossi, E. and Trevaskes, S. 2018. Procedural justice and the fair trial in contemporary Chinese criminal justice. *Governance and Public Policy in China* 2 (1–2), 1–92.

People's News Online. 2013. Zhonggong zhongyang bangongting yinfa: guanyu peiyang he jianxing shehui zhuyi hexin jiazhiguan de yijian (CCP central committee issues 'opinions on cultivating and practising socialist core values'). *Renminwang* (People's News Online). Available from: http://politics .people.com.cn/n/2013/1224/c1001-23925470.html.

2016. Xi Jinping zhuchi zhongyang zhengzhiju di 37 ci jiti xuexi (Xi Jinping chairs the 37th collective study session of the politburo). *Renminwang* (People's News Online). Available from: http://js.people.com.cn/n2/2016/1211/c359574-29444923.html.

People's Daily. 2018. Zhonggong zhongyang yinfa: shehui zhuyi hexin jiazhiguan rongru fazhi jianshe lifa xiufa guihua (The CCP central committee issues plan to integrate socialist core values into rule of law construction and legislation and revision of the law). *Renmin ribao* (People's Daily), 8 May. Available from: http://paper.people.com.cn/rmrb/html/2018-05/08/nw.D110000renmrb_20180508_3-01.htm.

Rosenzweig, J. 2017. State, society and the justice debate in contemporary China. In F. Sapio, S. Trevaskes, S. Biddulph and E. Nesossi, eds., *Justice: The China Experience*. Cambridge: Cambridge University Press, pp. 26–66.

Seeking Truth. 2017. Yong tiede jilü congyan zhidang (Using iron discipline to govern the party). Available from: www.qstheory.cn/CPC/2017-03/15/c_1120630273.htm.

Shen, Deyong. 2017. Jianchi yifa zhiguo he yide zhiguo xiang jiehe (Adhere to the integration of governing the country according to law and rule by moral virtues). Sina News, 20 April. Available from: http://news.sina.com.cn/sf/news/fzrd/2017-04-20/doc-ifyepsch1884020.shtml.

Smith, E. 2018. The rule of law doctrine of the Poliburo. *The China Journal* 79, 40–61.

State Council. 2019. Guowuyuan bangongting guanyu jiakuai tuijin shehui xinyong tixi jianshe goujian yi xinyong wei jichu dexinxing jianguan jizhi de zhidao yijian, guobanfa 2019, 35 hao (The general office of the state council on accelerating the construction of social credit system: guiding opinions on building a new credit-based regulatory mechanism). State Office, issued 2019, No. 35. Available from: www.gov.cn/zhengce/content/2019-07/16/content_5410120.htm.

Sun, Li. 2002. Dezhi yu fazhi de zhengdangxing fenxi – jianji zhongguo ji dongya fawenhua chuantong zhi jiansheng (An analysis of the validity of rule by moral virtue and rule by law – also an examination of legal cultural traditions of China and East Asia). *Zhongguo Shehui Kexue* (Social Sciences in China) 6, 95–105.

Trevaskes, S. 2018. A law unto itself: Chinese communist party leadership and *yifa zhiguo* in the Xi era. *Modern China* 44 (4), 347–73.

Wang, Qishan. 2014. Wang Qishan zai zhongyang jiwei sici quanhui shang fabiao jianghua (quanwen) (Wang Qishan speaks at the fourth plenary session of the central commission for discipline inspection (full text). Available from: www.chinanews.com/gn/2014/10-25/6716945.shtml.

Wang, Su, et al. 2018. Liangfa: shixian shanzhi de qianti (Benevolent laws: a precondition for good governance), *Guangming ribao* (Guangming Daily), 1 February. Available from: http://epaper.gmw.cn/gmrb/html/2015-02/01/nw.D110000gmrb_20150201_1-07.htm.

Xi, Jinping. 2015. Jiakuai jianshe shehui zhuyi fazhi guojia (Accelerating the process of constructing a socialist nation of the rule of law). *Qiushi* (Seeking Truth), 1 January. Available from: www.qstheory.cn/dukan/qs/2015-01/01/c_1113810966.htm.

Xinhua Net. 2016. Zhonggong zhongyang bangongting guowuyuan bangongting yinfa: guanyu jinyibu ba shehui zhuyi hexin jiazhiguan rongru fazhi jianshe de zhidao yijian (CCP central committee and state council issuing 'guiding opinions on further integrating socialist core values into the construction of rule of law'). *Xinhua* (Xinhua News), 15 November. Available from: http://news.xinhuanet.com/politics/2016-12/25/c_1120183974.htm.

2018. Li 'xin' chu 'bi' Xi Jinping zonglun xinxing zhengdang zhidu (Establishing the new and eradicating the demerits: Xi Jinping on the new-style political party system). *Xinhua* (Xinhua News), 10 March. Available from: www.xinhuanet.com/politics/2018-03/05/c_1122491671.htm.

Xinhua News Agency. 2014. Xi Jinping: Gudai zhuzhang lifa hezhi dezhu xingfu (Xi Jinping: ancient China supports governing through a combination of propriety and law and granting moral rules primacy over penal codes). *Xinhua* (Xinhua News), 13 October. Available from: http://theory.gmw.cn/2014-10/13/content_13524336.htm.

2018a. Zhongyang youguan bumen fuzeren jiu: 'shehui zhuyi hexin jiazhiguan rongru fazhi jianshe lifa xiufa guihua'da jizhe wen' (Responsible officials of relevant departments of the party central committee answer journalists' questions on plans to integrate socialist core values into the construction of rule of law, legislation and revision of laws). *Xinhua* (Xinhua News), 7 May. Available from: www.gov.cn/zhengce/2018-05/07/content_5288884.htm.

2018b. Xi Jinping: qieshi guanche luoshi xin shidai dang de zuzhi luxian quandang nuli ba dang jianshe de gengjia jianqiang youli (Xi Jinping: effectively implementing the Party's organisational path for the new era; the entire party working hard to make the party stronger and more powerful). *Xinhua*. (Xinhua News), 4 July. Available from: www.gov.cn/xinwen/2018-07/04/content_5303550.htm.

Xu, Xianming. 2017a. Xu Xianming: Jianchi yifa zhiguo he yide zhiguo xiang jiehe (Adhering to an integration of governing the country according to law and governing the country by moral virtue). *Qiushi* (Seeking Truth), 16 March. Available from: http://theory.people.com.cn/n1/2017/0316/c40531-29149761.html.

Xu, Yingyan. 2017b. Zuigaojian: ba shehui zhuyi hexin jiazhiguan rongru sifa ban'an quan guocheng (SPP: integrating socialist core values into the entire judicial and case handling procedures). *Jiancha ribao* (Procuratorate Daily), 26 April. Available from: www.spp.gov.cn/tt/201704/t20170426_188986.shtml.

Zhang, Fan. 2016. Fa an tianxia de run renxin – fade jiehe kaiqi guojia zhili xin jingjie (Law brings order and morals nurture the heart – opening up a new realm of governance with law–morality amalgam). *China Social Sciences Newspaper*, 16 December, 1.

Zhang, Wenxian. 2016. Xi Jinping fazhi sixiang yanjiu (zhong) – Xi Jinping fazhi sixiang de yiban lilun (On Xi Jinping's rule of law thought (2) – General theories of Xi Jinping's rule of law thought). *Law and Social Development* 3, 5–37.

Zhang, Xiaojun. 2019. The historical track of internal regulations of the communist party of China ruled by law. *China Legal Science* 7(3), 3–30.

Zhao, Dingxin. 2015. *The Confucian–Legalist State: A New Theory of Chinese History*. New York: Oxford University Press.

PART II

Ideology and the Party in Law and Organisation

6

Seeking Truthful Names

The External Implications of China's Internal Ideology and Organisation

MARGARET K. LEWIS

> We may still contrive to raise three cheers for democracy, although at present she only deserves two.
>
> (E. M. Forster 1951)

> The Party is the highest force for political leadership and the fundamental guarantee of the great rejuvenation of the Chinese nation. The Party exercises overall leadership over all areas of endeavour in every part of the country.
>
> (Xi Jinping, China Daily 2018a)

6.1 Introduction

In May 2018, the US government responded to the demand of China's aviation authority that air carriers adopt language regarding the status of Taiwan by railing against 'Orwellian nonsense [that is] part of a growing trend by the Chinese Communist Party to impose its political views on American citizens and private companies' (White House 2018). This language raised eyebrows as well as questions about how to best translate the forceful phrasing. It also underscored that ideology is not merely an internal concern: the 'political views' of the Party are of primary concern to people living in China, but they also matter to foreign audiences.

Characterising this incident as a ridiculous attempt at creating a totalitarian future has strong rhetorical effect. It does not, however, capture the complexities of how the ideology of the Chinese Communist Party (CCP or Party) is used in support of its organisation of power in the People's Republic of China (PRC or China). Nor does it clarify the varied ways that the Party-state is extending ideology beyond China's borders. An understanding of shifts in ideology – and its relationship to the design of the Party-state – is a necessary first step to appreciating the reverberations of those developments outside China.

Other chapters in this book explore the resurgence of ideology as a guiding force within China. This chapter shifts the focus from the internal to the external. It does this in two ways: first by examining how best to describe the organisation of power within China to audiences outside China and, second, by explaining why the PRC leadership's views regarding ideology and organisation matter to audiences outside China.

Section 6.2 tackles the 'what?' question of how power is structured in China today and the ideology that supports that structure, with ideology being defined in this book 'as a complex arrangement of ideas and assumptions that explains the world as it is and provides normative recommendations for political action' (Chapter 1, p. 5). Demystifying the complex Party-state structure, and recent shifts thereto, to non-specialists is all the more important because foreign audiences are currently engaged in heated policy debates. In the words of James Millward in an August 2019 *Washington Post* piece, the United States should 'both respectfully engage China and forthrightly confront the Chinese Communist Party' (Millward 2019). But to what extent are policymakers – let alone broader audiences outside China – differentiating between 'China' and the 'Party'? At a time when public-facing writing on China is sorely needed, specialists reading this book on the nuances of ideology should reflect on how we describe the organisation of power within China in our roles as teachers, commentators and policy advisors.

An accessible description of China's internal governing architecture is a foundation upon which to ask the 'so what?' question of why the PRC leadership's views about designing a government are relevant to people outside China (Section 6.3). Much has been written about whether there is a 'China model' (*zhongguo moshi* 中国模式) of *development* (Chen 2017; deLisle 2017). This chapter addresses an issue that is gaining greater attention: the PRC leadership's assertion that there is a China model of *governance* that is not just an alternative to, but actually superior to, a structure based on separation of powers (ChinaFile 2015).[1] The PRC leadership rejects both a separation of powers among government branches that check each other and the possibility of having multiple political parties vie for power.

[1] There is debate in the academic literature about the meaning of 'separation of powers' and its relationship to democracy and other aspects of government (Gittings 2018). For the purposes of this chapter, a general definition of separation of powers as dividing power among several distinct branches that check and balance each other's spheres of authority is sufficient to demonstrate the antithetical nature of governance in China. Likewise,

There is certainly no shortage of examples of multi-branch democracies[2] that are inefficient, contentious and downright messy – presenting a scorecard arguably worse than E. M. Forster's modest 'two cheers'. This presents an opportunity as China takes a more prominent position on the world stage. The China of today is not that of the 1960s when the Mao-era PRC was inwardly focused and foreign researchers sought out refugees for glimpses of internal developments (Cohen 2017). China is now projecting its strength economically, technologically, militarily and, as is the focus of this chapter, ideologically. The words that the PRC leadership uses to describe its structure of governance matter, just as its reaching beyond borders with money, surveillance technology and military hardware raises concerns.

In closing, this chapter turns to the prescriptive 'so what should be done?' question. It is unlikely that China will create an exportable 'new-style political-party system' (*xinxing zheng dang zhidu* 新型政党制度) for transplant in foreign soil. China's Party-state structure is rooted in a particular history that does not lend itself to an easy copy-and-paste abroad. And the PRC leadership has struggled to find the right tone in projecting soft power (Melik 2019). Public relations efforts like having Uighurs who are detained in government facilities sing for reporters 'If You're Happy and You Know It, Clap Your Hands' prompted outrage rather than assuaging foreign audiences' concerns (Schmitz 2019). Nonetheless, this chapter cautions that there are troubling implications of China's 'new-style' approach even if it is not directly adopted in other countries. Uniformity across countries is neither possible nor desirable, but too readily conceding the merits of a wide latitude for local variation in how countries structure power can gloss over what those variations mean in practice for the people being governed.

At the same time that acquiescing to the PRC leadership's phrasing raises concerns, the opposite extreme of headlines like 'When China Rules the World' can stoke emotion-driven responses (Hilton 2018). The curt rebuke of 'Orwellian nonsense' is also problematic because it fails to grapple with the power of ideology. The challenge then is not to

'democracy' – understood as a system whereby people choose their representatives through periodic, free elections – is in stark contrast to the Party's view of democracy as discussed in Section 6.2 herein.

[2] Although 'democracy' and 'separation of powers' are distinct concepts, they are related: the doctrine of separation of powers 'stands alongside that other great pillar of Western political thought – the concept of representative government – as the major support for systems of government which are labelled 'constitutional' (Vile 1967).

energise the Party's discourse such that it gains strength and becomes, as described by Louis Althusser, the air that human society breathes (Gloria Davies Chapter 3), but also not to dismiss it such that we ignore the influence that it can wield.

6.2 The Internal Situation

For readers who were taught civics based on a multi-branch government exercising mutual checks and balances, understanding the governing structure in China requires following Yoda's advice in the Empire Strikes Back that 'you must unlearn what you have learned'. China is not merely a 'one-party state' in that a single political party controls all government entities. Rather, it is a 'Party-state' in that there is both the Party (with its own complicated, massive structure) *and* the state. Or, as Li Ling explains in Chapter 7, China exhibits a 'party-state-ness' in which 'the Party is linked to the state but does not supplant it' yet 'the Party comes first' and the primacy of the Party's power is accomplished through organisational arrangement rather than legalised prerogatives. (Li Chapter 7, p. 189). Focusing on power distribution among state institutions can distract from the overarching question regarding the relationship between the state and Party.

Section 6.2.1 begins by using the image of a double-helix to sketch a historical backdrop of the interconnected relationship between the Party and the state. The PRC leadership's long-held rejection of a state structure based on separation of powers is logical when viewed from the perspective of the enmeshed nature of the Party-state and ultimate dominance of the Party.

China's Party-state has been enduring but not static. Section 6.2.2 turns to developments under Xi Jinping with respect to both the language used to describe China's governing architecture and the actual structure thereof. At the time of writing, the PRC leadership continues to concentrate power in Party institutions – a shift akin to emphasising the Party as the nucleus of an atom, with General Secretary Xi as the ultimate 'core' (*hexin* 核心) (Xinhua 2018a). This concentration is accompanied by a stern rejection of 'Western' models of governance and an embracing of China's own 'new-style political-party system'.

6.2.1 The Double Helix

There is no PRC without the Party. The CCP founded the PRC, has ruled it continuously for seventy years and faces no rival that is an even nascent threat to its lock on power. But it is not just that the formal government is controlled by people who are Party members. The Party itself has a gigantic, complex structure that directly applies to its approximately 90 million members and, indirectly, to everyone in China. For example, 'Unlike most higher education institutions in the world, all Chinese publicly funded institutions and independent institutions have a communist party secretary and several deputy party secretaries, and most privately funded institutions have a party secretary' (Jiang and Li 2012). The Party has stressed its leadership over universities: 'In order to better manage socialist higher education with Chinese characteristics, universities must not err from the Party line' (Xinhua 2017a). Only a small percentage of people studying and working in most universities are Party members, but the Party is omnipresent. Frank Upham wrote in his 2005 review of Zhu Suli's book on the workings of courts in the countryside, 'The Party is inextricably intertwined with governmental and commercial interests at every level of society down to the most remote village' (Upham 2005). Richard McGregor explains in his 2010 book, 'The tentacles of the state, and thus the party, go well beyond the government. As well as sitting above state-owned businesses and regulatory agencies, these party departments oversee key think-tanks, the courts, the media, all approved religions, and universities and other educational institutions, and maintain direct influence over NGOs and some private companies' (McGregor 2010: 15).

The interconnections between Party and state are not easily conveyed in visual depictions. One technique is to present side-by-side organisational charts (US–China Business Council). But that approach implies that Party and state are two stovepipes. Another is to use overlapping circles (i.e., a Venn diagram) with the Party's circle partially overlaying various state bodies (Lawrence and Martin 2013). This approach expresses how the Party permeates the state but can leave the viewer with the misimpression that there are areas of the state that are wholly untouched by the Party. The Party can inject itself into any aspect of governance, great or small. Yet another option is to create concentric circles with Xi Jinping at the centre and diminishing power radiating from that point (Fairbank Center 2018). This approach provides details on individuals' roles, but it can be perplexing for people not already familiar with the political landscape. It also does not capture the existence of state entities that are at least technically distinct from the Party.

An alternative way to conceptualise the significance of the hyphen in 'Party-state' is as the bonds between two strands in a double helix. As discussed in Section 6.2.2, there are important shifts occurring in the Party-state relationship. For decades following Deng Xiaoping's rise to power in the late 1970s, however, Party and state institutions largely operated as the twisting backbones in a DNA molecule that were bridged by a series of bonds to form an integrated system.[3] A entity could exist in the state strand or the Party strand, but it was never far removed from a bond that would connect it to the other side.

For example, although until 2018 the Party disciplinary mechanism was separate from the state's criminal justice system, a case could be transferred from one strand to the other, and there was coordination between the two (Li 2016). The linkages between Party and state are also conspicuous in the long-standing use of 'political legal committees' (*zhengfa weiyuanhui* 政法委员会). These committees coordinate the relationship among the public security bodies, courts and procuracy, and they act as a channel for the Party to intervene in specific cases (Peerenboom 2010).

Another example of the linkages between Party and state is the concurrent convening of the National People's Congress (NPC) and the Committee of the Chinese People's Political Consultative Conference (CPPCC) (PRC State Council Information Office 2018). The NPC is the unicameral national legislature that is dominated by Party members but holds the formal state power of enacting laws (NPC Observer 2018). The CPPCC is a political advisory body that state-run media describes as 'an important vehicle for multi-party cooperation and political consultation under the leadership of the [Party], and the key to socialist democracy' (Xinhua 2018b), but a critic explains it as 'a sort of vast invitation-only club – led by a member of the standing committee of the party's Politburo, working primarily through personal networks' (Lian 2018). These entities are distinct, but their simultaneous 'two sessions' (*liang hui* 两会) display the ties between Party and state (Xinhua 2018c).

There is both a Party constitution (or 'charter' – dangzhang 党章) and a state constitution. The NPC holds nominal power to amend and interpret the state constitution, but 'factual power of constitutional interpretation belongs to the party leadership. The CCP's power to

[3] Denise Y. Ho uses a DNA metaphor in a different way in her essay 'The Double Helix of Chinese History': 'So was the reform era yet another aberration in China's history, not unlike the Republican period? One way to approach this question is to imagine modern Chinese history as resembling the double-helix structure of DNA, comprising a strand of openness and one of authoritarianism' (Ho 2018).

initiate constitutional amendments indicates the sovereignty of the party over the Constitution' (Ahl 2019: 261). This combination of Party and state has been integral to the governing structure of the PRC.

The DNA analogy is admittedly imperfect in part because the Party and state have never been co-equal strands. The Party does not just penetrate into the state; it prevails. Nonetheless, while Party has always been above state – Party-state and not state-Party – the overtness of Party dominance has waxed and waned over the PRC's history. In 1949 when Mao Zedong established the PRC and ended Republic of China rule on the mainland, the country was in a shambles following decades of external threats and internal strife. Early nods towards building state institutions were abandoned in favour of the ideological fervour of the Anti-Rightest Campaign, Great Leap Forward and Cultural Revolution. It was not until after Mao's death in 1976 that energy was directed towards strengthening formal government bodies.

Deng Xiaoping included the necessity of upholding Party leadership in his 'Four Basic Principles' (*si xiang jiben yuanze* 四项基本原则) (Deng 1979). Yet the Deng era brought modest space to debate politics and an emphasis on building state capacity as China sought to modernise its economy. It also saw initial experimentation with village elections (O'Brian and Han 2009). The state backbone of the molecule gained strength and a bit of distance from the Party. The language of the 1982 PRC Constitution was also far less ideological than the 1954 and 1975 versions (Kellogg 2017: 348–9). The post-Mao emphasis on greater visibility of the legislative (NPC), executive (State Council) and judicial (Supreme People's Court [SPC] and subsidiary courts) organs gives the impression of a tripartite structure of separate powers. In reality, the relationship among these three entities is one of separation of functions. Even during the relatively open debates of the 1980s, China never came close to a structure within the formal government that empowered the legislative, executive and judicial bodies to check and balance each other's actions.

The 1980s also saw the high point for contemplating the separation of the Party and the government – not a dismantling of the Party, but rather a possible relaxation of bonds connecting the two strands. Reforms to the civil service and the allowance of increased power in the hands of central and local legislatures, among others initiatives, reflected Deng's desire to 'separate the party and government' (*dangzheng fenkai* 党政分开). This concept was included in a political work report issued during the 1987 13th Party Congress, the high-water mark for political reform during the

Deng era' (Johnson and Kennedy 2015). These discussions were halted in 1989 by the ideological crackdown following the violent physical crackdown on protestors in Tiananmen Square and far beyond. The Party once again reinforced its bonds with the state.

China's economic rise in the 1990s and greater integration into the international economy required a supporting state infrastructure and an overhaul of laws and regulations. Then General Secretary and President Jiang Zemin told a gathering of APEC leaders in 2001, 'Once inside the WTO, China will strictly comply with the universally acknowledged market rules, implement open, transparent and equality-based policies of trade and investment and endeavour to promote a multi-directional and multi-level opening-up in a wide range of areas' (PRC Ministry of Foreign Affairs 2001). Donald Clarke noted in 2003 the need for 'compliance and capacity-building efforts' but also commented that 'one cannot fail to be impressed with the amount of work that has been done by the government so far in identifying and revising – or abolishing where necessary – laws and regulations inconsistent with China's WTO obligations' (Clarke 2003: 104, 116). Randall Peerenboom observed in 2010 that 'collective independence of the Chinese courts has been strengthened through increased budgets, more streamlined and efficient processes, and efforts to increase the authority of the courts' (Peerenboom 2010: 74). The Party structure was still linked to state entities, but those bonds had become less conspicuous, and there was at least modest room for public discussion regarding adjustments to the relationship between Party and state. As Francis Fukuyama wrote in 2016:

> Since 1978, that Party-State hierarchical structure has been reconstructed and institutionalized in a broader and more modern form than what had existed prior to the Cultural Revolution. The Party has retreated from direct involvement in many areas of government, and regular state institutions have reclaimed authority, although the Party continues to command state and it is completely intertwined with the state.
>
> (Fukuyama 2016: 384)

Rumblings of a more overtly Party-centric discourse began to appear prior to Xi Jinping's rise. For instance, nods towards greater judicial independence were undercut in 2007 with the so-called 'Three Supremes' (*san ge zhi shang* 三个至上) that instructed judges and prosecutors to regard as supreme the Party's cause (*dang de shiye zhi shang* 党的事业至上), the people's interests (*renmin liyi zhi shang* 人民利益至上) and the Constitution and law (*xianfa falü zhi shang* 宪法法律至上) (Bandurski

2010). Tellingly, the supremes were always listed in this order. In 2009, Party-ordered study sessions on the 'Six Whys' emphasised that government based on separation of powers and multi-party elections was unsuitable for China (Six Whys 2009). In 2011, then Vice Premier Wu Bangguo told the NPC that 'we have made a solemn declaration that we will not employ a system of multiple parties holding office in rotation; diversify our guiding thought; separate executive, legislative and judicial powers; use a bicameral or federal system; or carry out privatization' (Wu 2011).

Looking back over the decades, the Party has delivered consistent messaging that it would not relinquish its monopoly on power. Nor would it empower state institutions to act without Party oversight, let alone operate as independent branches that could check each other's, and the Party's, actions. But the forcefulness of that message varied over time. After Xi Jinping assumed his position as CCP General Secretary, the tenor of the discussion changed.

6.2.2 The Atom

Much speculation accompanied Xi Jinping's assumption of the top leadership role. Perhaps he would be the leader to champion economic and political reforms that would inexorably push China in the direction of a market economy and separation of Party and state (Kristof 2013). Whatever optimism there was about the prospects for General Secretary Xi ushering in a political debate along the lines of that seen in the mid-1980s has been quashed. The PRC leadership has never recognised a constitutional structure that constrains the Party, but the Party's unfettered power was made all the more apparent with this 2018 addition to Article 1 of the PRC Constitution: 'The defining feature of socialism with Chinese characteristics is the leadership of the [CCP]' (Lawrence 2018). General Secretary Xi further cemented his power with the accompanying insertion of 'Xi Jinping Thought on Socialism with Chinese Characteristics for a New Era'. Nor is this phrasing just ideological bluster: structural changes are at work that are sapping strength from state institutions in favour of an energised Party with Xi as the 'core' (Xinhua 2018d).

In a departure from the double-helix structure with fluctuations in the strength of connecting bonds, what is emerging is akin to an atom. The Party stands more conspicuously than in decades as the massive nucleus at the centre of China's power structure. While state institutions still exist, these are comparatively lightweight particles orbiting the Party, and some are even being absorbed into the Party nucleus. As the Party moves to 'lead over everything' (*dang shi lingdao yiqie de* 党是领导 – 切的), a pressing question is whether formal state bodies will increasingly disappear through a form of electron capture into merged Party-state forms.

This shift has not happened overnight. Although a more overtly Party-centric discourse was gaining strength prior to Xi's ascendance (Minzner 2018), his comments in a December 2012 speech spurred a brief period of public debate regarding constitutional reform (Zhao 2012). Scholars have long discussed the significance of the PRC Constitution and constitutions in authoritarian states more generally (Ginsburg and Simpser 2013). Hope that the 2013 debate would push the rights contained in the Constitution from aspirational to operational was, however, short lived. In Chapter 2, Rogier Creemers describes the difference between the rejected term 'constitutional governance' (*xian zheng* 宪政) and the phrasing adopted by the Fourth Plenum of the 18th CCP Congress of 'governing the country according to the Constitution' (*yi xian zhi guo* 依宪治国) as 'represent[ing] a world of difference within Chinese circles, as one entails political correctness, the other dissent' (Creemers Chapter 2, p. x). Thomas Kellogg concluded in 2016 that 'the [2013 constitutional] debate, and the Party's response to it, highlighted the leadership's view of the constitution as a political tool, rather than a legal blueprint' (Kellogg 2017: 343). This assessment holds today.

In 2013, the Party also issued 'A Communiqué on the Current State of the Ideological Sphere' (*guanyu dangqian yishi xingtai lingyu qingkuang de tongbao*关于当前意识形态领域情况的通报), which soon became known for its numeral identifier as Document Nine. The directive warned:

> Western Constitutional Democracy has distinct political properties and aims. Among these are the separation of powers, the multi-party system, general elections, independent judiciaries, nationalized armies, and other characteristics . . . . [Critics'] goal is to use Western constitutional democracy to undermine the Party's leadership, abolish the People's Democracy, negate our country's constitution as well as our established system and principles, and bring about a change of allegiance by bringing Western political systems to China.
>
> (ChinaFile 2013)

The observer of elite PRC politics, Willy Lam, noted in March 2013 how structural changes to the Party-state 'mark a departure from the dictums of late patriarch Deng Xiaoping about the devolution of powers and in particular, the separation of party and government, which was written into the Political report to the 13th Party congress of 1987. President Xi, however, obviously favors a different approach to governance' (Lam 2013). Researchers at the Center for Strategic and International Studies (CSIS) similarly noted Xi's increasing reliance on coordinating policy bodies (*lingdao xiaozu* 领导小组 – leading small groups), signalling a shift towards Party entities at the expense of state institutions (Johnson et al. 2017).

A sampling of quotes from high-ranking officials underscores how the discourse of Party dominance gained ground leading up to the 19th Party Congress in October 2017. In 2015, Wang Qishan – then head of the Party's disciplinary arm – was asked if the PRC Constitution could follow the 'rule of law' and judicial independence, to which he replied, 'Impossible. The administration of justice must come under the Party's leadership. That's China's special characteristic' (Wang 2015). In March 2017, Wang reiterated, 'There is no such thing as separation between the party and the government. There is only a division of functions' (Shi 2017). In November 2017, he added that separation of Party and government had resulted in weakening the Party's leadership and construction (Wang 2017).

Court leaders repeated these sentiments, including in January 2017 when the President of the SPC cautioned that China 'should resolutely resist erroneous influence from the West: "constitutional democracy," "separation of powers" and "independence of the judiciary"' (Forsythe 2017). This message was firmly delivered to the bar when, in August 2017, the Minister of Justice told a gathering of defence lawyers that separation of powers does not suit China (RFA 2017). The Minister added in January 2018 when speaking to lawyers that the Party was the 'soul of the country's legal system' (Xinhua 2018e).

The rhetoric of unquestionable dominance of Party over state was thus on the rise by the time of the 19th Party Congress in October 2017. General Secretary Xi proclaimed at the meeting, 'Every one of us in the Party must do more to uphold Party leadership and the Chinese socialist system, and resolutely oppose all statements and actions that undermine, distort, or negate them' (Xi 2017). He repeated this message in the intervening months between the Party Congress and the March 2018 meetings of the NPC and CPPCC. In January 2018, for instance, he again stressed the Party's 'absolute leadership' over political-legal work (Xinhua 2018f). At his speech closing the NPC meeting, General Secretary Xi declared, 'The leadership of the [CCP] is the defining feature of socialism with Chinese characteristics. The Party is the highest force for political leadership and the fundamental guarantee of the great rejuvenation of the Chinese nation. The Party exercises overall leadership over all areas of endeavour in every part of the country' (China Daily 2018a).

China watchers debated the significance of the March 2018 constitutional amendment allowing the PRC president to serve more than two terms. At a minimum, it was another manifestation of Xi's move to break with established norms and leave open the option to dominate politics for years to come. The subsequent squelching of criticism of the constitutional amendment further emphasised that the fleeting tolerance in 2013 for even academic debate was firmly in the past. A university lecturer was dismissed in May 2018 after students reported that she made ideologically incorrect comments regarding the amendments (RFA 2018). In March 2019, constitutional law professor Xu Zhangrun was banned from teaching and put under investigation for writing essays critical of Xi Jinping (ChinaFile 2019).

The 2018 'Plan of Deepening Reform of Party and State Institutions' (*Shenhua dang he guojia jigou gaige fang'an* 深化党和国家机构改革方案) received less notice outside China yet marked a shift in the division of functions between Party and state. A stated purpose was to 'resolutely preserve the authority and centralized and unified leadership of the party Central Committee with Comrade Xi Jinping as the core' (Xinhua 2018g). The Plan brought 'influential state agencies . . . under direct party management under the new structure' (Merics 2018). For example, as discussed by Li Ling (Chapter 7), a merger of the state anti-corruption bodies with the corollary Party bodies has created a super entity called the 'National Supervision Commission' (NSC) (*guojia jiancha weiyuanhui* 国家监察委员会) with reach beyond Party members to people even loosely affiliated with the government. Further entangling Party and state, the first head of the NSC is a former deputy of the Party's Central Commission for Discipline Inspection (CCDI), leading a former editor of a Party newspaper to note, 'The authority of the CCDI will definitely reign over that of the supervisory commission' (Gan 2018).

The ideological push accompanying the Commission's creation reinforced that the goal was not to loosen the Party's grip in favour of an independent state institution but rather to absorb state functions into the Party. A string of articles on topics like realising 'absolute Party leadership over political-legal work' (Legal Daily 2018) and 'why "western" judicial independence doesn't work for China' (Fan 2018) continued the momentum of this Party-centric discourse. *Qiushi*, a major Party journal, published a question-and-answer format article on why 'Western' judicial independence is not right for China (Qiushi 2018). It explained that judicial independence does not have 'universal applicability' (*shijie pubian shiyongxing* 世界普遍适用性), and transplanting it to developing countries without regard for national conditions can result in 'judicial corruption and other chaos' (*sifa fubai deng luanju* 司法腐败等乱局). More pointedly, copying Western judicial systems would mean negating the Party's leadership.

This does not mean that the Party actually reviews every action by judges and other people holding positions in the state structure. Taisu Zhang and Tom Ginsburg contend in an article written in 2018 that '[i]t is probably safe to say that the courts have never in PRC history been as independent, professional, and powerful as they currently are' (Zhang and Ginsburg 2018: 311). They add, however, that 'the Party leadership's control over the courts has arguably increased under Xi, as has its control over all governmental and Party organs. It has simply chosen not to exercise this control in ways that interfere with legal professionalism' (Zhang and Ginsburg 2018: 332). There is an ever-present potential for Party intervention that can influence decision-making even in the absence of concrete Party directives.

Xi Jinping reiterated this dominance in a February 2019 article in *Qiushi* titled 'Strengthening the CCP's Leadership over Governing the Nation in Accordance with the Law' (*jiaqiang dang dui quanmian yi fa zhi guo de lingdao* 加强党对全面依法治国的领导) (Qiushi 2019a). There is no shortage of laws in the PRC today, but Fu Hualing describes the PRC leadership's 'dilemma in which, on the one hand, China has initiated the most repressive campaign against political dissidents, real or perceived . . . and, on the other, has jump-started the most systematic and structural legal reform, unprecedented since Chinese reform started 40 years ago' (Fu 2019). Extensive, detailed formal laws coexist with the understanding that the Party can and will intervene when its interests could possibly be threatened.

Senior officials in the NPC have likewise affirmed allegiance to the Party and, in particular, Xi Jinping: 'Stressing that upholding the Party's leadership is a political principle for people's congresses, the statement said the NPC Standing Committee should firmly safeguard the authority and core status of Xi, as well as the authority and centralised, unified leadership of the [Party] Central Committee with Xi at the core' (Xinhua 2018h).

While the PRC leadership has fortified the Party's dominance and the accompanying rejection of governing structures based on multiple political parties and separation of powers, it has not been clear on the details of the system it is espousing. It is certainly not describing the system as a dictatorship, resilient authoritarianism (Nathan 2003), fragmented authoritarianism (Johnson and Kennedy 2015), or other unflattering terms that have been used by outside observers. General Secretary Xi has instead heralded his governing structure as a 'new-style political-party system' (*xinxing zheng dang zhidu* 新型政党制度) (CRI.CN 2018), which *People's Daily* described as 'growing from China's soil' (People's Daily 2018a).

The contours of the proposed system are murky, but the official emphasis on the phrase is clear. In March 2018, *China Daily* stressed the unifying role of the Party when addressing the question 'What is "new" in new-style political-party system?': 'It unites all political parties and people without party affiliation toward a common goal and struggle, effectively preventing the flaws of the absence of oversight in one-party rule or power rotation and nasty competition among multiple political parties' (China Daily 2018b). *People's Daily* added that characteristics of the 'new' system include concentrating power to handle major issues, promoting social development through scientific and democratic policy decisions, and achieving the broadest possible consensus under the leadership of the Party (People's Daily 2018a).

Praise for this system in the Party-state media abounds. In June 2018, *People's Daily* ran a piece on how the new-style political-party system fits the 'Chinese cultural spirit' (*zhonghua wenhua jingshen* 中华文化精神) (He 2018). In July 2018, the Chinese Social Sciences Net – sponsored by the prestigious Chinese Academy of Social Sciences – reprinted an article on the 'superiority' (*youxuexing* 优越性) of the system (Zhu 2018). A July 2018 article in *Beijing Daily* comparing the new-style political-party system from an international perspective explained that it avoids the negative aspects of multiple parties rotating into power and instead is marked by 'leadership' (*lingdao* 领导) and 'cooperation' (*hezuo* 合作) (Beijing Daily 2018). And, in August 2018, a Party news website posted a piece titled, 'New-Style Political-Party System is a Great Political Creation' (Gao and Xu 2018). The Party-state continued to laud the system in 2019, with two April articles in *Qiushi* describing the system and its creation (Qiushi 2019b; 2019c). In May 2019, an article on the Party's website extolled how the system can 'realize the fundamental interests of the broad masses in a true, extensive, and enduring manner' (Zhu 2019).

Whatever one's view of the significance of these developments, it is indisputable that the PRC leadership is emphatic in its rejection of what it sees as foreign (and particularly 'Western') ideas of separation of powers. The Party is the nucleus and – while state electrons orbiting that core might go about daily work without constant, specific instructions from the centre – the Party's dominance looms.

Moreover, the locus of power is increasingly not in the collective Party leadership. In May 2018, the Party's *Study Times* reminded readers once again who is ultimately in charge: 'Defending the core status of General Secretary Xi Jinping, defending the authority of the party center, and obeying the centralised unitary leadership of the party center are the priority tasks of party political development' (Study Times 2018). In August 2019, the Party's Central Committee on Governing the Nation in Accordance with the Law (*zhongyang quanmian yifa zhiguo weiyuanhui* 中央全面依法治国委员会) issued a new document aimed at further enhancing the Party's comprehensive management that proclaimed, 'Over the past three years, under the strong leadership of the central Party with Comrade Xi Jinping as the core, along with the combined efforts of relevant organs in all places, implementation has achieved outstanding results' (Law-Based Governance Committee 2019).[4] Nonetheless, it called for even greater efforts because of persisting problems and set forth a litany of areas for enhanced work, indicating a further muddling of Party and state.

Chinese journalist Qian Gang succinctly summed up this deluge of documents, speeches and commentaries addressing Xi's view on organising power: following Xi's August 2018 speech in which he emphasised the correctness of Party ideology as well as the importance of safeguarding the Party's centralised and unified leadership (Xinhua 2018i), Gang noted, 'Party discourse notwithstanding, this is a far more direct injunction: Listen to me, follow me' (China Media Project 2018).

6.3 The External Implications

Invigorated Party ideology and a fortified Party-centric governing structure of course have the most significant and lasting impact on people living in China. PRC citizens generally have limited, if any, opportunity to live permanently outside of China. They must navigate the system in which their lives are enmeshed. At the same time, domestic political developments are also important to audiences beyond China's borders, first because caring about the situation of people in other countries is the

[4] '三年来，在以习近平同志为核心的党中央坚强领导下，在各地各有关部门共同努力下，执行工作取得了显著成效.'

principled thing to do. Second, from a pragmatic perspective, people who have business with China or are, for instance, negotiating trade deals with China increase their chances of achieving their goals by identifying counterparts who have actual power, which requires an understanding of the complex Party-state.

But the Party-state's ideology matters even to more diffuse foreign audiences who will never have direct dealings with China. Opinions vary on the significance of the shift from Deng Xiaoping's principle of 'hiding strength and biding time' (*tao guang yang hui* 韬光养晦) to Xi Jinping's foreign policy directive of 'striving for achievement' (*fenfa youwei* 奋发有为) (Kania 2018; Zhang 2018). And while there is debate about whether the ideological hardening internally and increased presence externally are signs of confidence or insecurity (Cohen 2015), either way it is incontrovertible that China is displaying a more assertive stance economically (e.g., through the Belt and Road initiative), technologically (e.g., by exporting surveillance technologies) and militarily (e.g., through development of features claimed by China in the South China Sea). Attention is also increasing on the Party-state's involvement in funding foreign universities and in shaping international institutions.

All of these actions outside China's borders are of great importance, but this chapter is about words. Section 6.3 focuses on the PRC leadership's outward push of its ideology, specifically regarding governance. The ability to back up words with action is critical to giving those words power in the international sphere, but the point here is to begin by understanding what the PRC leadership is saying (Section 6.3.1). In the simplest terms, the Party-state has a message to the world about how states organise power, and the world would be wise to more pointedly push back against its claims. Dismissing the Party-state's discourse as gibberish is imprudent, as is the opposite extreme of demonising an amorphous China threat.

Section 6.3 concludes by encouraging that audiences outside China respond, in part, by seeking truthful names: scrutinise what is occurring within China and then adopt language that is in accordance with the information that inquiry unveils (Section 6.3.2). Enhanced attention to facts and words is not, standing alone, a sufficient response to a bolder China, but it is an important first step. Clarity can help lay a foundation for clear-eyed action.

6.3.1 Ideology's External Push

That the PRC's rising power might in itself embolden the governments of other non-democratic states has been widely discussed. Andrew Nathan explained in 2015, '[A]s the prestige of the Chinese model grows, even without Chinese efforts to propagate it, other authoritarian governments are encouraged by the idea that authoritarianism is compatible with modernization, and they try to adapt, to varying degrees' (Nathan 2015: 158). Scholars cautioned shortly after Xi's elevation that China might transition from being a point of reference towards a more 'missionary' or 'proselytizing' stance regarding its system of governance (Nathan 2015: 158; Perry 2015: 904). There is a wide range of opinions on China's external influence, with FBI Director Christopher Wray stating that the US government is trying to 'view the China threat as not just a whole-of-government threat but a whole-of-society threat' (Redden 2018). In contrast, Jessica Chen Weiss takes a more measured tone that, although China's actions abroad have 'undermined liberal values[,]' 'those developments reflect less a grand strategic effort to undermine democracy and spread autocracy than the Chinese leadership's desire to secure its position at home and abroad' (Weiss 2019a: 94).

The PRC leadership's game plan is unclear, as is the extent to which there is a concrete 'to do' list of future steps for transmitting its views on governance abroad. But the push to expand its voice outside China is apparent, such as by rebranding China Central Television's (CCTV's) English-language stations as China Global Television Network (CGTN) with articles like 'Xi's Concept of "Community of Shared Future for Mankind" Endorsed at BRICS Governance Seminar' (CGTN 2018) and 'Hungarian Version of President Xi's Book on Governance Launched' (CGTN 2017). Moreover, even if the intention is not to transplant variants of China's governing structure to other countries, at a minimum the PRC leadership is promoting its 'new-style political-party system' not only as best for China but also as a contribution to the world (Xinhua 2018j). Despite reassurances that '[w]e will not ask other countries to copy the Chinese practice' (Xinhua 2017b), General Secretary Xi has stated that China's style of governance contributes 'China's wisdom' to the development of political parties around the world (CRI.CN 2018). State-run media reinforced this sentiment with, for instance, Xinhua using the headline, 'China's Party System is [a] Great Contribution to Political Civilization' (Xinhua 2018k). The CCP's gathering of representatives of political parties from 120 countries at a 'World Political Parties Dialogue' in December 2017 displayed a more high-profile role for China on the international stage. The 'Beijing Initiative of Chinese Communist Party and the World's Political Parties High-level Dialogue' published at the meeting's close stated 'that the CCP is not only a political party that seeks happiness for the Chinese people but also a political party that strives for the cause of human progress. It not only pays attention to the welfare of its own people, but also has a world vision and shoulders the responsibility that a big party is meant to take' (Xinhua 2017c).

It is unlikely that other countries will, or even could, 'copy the Chinese practice' because of the particular mix of factors required, including a longstanding, dominant party structure that is distinct from yet intertwined with formal state institutions and which is led by a strong central leadership. The more pressing issue is that the PRC leadership's discourse on governance celebrates the consolidation of power as a superior form of government to one based on multiple parties and multiple branches of government. The PRC's approach certainly allows for streamlined decision-making. In contrast to the extensive procedural requirements for public works in the United States, I recall the shock of a group of congressional staffers visiting Xiamen when they learned of the rapid planning and construction of the Xiang'an Tunnel that reduced travel time from ninety to nine minutes (Arup).

The PRC leadership's discourse further legitimises systems in which people are denied a direct voice in government. Xi asserted that China's system 'pools ideas and suggestions through institutional, procedural, and standardized arrangements and develops a scientific and democratic decision making mechanism' (Xinhua 2018k). In March 2018, People's Daily proclaimed that only the Party could fully promote democracy (People's Daily 2018b). This claim is not new. The Party since Mao has been based on the idea of the 'People's democratic dictatorship' in which the Party-state represents the people even though there is no direct electoral mechanism for the people to express their support. Elizabeth Perry wrote in 2015, 'In China, populist conceptions of democracy, for which the litmus test of a "democratic" government is whether it benefits the people and reflects the will of the people, seem consistently to trump electoral conceptions' (Perry 2015: 908). Wang Shaoguang wrote in 2014, 'Many people in the West arrogantly believe that only their understanding of democracy is true, and that there is only one correct understanding of democracy: this is a form of cultural hegemony' (Wang 2014). Today, 'democracy' – understood in this non-electoral conception – is even included among the Party's twelve 'Socialist Core Values' （*shehuizhuyi hexin jiazhiguan* 社会主义核心价值观） (Lin and Trevaskes Chapter 5).

What exact conditions are necessary for a country to be deemed a 'democracy' is contested. David Van Reybrouck, for example, has bemoaned that '[t]he words "elections" and "democracy" are nowadays synonymous for almost everyone. We have become convinced that the only way to choose a representative is through the ballot box' (Van Reybrouck 2018: 38). He instead proposes use of a 'sortitive' or 'deliberative democracy' that involves a group of people being chosen by lots (Van Reybrouck 2018: 38). And Daniel Bell has argued that the PRC's 'political meritocracy' could help remedy flaws of electoral democracy (Bell 2015). Even granting some leeway as to the core elements of democracy, the PRC leadership's version of democracy falls totally outside the parameters generally recognised by mainstream social scientists (O'Brien and Han 2009: 362; Perry 2015: 905). As Deane Neubauer wrote in 1967, 'By definition, political democracy in nation-states requires some minimal level of citizen participation in decision making' (Neubauer 1967: 1002). In contrast, China received a score of negative one out of forty in Freedom House's 2019 report for 'political rights and civil liberties' because discretionary negative points for policies aimed at altering the demography of ethnic minority regions pushed the score from the previous year's zero into the sub-zero zone (Freedom House 2019a).

The PRC leadership refutes this assessment and instead claims that it has figured out a better model where the messiness of multiple parties and multiple branches is discarded in favour of centralisation and cohesion. It is advertising this view to the world. For authoritarian-leaning leaders in other countries, this message can serve as a welcome affirmation and a 'helping hand': 'The country's four decades of rapid economic growth have demonstrated that development does not require democracy' (Weiss 2019a: 95). Leaders from countries known for repression of civil and political rights – such as Russia, Saudi Arabia, Philippines and Tajikistan – have openly backed the Party-state's repression of civil and political rights, as seen in a July 2019 letter signed by thirty-seven countries supporting China's human rights record, including in Xinjiang (Xinhua 2019).

6.3.2 *External Push-Back on Ideology*

Having addressed the 'so what?' question of why the PRC leadership's proclaiming of a better form of governance matters, the prescriptive 'so what should be done?' question follows.

One potential answer is to do nothing, or at least nothing more than call out the rhetoric as 'Orwellian nonsense' and then hope the world sees that the 'emperor has no clothes' (or 'has no separation-of-powers', as the case may be). The merits of this passive approach are questionable, first because democracy is vulnerable. Democracy has not been the dominant form of government through history, and the past decade has seen momentum lag. Larry Diamond noted in 2015, 'Since 2006, there has been no net expansion in the number of electoral democracies, which has oscillated between 114 and 119 (about 60 percent of the world's states)' (Diamond 2015: 142). Freedom House tellingly titled its 2018 global report 'Democracy in Crisis,' reflecting the finding that '[f]or the 12th consecutive year . . . countries that suffered democratic setbacks outnumbered those that registered gains' (Freedom House 2018). The 2019 report took on an even darker tone with the title 'Democracy in Retreat' (Freedom House 2019b).

One response to the external push of a China governance model is for countries that are democratic to better themselves both for the benefit of people living in those countries as well as because it is easier to inspire people to strive for democracy when the goal looks worthy of emulation (Nathan 2018; Weiss 2019b). This effort can proceed simultaneously with – not just as an alternative to – an appraisal of the merits of China's governance structure. Nor should the many problems faced by democracies distract from the distinct task of evaluating what the PRC leadership is promoting. Even if the applause for democracy declines, whether China's system deserves any cheers is a separate question.

An assessment of Party ideology is timely because the PRC leadership is now presenting its form of governance as a source of inspiration, not merely as a uniquely Chinese system that the rest of the world should respect and leave alone. It is advancing a discourse that embraces local variation as an expression of sovereignty while offering up its system as a desirable model. The logical and expected question to a country's marketing of its system is then 'why should we follow your example?'

This chapter endorses a two-step response: examine closely what is actually going on in China and, then, use language that conveys what is observed. The PRC leadership is making strong claims about the merits of its governance system, and the international community should 'seek truth from facts' to evaluate those claims. If indeed the PRC leadership has developed a superior form of governance, then it should withstand independent appraisals. Yet quite the opposite is occurring: the Party-state is blocking the sunlight of outside scrutiny. Formidable constraints on access to information demonstrate how the PRC leadership is constructing a membrane around China that seeks to both selectively admit information from external sources and selectively transmit information about its internal situation. On the inbound side, Kecheng Fang wrote in August 2019, 'China's propaganda system not only censors information, but it also proactively produces and disseminates information. Here's an example. While silent on allegations of excessive force from the Hong Kong police, China's state media cherry-picked cases in which police officers were hurt and amplified the disruption to the city' (Fang 2019). On the outbound side, for instance, the 2016 visit to China by UN Special Rapporteur Philip Alston was marred by the Party-state's efforts to control his meetings and schedule, resulting in what he termed a highly 'choreographed visit' instead of the unfettered access that is expected for visiting rapporteurs (Human Rights Watch 2017). He documented a number of difficulties, including that he 'was regularly followed by security officers posing as private citizens, thus making it virtually impossible to meet privately with civil society organizations and individuals' (Alston 2017: para. 6). These obstacles hindered his ability to provide external audiences with a comprehensive assessment of the internal situation.

General Secretary Xi has cited one benefit of the 'new-style' government as it 'truly, extensively and in the long term represents the fundamental interests of all people and all ethnic groups and fulfils their aspirations' (Li 2018). State-run media reports provide a glowing picture of ethnic minorities' living conditions: in April 2018, Xinhua reported that, in the northwest region of Xinjiang, 'the economy is growing steadily and healthily; people's livelihoods keep improving; and the exchange and integration of ethnic groups have increased' (Xinhua 2018l). In contrast to this claim, scholars, journalists and NGOs have made great efforts to document the realities of the repression behind the arbitrary detentions and other rights-depriving practices aimed at Uighurs and other Muslim minority groups in Xinjiang (Batke 2019a; Zenz 2019). Initiatives to obtain information on the situation in Xinjiang have been frustrated by restrictions on NGO activities (ChinaFile 2018) and the media (China Digital Times 2018), as well as by visa denials for journalists (Guardian 2018) and scholars who write on the issue (Millward 2017). Reporting, nonetheless, continues through use of technology and dogged investigative journalism (Dou et al. 2018).

Nor are challenges to obtaining information limited to the most sensitive areas like Xinjiang and Tibet. In their survey of over 500 China scholars, Sheena Greitens and Rory Truex found that 26 per cent of scholars who conduct archival research reported being denied access and that respondents noted how digitisation had resulted in sanitation of previously accessible materials (Greitens and Truex 2019). One respondent commented, 'It has become incredibly difficult to conduct archival research in China. From 2012 to 2018, it has become increasingly difficult. I think it will soon be impossible' (Greitens and Truex 2019: 8). These challenges are not new: outside of archival research, 'we do not find strong evidence that repressive experiences among inter-national scholars have become more common under Xi Jinping习近平 (2012–present) . . . . We do not, however, interpret our data as saying that there has been no change to China's research environment' (Greitens and Truex 2019: 11).

There has been a marked change in the environment for foreign NGOs, with the China NGO Project concluding in January 2019 that 'the Foreign NGO Law has been largely successful in allowing provincial Public Security Bureaus to act as gatekeepers for foreign NGOs seeking to work in China and funnel their activities toward the government's preferred ends' (Batke 2019b). The Foreign Correspondents' Club of China's 2018 report was also bleak: 'Fifty five percent of respondents said they believed conditions deteriorated in 2018 – the largest proportion since 2011, when foreign media coverage of pro-democracy protests prompted an extensive government backlash. Not a single correspondent said conditions improved last year' (FCCC 2019).

The importance of striving to get facts right even in the face of daunting obstacles may seem trite. But the regularity with which there is a lack of specificity when explaining developments in China warrants emphasising this point. Shazeda Ahmed, who studies Internet policy in China, writes, 'Almost every day, I receive an email from Google Alerts about a new article on China's "social credit system." It is rare that I encounter an article that does not contain several factual errors and gross mischaracterizations' (Ahmed 2019). This does not mean that social credit initiatives in China are benign. The problem is that inaccuracies hinder the ability to figure out what is actually occurring (because we think we have already reached an answer), tend towards creating a general 'China is bad' narrative (instead of a precise critique) and provide the Party-state propaganda forces an easy retort that foreign observers are indeed mistaken.

The next step after obtaining information is to find words that capture what was found. Outside audiences should reflect carefully on how the words they choose can embolden or, conversely, deflate the PRC leadership's international 'discourse power' (*huayu quan* 话语权) (Xinhua 2016). Repeating the language preferred by the PRC leadership will not give it magic powers, but it can gradually align the international discourse with the Party's ideology. For example, when then US Secretary of State Rex Tillerson visited Beijing, he commented that 'the U.S. side is ready to develop relations with China based on the principle of no conflict, no confrontation, mutual respect, and win-win cooperation'. An article in *The New Yorker* warned, 'Who could argue with such inoffensive sentiments? Tillerson's words, however, echoed a curious antecedent. On numerous occasions, China's President has used almost the same phraseology' (Beech 2017). Similarly, PRC state media applauded in 2017 when '[f]or the first time, the concept [of common destiny], which was proposed by President Xi Jinping in 2012, was incorporated in a UN resolution' (China Daily 2017). Andréa Worden describes China's requests for 'studies' related to proposed resolutions before the UN Human Rights Council as 'not academic exercises, but rather, with the PRC member of the obscure [Human Rights Council Advisory Committee] chairing the drafting groups for both studies, a means to further entrench the Chinese Party-state's human rights agenda and discourse into the work of the [Human Rights Council]' (Worden 2019).

As for specific suggestions on phrasing, use PRC 'government' only when referring to formal state institutions because the locus of power is in the Party, not the state. Accordingly, 'Party-state' better expresses the actual structure of power as being held by the Party but intertwined with formal state institutions. Integrating 'Party' into the non-specialist conversation about China is especially helpful in describing China, given the shift towards the Party-centric 'atom' described above. At the same time, use 'communist' sparingly – such as when giving the official name of the Party – because, whatever China's economic and social system is today, it has little resemblance to textbook communism (Clarke 2018).

'PRC leadership', though somewhat vague, conveys that there is a centralised group of decision-makers who are not merely government officials: they regularly hold Party and state positions simultaneously. Chief among this leadership is Xi Jinping, whom this chapter has identified as 'General Secretary Xi' to reflect his most important title, CCP General Secretary (*zong shuji* 总书记). The more common title used in English-language publications is 'President Xi,'[5] which is his lesser role as

[5] For example, the Jamestown China Brief announced in March 2018 that it would 'from now on refer to Xi Jinping as "CPC General Secretary Xi" rather than "PRC President Xi", because it's probably better to use the title that matters' (Schrader 2018).

the PRC head of state (*zhonghu renmin gongheguo zhuxi* 中华人民共和国主席). If Xi Jinping is on a state visit to a foreign country, then it makes sense to use 'President Xi' as that more accurately describes the role in which he is engaging with the other country. In contrast, 'General Secretary Xi' captures his primary role in China's power structure.

Describing entities and concepts in terms that reflect the actual situation, not the language that is more familiar to audiences outside China, extends beyond descriptions of the PRC's governing architecture. For example, 're-education' and other euphemisms can too easily provide a pleasant gloss when the reality is 'detention'.[6] And the word 'reform' is laden with values that might not be shared by the PRC leadership and the external observers using that same term (Feigenbaum 2018). 'Change' is a more neutral word that simply indicates a shift from one state of being to another. Charles Parton similarly pointed out Confucius's warning when criticising use of 'hackneyed language':

> If names be not correct, language is not in accordance with the truth of things. If language be not in accordance with the truth of things, affairs cannot be carried on to success . . . What the superior man requires is just that in his words there may be nothing incorrect.
>
> (Parton 2018)[7]

And while the existence of a single objective 'truth' can be debated, there is at least room for foreign audiences to be more discerning in how they describe the Party-state's ideology and organisation. This is a foundational step to address thoughtfully the outward push of the Party-state's ideology on governance and carry on to success an appraisal thereof.

[6] Use of euphemistic language is by no means limited to China and, likewise, this call for language in accordance with the truth of things is not limited to China. The Special Rapporteur on Extreme Poverty and Human Rights made this point in a 2015 report: '[T]he use of a human rights framework and discourse actually makes an enormous difference, which is of course precisely why the [World] Bank is so resistant to using it and so attached to the never-ending search for surrogate language that enables it to get at the same concerns' (Alston 2015: para. 65).

[7] Alternative translations of this passage from *The Analects* (13:3) include, 'If names aren't rectified, speech doesn't follow from reality. If speech doesn't follow from reality, endeavors never come to fruition' (Hinton 2013) and 'If names are not rectified, then language will not be appropriate, and if language is not appropriate, affairs will not be successfully carried out' (deBary and Bloom 1999).

6.4 Conclusion

This chapter does not want to oversell what this approach of seeking truthful names will accomplish. Foreign scholars and policy makers have long debated the ability and wisdom of trying to change China's legal, economic and political systems, with the results to date cautioning that outside pressure often carries little weight and can at times be counterproductive (Kroncke 2015). Taking a more vocal stance towards the PRC leadership's assertion of the merits of its governance style may do little if anything to change how the Party rules China. It can, however, check the Party's preferred discourse from infusing conversations outside China and prompt discussions about the fundamental elements of government needed to create conditions 'whereby everyone may enjoy his civil and political rights' (International Covenant on Civil and Political Rights).

An invigorated analysis by foreign audiences can also provide moral support to people inside China who disagree with aspects of the Party's rule. While efforts to measure public opinion in China are worthy of scepticism, 'various multinational opinion surveys consistently find a "high level of regime support" in China, even after factoring in the possibility that some people hide their dissatisfaction for fear of political repercussions' (Thomas 2019). Yasheng Huang, for example, wrote in August 2019 that the PRC leadership 'has managed the public relations feat of casting the trade war with America as a war not on China, but on China's people' (Huang 2019). Ian Johnson observed after watching the National Day parade in Beijing on 1 October 2019, 'Realizing that some of these emotions are genuine is important because we can't understand China if we think the party only rules through the authoritarian methods that reporters understandably focus on' (Johnson 2019).

But there are other views, too, that are largely unheard. Xi's consolidation of power, emphasis on the Party's primacy and fierce repression of dissenting voices means that any seeds of opposition will have little hope of sprouting under his rule. To question the Party's ideology is to put oneself, and family, at risk of reprisal. That people who disagree would stay quiet when faced with this reality is understandable. The renowned law professor He Weifang quoted the poem 'We are Wooden People' to express what he sees as the spirit of the times: 'We are wooden people, forbidden to speak, not allowed to laugh, not even permitted to move . . . . If I am to die, I will die on the path to my humanity' (Buckley

2018). Foreign observers cannot speak for people living in China, but they can help find channels for their voices to reach beyond China's borders. They can also be forthright in their own assessments of the Party-state, not only seeking truthful names but also speaking truthful names.

References

Ahl, B. 2019. Judicialization in authoritarian regimes: the expansion of powers of the Chinese Supreme People's Court. *International Journal of Constitutional Law* 17(1), 252–77.

Ahmed, S. 2019. The messy truth about social credit. *ChinaFile*, 22 April. Available from: www.chinafile.com/reporting-opinion/viewpoint/messy-truth-about-social-credit.

Alston, P. 2015. U.N. Secretary-General, Report of the Special Rapporteur on extreme poverty and human rights, U.N. Doc. A/70/274, 4 August.

2017. Report of the Special Rapporteur on extreme poverty and human rights on his mission to China. A/HRC/35/26/Add.2, 28 March.

Arup. First subsea tunnel in mainland China. Last visited September 2019. Available from: www.arup.com/projects/xiamen-xiangan-tunnel.

Bandurski, D. 2010. Three Supremes 三个至上. *China Media Project*, 12 November. Available from: http://chinamediaproject.org/2010/11/12/three-supremes-%E4%B8%89%E4%B8%AA%E8%87%B3%E4%B8%8A/.

Batke, J. 2019a. Where did the one million figure for detentions in Xinjiang's camps come from? *ChinaFile*, 8 January. Available from: https://perma.cc/6E35-A92W.

2019b. Two years of the Foreign NGO Law: how did 2018's registrations and filings stack up against 2017's? *ChinaFile*, 3 January. Available from: https://perma.cc/WK22-RHBK.

Beech, H. Rex Tillerson's deferential visit to China. *New Yorker*, 21 March. Available from: www.newyorker.com/news/news-desk/rex-tillersons-deferential-visit-to-china.

Beijing Daily. 2018. Zai guoji bijiaozhong lijie he jianchi xinxing zheng dang zhidu (Uphholding and understanding the new-style political-party system in the context of international comparison). *Beijing ribao* (Beijing Daily), 11 July. Available from: www.globalview.cn/html/zhongguo/info_25678.html.

Bell, D. 2015. *The China Model: Political Meritocracy and the Limits of Democracy.* Princeton: Princeton University Press.

Buckley, C. 2018. Chinese legal maverick, facing political gales, bides his time. *New York Times*, 18 May. Available from: www.nytimes.com/2018/05/18/world/asia/china-rights-he-weifang.html.

CGTN. 2018. Xi's concept of 'community of shared future for mankind' endorsed at BRICS governance seminar, 8 July. Available from: https://news.cgtn.com/news/3d3d414e3563544e78457a6333566d54/index.html.

2017. Hungarian version of President Xi's book on governance launched, 25 April. Available from: https://news.cgtn.com/news/3d416a4d78597a4d/index.html.

Chen, Weitseng, ed. 2017. *The Beijing Consensus? How China Has Changed Western Ideas of Law and Development*. Cambridge: Cambridge University Press.

China Daily. 2017. Concept of common destiny embraced. *China Daily*, 20 February. Available from: http://usa.chinadaily.com.cn/epaper/2017-02/20/content_28266917.htm.

2018a. Speech delivered by President Xi at the NPC closing meeting. *China Daily*, 22 March. Available from: www.chinadaily.com.cn/hkedition/2018-03/22/content_35894512.htm.

2018b. Xinxing zheng dang zhidu xin zai nar? Xi Jinping zong shuji zenme shuo (What is new about the new-style political-party system? General Secretary Xi Jinping explains). *Zhongguo ribaowang* (China Daily online), 6 March. Available from: http://language.chinadaily.com.cn/2018npc/2018-03/06/content_35794078.htm.

China Digital Times. 2018. FCCC: Foreign reporting conditions declined in 2017, 31 January. Available from: https://chinadigitaltimes.net/2018/01/fccc-foreign-reporting-conditions-declined-2017/.

China Media Project. 2018. Qian Gang, signals from Xi's speech on ideology. *China Media Project*, 23 August. Available from: http://chinamediaproject.org/2018/08/23/signals-from-xis-speech-on-ideology/.

ChinaFile. 2013. Document nine: a ChinaFile translation. *ChinaFile*, 8 November. Available from: www.chinafile.com/document-9-chinafile-translation.

2015. Is there a China model? *ChinaFile*, 16 October. Available from: www.chinafile.com/conversation/there-china-model.

2018. The China NGO Project, will 2018 be the year of a silent foreign NGO exodus? *ChinaFile*, 23 May. Available from: www.chinafile.com/ngo/latest/will-2018-be-year-of-silent-foreign-ngo-exodus.

2019. What does the punishment of a prominent intellectual mean for intellectual freedom in China? *ChinaFile*, 28 March. Available from: https://perma.cc/T8FR-5MLQ.

Clarke, D. 2003. China's legal system and the WTO: prospects for compliance, *Washington University Global Studies Law Review* 2(1), 97–118.

2018. Jiang Shigong on Xi Jinping and socialist with Chinese characteristics: an empty vessel. *The China Collection*, 28 May. Available from: http://thechinacollection.org/jiang-shigong-xi-jinping-socialism-chinese-characteristics-empty-vessel/.

Cohen, J. 2015. The insecurity underpinning Xi Jinping's repression. *Washington Post*, 23 September. Available from: https://perma.cc/MSF4-M3B8.

2017. Hong Kong in 1963–1964: adventures of a budding China watcher. *Hong Kong Law Journal* 47(1), 291–310.

CRI.CN. 2018. Lianghui – gaige xin zhengcheng: xinxing zheng dang zhidu wei shijie zheng dang zhengzhi fazhan gongxian zhongguo zhidu (The two sessions: reform a new journey: the new-style political-party system is China's contribution to the world for the development of political parties). *Guoji zaixian* (CRI News), 8 March. Available from: http://news.cri.cn/20180308/962b9850-3a41-45ac-57c0-a4afdaa2d9e4.html.

de Bary, T. and Bloom, I. 1999. *Sources of Chinese Tradition*. New York: Columbia University Press, 1999.

deLisle, J. 2017. Law in the China model 2.0: legality, developmentalism and Leninism under Xi Jinping, *Journal of Contemporary China* 26(103), 68–84.

Deng, Xiaoping. 1979. 四项基本原则, 30 March.

Diamond, L. 2015. Facing up to the democratic recession. *Journal of Democracy* 26(1), 141–55.

Dou E., Page, J. and Chin J. 2018. China's Uighur camps swell as Beijing widens the dragnet. *Wall Street Journal*, 17 August. Available from: www.wsj.com/articles/chinas-uighur-camps-swell-as-beijing-widens-the-dragnet-1534534894.

Fairbank Center. 2018. How the CCP rules: China's leaders of party and state, March. Available from: https://medium.com/fairbank-center/infographic-chinas-leaders-of-party-and-state-after-the-13th-npc-and-cppcc-92383d3a1fe5.

Fan, Mingzhi. 2018. Xi fang 'sifa duli' wei shenme zai zhongguo zou bu guo (Why western 'judicial independence' can't work in China). *Qiushi* (Seeking Truth). 15 January. Available from: www.qstheory.cn/dukan/qs/2018-01/15/c_1122241714.htm.

Fang, Kecheng. 2019, What is China's propaganda machine saying about the Hong Kong protests? *Washington Post (Monkey Cage)*, 19 August. Available from: https://beta.washingtonpost.com/politics/2019/08/19/what-is-chinas-propaganda-machine-saying-about-hong-kong-protests/.

FCCC. 2019. Under watch: FCCC 2018 report on media freedoms in China. Available from: www.dropbox.com/s/h2h00yicr2eusyt/under%20watch.pdf?dl=0.

Feigenbaum, E. 2018. A Chinese puzzle: why economic 'reform' in Xi's China has more meanings than market liberalization. *Macropolo*, 26 February. Available from: https://perma.cc/G3HG-ZWFF.

Forster, E. M. 1951. *Two Cheers for Democracy*. Edward Arnold & Co.

Forsythe, M. 2017. China's chief justice rejects an independent judiciary, and reformers wince. *New York Times*, 18 January. Available from:

www.nytimes.com/2017/01/18/world/asia/china-chief-justice-courts-zhou-qiang.html?_r=0.

Freedom House. 2018. Democracy in crisis: freedom in the world 2018. Available from: https://freedomhouse.org/sites/default/files/FH_FITW_Report_2018_Final_SinglePage.pdf.

2019a. Freedom in the world 2019, China. Available from: https://freedomhouse.org/report/freedom-world/2019/china.

2019b. Democracy in retreat. Available from: https://freedomhouse.org/report/freedom-world/freedom-world-2019.

Fu, Hualing. 2019. Duality and China's struggle for legal autonomy. *China Perspectives* 2019(1). Available from: www.cefc.com.hk/issue/china-perspectives-20191/.

Fukuyama, F. 2016. Reflections on Chinese governance. *Journal of Chinese Governance* 1(3), 379–91.

Gan, N. 2018. Surprise choice for China's anti-graft watchdog signals Communist Party's authority over the state. *South China Morning Post*, 18 March. Available from: www.scmp.com/news/china/policies-politics/article/2137735/yang-xiaodu-surprise-choice-head-chinas-new-powerful.

Gao, Guosheng, and Xu, Feng. 2018. *Xinxing zheng dang zhidu shi weida de zhengzhi chuangzao.* (The new-style political-party system is a great political creation). *Zhongguo gongchandang xinwen* (CPCNews.Cn), 11 August. Available from: http://theory.people.com.cn/n1/2018/0811/c40531-30222967.html.

Ginsburg, T. and Simpser, A. (2013). Introduction. In T. Ginsburg and A. Simpser, eds., *Constitutions in Authoritarian Regimes*. Cambridge: Cambridge University Press, pp. 1–18.

Gittings, D. 2018. Separation of powers and deliberative democracy. In R. Levy et al., eds. *The Cambridge Handbook of Deliberative Constitutionalism*. Cambridge: Cambridge University Press, pp. 113–24.

Greitens, S. C., and Truex, R. 2019. Repressive experiences among China scholars: new evidence from survey data. *The China Quarterly*, 1–27. doi: 10.1017/S0305741019000365. Details at: www.cambridge.org/core/journals/china-quarterly/article/repressive-experiences-among-china-scholars-new-evidence-from-survey-data/C1CB08324457ED90199C274CDC153127.

Guardian. 2018. China 'ejects' US journalist known for reporting on Xinjiang repression. *The Guardian*, 22 August. Available from: www.theguardian.com/world/2018/aug/22/china-ejects-us-journalist-known-for-reporting-on-xinjiang-repression.

He, Xingliang. 2018. Qihe zhonghua wenhua jingshen de xinxing zheng dang zhidu (A new-style political-party system that is compatible with the spirit of Chinese culture). *Renmin Ribao* (People's Daily), 3 June. Available from: http://china.chinadaily.com.cn/2018-06/03/content_36318196.htm.

Hilton, I. 2018. When China rules the world. *Prospect*, 14 May. Available from: www.prospectmagazine.co.uk/magazine/when-china-rules-the-world.

Hinton, D. 2013. *The Four Chinese Classics: Tao Te Ching, Analects, Chuang Tzu, Mencius*. Berkeley: Counterpoint Press.

Ho, D. 2018. The double helix of Chinese history. *Project Syndicate*, 15 March. Available from: www.project-syndicate.org/commentary/china-xi-authoritarianism-and-reform-by-denise-y-ho-2018-03.

Huang, Yasheng. 2019. Trump has succeeded. Now lots of Chinese people are buying Huawei phones. *New York Times*, 9 August. Available from: https://perma.cc/V2D3-UCW2.

Human Rights Watch. 2017. The costs of international advocacy: China's interference in United Nations human rights mechanisms, September. Available from: www.hrw.org/report/2017/09/05/costs-international-advocacy/chinas-?interference-united-nations-human-rights.

International Covenant on Civil and Political Rights, Dec. 16, 1966, S. Treaty Doc. No. 95-20, 6 I.L.M. 368 (1967) 999 U.N.T.S. 171.

Jiang, Hua, and Li, Xiaobin. 2012. Party secretaries in Chinese higher education institutions, who are they? *Journal of International Education and Leadership* 2(2), 1–13.

Johnson, C. and Kennedy, S. 2015. China's un-separation of powers: the blurred lines of party and government. *Foreign Affairs*, 24 July. Available from: www.foreignaffairs.com/articles/china/2015-07-24/chinas-un-separation-powers.

Johnson, C., Kennedy, S. and Qiu, M. 2017. Xi's signature governance innovation: the rise of leading small groups. *CSIS*, 17 October. Available from: www.csis.org/analysis/xis-signature-governance-innovation-rise-leading-small-groups.

Johnson, I. 2019. China, where state pomp comes with real feeling. *New York Times*, 3 October. Available from: www.nytimes.com/2019/10/03/opinion/china-national-day-.html.

Kania, T. 2018. The right to speak: discourse and Chinese power. *Center for Advanced China Research*, 27 November. Available from: https://perma.cc/PTU2-E89N.

Kellogg, T. 2017. Arguing Chinese constitutionalism: the 2013 constitutional debate and the 'urgency' of political reform. *University of Pennsylvania Asian Law Review* 11, 337–407.

Kristof, N. 2013. Looking for a jump-start in China. *New York Times*, 5 January. Available from: www.nytimes.com/2013/01/06/opinion/sunday/kristof-looking-?for-a-jump-start-in-china.html.

Kroncke, J. 2015. *The Futility of Law and Development: China and the Dangers of Exporting American Law*. New York: Oxford University Press.

Lam, W. 2013. Centralized power key to realizing Xi's 'China dream'. *Jamestown China Brief*, 28 March. Available from: https://jamestown.org/wp-content/uploads/2013/03/cb_03_25.pdf?x87069.

Law-Based Governance Committee. 2019. Guanyu jiaqiang zonghe zhili cong yuantou qieshi jiejue zhixing nan wenti de yijian (Opinions on strengthening comprehensive management to solve difficulties in implementation right from the source). *Zuigao renmin fayuanwang* (SPC online), 22 August. Available from: https://perma.cc/52EB-AB8S.

Lawrence, S. 2018. China's communist party absorbs more of the state. *Congressional Research Service*, 23 March. Available from: https://perma.cc/HYH2-YK3F.

Lawrence, S. and Martin, M. 2013. Understanding China's political system. *Congressional Research Service*, 20 March. Available from: https://fas.org/sgp/crs/row/R41007.pdf.

Legal Daily. 2018. Zhongyang zhengfawei qidong zhanluexing quanjuxing yinlingxing de shi da wenti duice yanjiu (Central political-legal committee launches a strategic, comprehensive, leading ten-big-questions countermeasures study), 3 April. Available from: www.legaldaily.com.cn/index_article/content/2018-04/03/content_7513316.htm?node=5955.

Li, Ling. 2016. The rise of the discipline and inspection commission, 1927–2012: anticorruption investigation and decision-making in the Chinese Communist Party. *Modern China* 42(5), 447–82. Available from: http://journals.sagepub.com/doi/pdf/10.1177/0097700416631047.

Li, Zhen. 2018. Renlei zhengzhi wenming zhongda gongxian (A major contribution to human political civilisation). *Renmin Ribao Haiwai Ban* (People's Daily Overseas Edition), 13 March. Available from: http://paper.people.com.cn/rmrbhwb/html/2018-03/13/content_1841282.htm.

Lian, Yizheng. 2018. China has a vast influence machine, and you don't even know it. *New York Times*, 21 May. Available from: www.nytimes.com/2018/05/21/opinion/china-overseas-intelligence-yang.html.

McGregor, R. 2010. *The Party: The Secret World of China's Communist Rulers*. New York: HarperCollins.

Melik, K. 2019. China has a soft power problem. *Wall Street Journal*, 5 September.

Merics. 2018. China update, 22 March. Available from: www.merics.org/en/newsletter/china-update-62018.

Millward, J. 2017. Being blacklisted by China, and what can be learned from it. *Medium*, 28 December. Available from: https://medium.com/@millwarj/being-blacklisted-by-china-and-what-can-be-learned-from-it-faf05eb8e1e2.

2019. We need a better middle road on China. Here's how we can find it. *Washington Post*, 6 August. Available from: www.washingtonpost.com/opinions/2019/08/06/better-middle-road-china/.

Minzner, C. 2018. *End of an Era*. New York: Oxford University Press.

Nathan, A. 2003. Authoritarian resilience. *Journal of Democracy* 14(1), 6–17.

2015. China's challenge. *Journal of Democracy* 26(1), 157–70.

2018. Is American policy towards China due for a 'reckoning'? *ChinaFile*, 15 February. Available from: www.chinafile.com/conversation/american-policy-toward-china-due-reckoning.

Neubauer, D. 1967. Some conditions of democracy. *American Political Science Review* 61(4), 1002–9.

NPC Observer. 2018. Exclusive: demographics of the 13th NPC (Updated), 11 March. Available from: https://npcobserver.com/2018/03/10/exclusive-demographics-of-the-13th-npc/.

O'Brien K. and Han, R. 2009. Path to democracy? assessing village elections in China. *Journal of Contemporary China* 18(6), 359–78.

Parton, C. 2018. Hackneyed language hampers the west's ties with China. *Financial Times*, 9 May.

Peerenboom, R. 2010. Common myths and unfounded assumptions: challenges and prospects for judicial independence in China, in R. Peerenboom, ed., *Judicial Independence in China*. Cambridge: Cambridge University Press, pp. 69–94.

People's Daily. 2018a. Zhongguo xinxing zheng dang zhidu dai gei shijie de qishi (An inspiration brought to the world by the new-style political-party system). *Renmin Ribao* (People's Daily), 10 March. Available from: http://world.people.com.cn/n1/2018/0310/c1002–29859416.html.

2018b. Xuan Li (pseudonym), Baozheng dang he guojia chang zhi jiu an de zhongda zhidu anpai (Major institutional arrangements to ensure the long-term stability of party and state). *Renmin Ribao* (People's Daily), 1 March. Available from: http://politics.people.com.cn/n1/2018/0301/c1001–29840344.html.

Perry, E. 2015. The populist dream of Chinese democracy. *Journal of Asian Studies* 74(4), 903–15.

PRC Ministry of Foreign Affairs. 2001. President Jiang Zemin delivered a speech at APEC economic leaders' meeting: strengthen cooperation and meet new challenges together in the new century, 21 October. Available from: www.fmprc.gov.cn/mfa_eng/wjdt_665385/zyjh_665391/t25043.shtml.

PRC State Council Information Office. 2018. China's top political state bodies to meet in early March, 31 January. Available from: www.scio.gov.cn/m/32618/Document/1618564/1618564.htm.

Qiushi. 2018. Qingxing! Xifang sifa duli zai wo guo zou bu tong (Wake up! Western judicial independence can't work in China). *Qiushi* (Seeking Truth). No. 2. Available from: www.qstheory.cn/zhuanqu/qsdd/2018-01/22/c_1122296965.htm.

2019a. Qiaqiang dang dui quanmian yifa zhiguo de lingdao (Strengthening the party's leadership over the overall rule of law). *Qiushi* (Seeking Truth), 15 February. Available from: https://perma.cc/6JYW-9RLG.

2019b. Xinxing zheng dang zhidu zai he chu? (In what ways is the new-style political-party system new?). *Qiushi* (Seeking Truth), 17 April. Available from: www.qstheory.cn/laigao/ycjx/2019-04/17/c_1124380319.htm.

2019c. Xinxing zheng dang zhidu shi ruhe chuangzao de? (How was the new-style political party system created?). *Qiushi* (Seeking Truth), 12 April. Available from: www.qstheory.cn/wp/2019-04/12/c_1124356997.htm.

Redden, E. 2018. The Chinese student threat? *Inside Higher Ed*, 15 February. Available from: https://perma.cc/GL2B-JUYL.

RFA. 2017. Sifabu wei weiquan lüshi shouke zai fouding 'san quan fen li' (Ministry of justice instructs rights lawyers to negate the separation of power). RFA News, 31 August. Available from: www.rfa.org/mandarin/yataibaodao/renquanfazhi/xl1-08312017103425.html.

2018. Chinese lecturer fired for raising presidential term-limit in class. 21 May. Available from: www.rfa.org/english/news/china/lecturer-05212018105710.html.

Schmitz, R. 2019. Reporters notebook: Uighurs held for 'extremist thoughts' they didn't know they had. *NPR*, 7 May. Available from: www.npr.org/2019/05/07/720608802/reporters-notebook-uighurs-held-for-extremist-thoughts-they-didnt-know-they-had.

Schrader, M. 2018. *Twitter*. Available from: https://twitter.com/tombschrader/status/979056963098116096.

Shi, Jiangtao. 2017. 'No separation of powers': China's top graft-buster seeks tighter party grip on government. *South China Morning Post*, 6 March. Available from: www.scmp.com/news/china/policies-politics/article/2076501/no-separation-powers-chinas-top-graft-buster-seeks.

Six Whys. 2009. 'Liuge' weishenme: dui jige zhongda wenti de huida – chuban fashe. Gov.cn (PRC Government Website). 30 May. Available from: http://www.gov.cn/jrzg/2009-05/30/content_1327352.htm.

Study Times. 2018. Zuo weihu hexin weihu quanwei de biaoshuai (A model for sustaining core maintenance of authority). *Xuexi Shibao* (Study Times), 21 May. Available from: http://news.sina.com.cn/c/xl/2018-05-21/doc-ihaturft4481428.shtml.

Thomas, N. 2019. These numbers show why U.S. policy makers are misjudging popular support for China's government. *Market Watch*, 2 October. Available from: www.marketwatch.com/story/these-numbers-show-just-how-much-the-lives-of-everyday-chinese-have-improved-in-recent-decades-2019-10-02.

Upham, F. 2005. Who will find the defendant if he stays with his sheep? justice in rural China, *Yale Law Journal* 114(7), 1675–718.

U.S.–China Business Council. Chinese Government. Available from: www.uschina.org/resources/chinese-government .

Van Reybrouck, D. 2018. *Against Elections*. New York: Seven Stories Press.

Vile, M. J. C. 1967. *Constitutionalism and the Separation of Powers*. Oxford: Clarendon Press.

Wang, Shaoguang. 2014. *Representative and Representational Democracy*. Reading the China Dream, Mark McConaghy and Shi Anshu, trans. Available from: www.readingthechinadream.com/wang-shaoguang-representative-and-representational-democracy.html.

Wang, Qishan. 2015. Wang Qishan zuixin biaotai: women ren jianjue ye hen shenzhong (Wang Qishan's latest statement: we are very determined and very cautious). *Gongshi Wang* (Consensus online), 28 April. Available from: www.gelora45.com/news/WangChiShan_KamiTeguhDanHatihati_Th.pdf.

2017. Wang Qishan, kaiqi xin shidai ta shang xin zhengcheng (Wang Qishan, beginning a new era, embarking on a new journey). *Renmin Ribao* (People's Daily), 7 November. Available from: http://cpc.people.com.cn/n1/2017/1107/c64094-29630544.html.

Weiss, J. 2019a. A world safe for autocracy? China's rise and the future of global politics. *Foreign Affairs* 98(4), 92–102.

2019b. Testimony before the U.S. House of Representatives Permanent Select Committee on Intelligence, hearing on 'China's digital authoritarianism: surveillance, influence, and political control'. 16 May. Available from: https://perma.cc/CHT3-MS5C.

White House. 2018. Statement from the press secretary on China's political correctness. 5 May. Available from: www.whitehouse.gov/briefings-statements/statement-press-secretary-chinas-political-correctness/.

Worden, A. 2019. The Human Rights Council Advisory Committee: a new tool in China's anti-human rights strategy. *Sinopsis*, 6 August. Available from: https://perma.cc/A3RW-WATB.

Wu, Bangguo. 2011. 2011 Report on the word of the National People's Congress, 10 March. Available from: https://china.usc.edu/wu-bangguo-2011-report-work-national-people%E2%80%99s-congress-march-10-2011.

Xi, Jingping. 2017. Full text of Xi Jinping's report at the 19th CPC National Congress. *China Daily*, 18 October. Available from: www.chinadaily.com.cn/china/19thcpcnationalcongress/2017-11/04/content_34115212.htm.

Xinhua. 2016. Bawo guoji huayu quan youxiao chuanbo zhongguo shengyin – Xi Jinping wai xuan gongzuo silu linian tanxi (Grasping the right to international discourse power to effectively spread China's voice: analysis of the ideas of Xi Jinping's outreach work). *Xinhua* (Xinhua News), 6 April. Available from: https://perma.cc/6N34–3W27.

2017a. CPC meeting stresses party's leadership over universities, 28 June. Available from: http://en.people.cn/n3/2017/0628/c90000–9234455.html.

2017b. We will not 'export' Chinese model: Xi, 1 December. Available from: www.xinhuanet.com/english/2017-12/01/c_136793833.htm.

2017c. Zhongguo gongchandang yu shijie zheng dang gaoceng duihuahui (High-level dialogue between the CCP and worldwide political parties).

Xinhuawang (Xinhua online), 3 December. Available from: www.xinhuanet.com/world/2017-12/03/c_1122050731.htm.
2018a. Xi as core. 13 January. Available from: www.xinhuanet.com/english/2018-01/13/c_136893080.htm.
2018b. China focus: member list of 13th CPPCC National Committee released. 25 January. Available from: www.xinhuanet.com/english/2018-01/25/c_136924802.htm.
2018c. Landmark two sessions set course for 'new era'. 20 March. Available from: www.china.org.cn/china/NPC_CPPCC_2018/2018-03/20/content_50729765.htm.
2018d. Safeguarding Xi's core position is the key: communique. 13 January. Available from: www.xinhuanet.com/english/2018-01/13/c_136893080.htm.
2018e. Chinese justice minister stresses CPC leadership of lawyers. 19 January. Available from: www.xinhuanet.com/english/2018-01/19/c_136908219.htm.
2018f. China focus: Xi stresses party's 'absolute leadership' over political, legal work, 22 January. Available from: www.xinhuanet.com/english/2018-01/22/c_136915374.htm.
2018g. Zhonggong zhongyang yinfa 'shenhua dang he guojia jigou gaige fang'an' (The central committee of the CCP issues 'deepening party and state reform plan'). *Xinhuawang* (Xinhua online), 21 March. Available from: www.xinhuanet.com/politics/2018-03/21/c_1122570517.htm.
2018h. Senior legislators study Xi's thought on people's congress system. 22 May. Available from: www.xinhuanet.com/english/2018-05/22/c_137198491.htm.
2018i. Xi Jinping: ju qizhi ju minxin yu xinren xing wenhua zhan xingxiang geng gao wancheng xin xing shi xia xuanchuan sixiang gongzuo shiming renwu (Xi Jinping: raising the banner and gathering people to cultivate an image of the new person so as to better accomplish the mission of propaganda and ideological work under the new situation). *Xinhuawang* (Xinhua online), 22 August. Available from: www.xinhuanet.com/politics/2018-08/22/c_1123310844.htm.
2018j. Zhongguo xinxing zheng dang zhidu gei shijie de qishi (The revelation brought to the world by China's new-style political-party system). *Xinhuawang* (Xinhua online), 10 March. Available from: www.xinhuanet.com/world/2018-03/10/c_129826579.htm.
2018k. China's party system is great contribution to political civilization: Xi. 5 March. Available from: www.xinhuanet.com/english/2018-03/05/c_137015955.htm.
2018l. Religious extremism notably curbed in Xinjiang: senior Chinese official. Xinhua, 14 March. Available from: www.xinhuanet.com/english/2018-04/14/c_137111356.htm.
2019. Ambassadors from 37 countries issue joint letter to support China on its human rights achievements. 13 July. Available from: https://perma.cc/Y6LX-S7YS.

Zenz, A. 2019. 'Thoroughly reforming them towards a healthy heart attitude': China's political re-education campaign in Xinjiang. *Central Asian Survey* 38(1).

Zhang, L. 2018. What does 'great power diplomacy with Chinese characteristics' Mean? *Carnegie-Tsinghua Center for Global Policy*, 20 April. Available from: https://perma.cc/CP57-S7FH.

Zhang, Taisu, and Ginsburg, T. 2019. China's turn toward law. *Virginia Journal of International Law* 59(2), 306–89.

Zhao, Yinan. 2012. Uphold constitution, *Xi says. China Daily*, 5 December. Available from: http://usa.chinadaily.com.cn/china/2012-12/05/content_15985894.htm.

Zhu, Lingjun. 2019. Zhongguo gongchandang shi women de xiang shiye de lingdao hexin (The CCP is the core of leadership for all of our causes). *Zhongguo gongchandang xinwen* (CPCNews.Cn), 23 May. Available from: https://perma.cc/556L-KTNK.

Zhu, Xiqun. 2018. Xinxing zheng dang zhidu de youshixing ji fazhan wanshan (The superiority of the new-style political-party system and its developmental perfection). *Renmin Luntan – Xueshu Qianyan* (People's Forum: Academic Frontier), April edition, reprinted 16 July. Available from: www.cssn.cn/zzx/zwzzzd_zzx/201807/t20180716_4504285.shtml.

7

The 'Organisational Weapon' of the Chinese Communist Party

China's Disciplinary Regime from Mao to Xi Jinping

LING LI

7.1 Introduction

It was more than six decades ago that the term 'organisational weapon' was first coined by the late professor Phillip Selznick and presented in the book title of his study of Bolshevik strategy and tactics. Considered as a 'weapon' of the Communist Party of the Soviet Union (CPSU) was its modus operandi, driven by the desires of power-seizure and societal transformation (Selznick 1952: 4–7). Labelling it a 'combat party', Selznick asserted that the communist party, guided by its ideology, set out to seize power not through a traditional revolutionary approach, such as overthrowing a ruler through a popular uprising or a military coup, but through institutional subversion (Selznick 1952: 6). The instrument to accomplish this was the organisation of the communist party, an organisation comprising an elite of reliable agents who were skilfully trained, thoroughly indoctrinated and rigidly disciplined to carry out whatever mission was given to them. Through the activities of these agents, the communist party could progressively develop a network of power in a targeted society from the bottom up by infiltrating established institutions and groups, neutralising opposition and gaining control over positions of power in these establishments, and ready itself to displace the constitutional authority of the state when the time came to do so (Blumer 1952: 631).

Written in 1952, long after the 1917 Russian Revolution, this image of the communist party conveyed by Selznick in his book is static and incomplete. Relying on Leninist literature and reports of activities from underground communist parties in the United States, Great Britain, China and Germany in the first-half of the 20th century (Blumer 1952: 14–16), Selznick's focus was limited to the very early phase of developments of communist parties, that is, prior to their successful seizure of power. This narrow focus produced an incisive explanation of the mode of operation (or modus operandi) of revolutionary communist parties at their inceptive stage but not of established communist parties when their power has been secured. This gap prevents a more complete understanding of the operation of the community party because the party's goals are diametrically opposite at these two stages: one is to subvert power (at the inceptive stage) and the other is to retain power (at the established stage).

In this chapter, I focus on the 'organisational weapon' of the Chinese Communist Party (CCP or Party) and analyse how the Party uses administrative arrangements and manipulations to preserve its political monopoly and control over the Chinese state. To this end, I use the evolvement of the Party's disciplinary regime from the Mao to the Xi eras as an example and the empirical basis for my analysis. Moreover, with this exercise, I also intend to draw attention to the distinctions between one type of single-party state and another, not based on the substances of their policies and programs but on how they operate. The rest of this chapter is organised in two sections. Section 7.2 discusses the conceptual qualities of the mode of operation of China's Party-state from a comparative perspective. Section 7.3 involves two tasks. The first is to conduct a historical analysis of the evolution, in terms of its mode of operation, of the Party-state's disciplinary regime from 1949 till the present. The second task is to use this historical analysis to contextualise and highlight the significance of Xi Jinping's institutional reform related to the National Supervision Commission (NSC).

7.2 Conceptual Qualities of China's Party-State

A useful starting point to understand the conceptual qualities of the communist regime of the People's Republic of China (PRC or China) is by way of comparison. Conceptually distinguishing it from other regime types requires two steps. The first step is to divide different regime types based on constitutional foundation. In this regard, a communist regime bears two characteristics. First, it is an authoritarian state where the authoritarian ruler does not claim ownership of the state but lays the constitutional foundation of the regime on a claim of popular sovereignty. Second, although it is a state which is constituted upon principles of popular sovereignty, that sovereignty is subjugated to the legitimated monopolistic control by one single political group. The first characteristic would immediately set apart communist regimes from traditional hereditary regimes, and the second would differentiate them from electoral democracies, including 'hybrid' or competitive authoritarian regimes where political competition is permitted but the electoral process is heavily manipulated and the results skewed. However, this criterion does not distinguish communist regimes from other types of autocratic 'republics' such as Nazi Germany, whose constitution recognised both the popular sovereignty and the monopolistic power of a single political group or person. For that, we need to take the second step, which is based on the mode of operation of their autocratic rule.

The mode of operation of communist regimes demonstrates a certain character that I call 'party-state-ness'. This party-state-ness has the following features. First, its political system is organised under a dual party-state structure, which consists of two self-contained administrative substructures: one of the party and one of the state. Second, the party structure operates in parallel to the state structure, which means that the party is linked to the state but does not supplant it. Third, in the dual party-state structure, the party comes first and the supremacy of the party is realised through organisational arrangements rather than through law. This means that the constitution recognises popular sovereignty as the primary source of legitimacy of public offices; it upholds the rule of law and renders no above-the-law prerogative either to the party or to any of its offices (Li and Zhou 2019). These features are found uniquely in communist regimes, which distinguishes them from the Nazi regime, which was also run by a single party, a point which I will turn to next.

7.2.1 'Dual State'

'Dual state' is an important concept conceived by Ernst Fränkel to describe the form of governance in Nazi Germany during 1933–38. Fränkel's dual state consists of a 'normative state' (*Rechtstaat*), which refers to 'an administrative body endowed with elaborate powers for safeguarding the legal order as expressed in statutes, decisions of the courts and activities of the administrative agencies', and a 'prerogative state', referring to the 'governmental system which exercises unlimited arbitrariness and violence unchecked by any legal guarantees' (Fränkel 2017: xiii). The normative state protected only the 'constructive forces' from the Gestapo, and its main task was to maintain economic life (Fränkel 2017: 96). To that end, economic estates (*Wirtscharftestände*) were created to prevent interference from the prerogative state and to provide business, trade and industry with a measure of self-governance (Fränkel 2017: 97).

The appeal of Fränkel's dual state is evident. It provides a simplified outlook of a complex society ruled incongruously by both law-and-order and arbitrariness-and-terror. It is no wonder that inspiration from Fränkel's dual state theory soon led parallels to be drawn between fascist and Leninist regimes. In Robert Sharlet's contribution to the same volume where T. H. Rigby promoted his mono-organisational thesis, he employed the term 'prerogative state' to represent the sphere of the Soviet state that was governed by the 'rule of force', namely, the CPSU, and the 'normative state', the one governed 'through a system of sanctioned legal norms prescribing the permissible boundaries of interpersonal relations and citizen-state relations' (Sharlet 1975: 156). A similar characterisation of the Soviet legal system can be found elsewhere (Osakwe 1985). Indeed, we can certainly identify the quality that both fascist and Leninist regimes share, namely, the vulnerability of law to the power of coercion. However, to apply the dual state theory to Leninist regimes, especially China, obscures an important distinction between the two regime types: the mode of operation of autocratic rule.

In the case of Nazi Germany, the National Socialist German Worker's Party (the Nazi Party) was deeply incorporated into the state constitutional order. As soon as the Nazi Party came to power in 1933, it altered the constitutional order through the notorious Enabling Act (*Gesetz zur Behebung der Not von Volk und Reich*) in 1933, which gave the government led by the Nazi Party the power to enact decrees which might 'deviate from the constitution'. In January 1934, the Reconstruction Act (*Gesetz zum Neuaufbau des Reichs*) was introduced, which conferred upon Hitler's cabinet the *Pouvoir constitué* without limitations.[1] Only six months later, following the death of President Paul von Hindenburg, another important statute, namely, the Succession Act (*Gesetz über das Staatsoberhaupt des deutschen Reichs*) was introduced. This Act conferred de jure the power that was previously retained by the presidential office, at least in name, to Hitler as the Reichskanzler, an

[1] The power was used, for instance, to turn a federal republic into a unitary and centralised state by transferring the sovereign powers of the previously autonomous *Ländes* (provinces) to the Reich and reducing the provincial governments to agencies of the Reich Government.

office that Hitler had been holding since 1933, and hence rendered him the complete dictatorship by law.

With the immense legislative power vested in Hitler's office as the Reichskanzler, a number of laws were passed in quick succession that embedded the Nazi Party in the state system and ensured its legitimate political domination. For example, the Law to Safeguard the Unity of Party and State in 1933 (hereafter the Unity Law) recognised the Nazi Party as 'a corporation under public law', whose organisation would be determined by the Führer. It also made the paramilitary organisation of the *Sturmabteilung* (SA) effectively a state institution by promoting its political leader to the Reich cabinet[2] and demanded loyalty from members of the Nazi Party and the SA to Hitler himself. Section Eight of the Unity Law (1933) also stipulated that the Reich Chancellor, as Führer of the Nazi Party and the supreme commander of the SA, would issue regulations needed for the execution and augmentation of this law, particularly with respect to the judical organisation and procedure of the Nazi Party and the SA. Later, a decree of the Reich Minister of Justice, dated 17 February 1934, conferred state authority to the ranks of the Nazi leadership corps by providing that 'the supreme offices of the *Reichsleitung* (Nazi Party political positions at the national level) are equal in rank to the supreme Reich Government authorities' (Jackson 1945). On 15 September 1935, the Reichstag applied the final touches to the fusion of the Nazi Party and the state with the passage of the Reich Flag Law, which made the Swastika flag of the Nazi Party the official flag of the Reich (RGBL 1935).

Vested with unlimited legislative and administrative power, the Nazi Party could carry out its actions directly from the state offices that they occupied. Both the prerogative and normative states in Fränkel's dual state were inseparable, as stated in Section 1 of the Unity Law (1933), and their shared seat of power rested primarily in the state system of the Reich. The party system functioned more as a platform for electoral campaigns and a channel of internal communication.

In contrast, in the PRC, the legitimacy of the Party's rule is not derived from the state's constitutional authorisation. The Constitution makes references to the Party mostly in the narratives of the preface. In such references, the Party appears only in its collectivity and in the most

[2] Other than the Chief of Staff of the SA, the Deputy of the Führer (vice-Party leader) was also introduced to the Reich cabinet as a Nazi Party political leader without a portfolio in the state structure.

abstract form, for instance, 'shall adhere to the Party's leadership', which would be generally considered empty and unenforceable slogans in normal circumstances. With the exception of the 1975 and 1978 Constitutions that followed the disruptive Cultural Revolution, where a provision was introduced that conferred power to the Chairman of the Party Central Committee as the commander-in-chief of the military force (the relevant provision was removed in 1982), the Constitution has otherwise never rendered any power of substance, let alone prerogatives, to any particular office of the Party. To the contrary, the Party had long pledged in the Constitution to operate under the confines of the Constitution and statutes of the state. At the same time, the structural integrity of the state system was maintained in the post-1982 constitutional order: a Party leader would not be given state authority without holding a state office, and only state institutions were entitled to exercise enforcement power, especially coercive power.

This is not, however, to suggest that the Party has in fact subjugated itself to state power. Instead, I make the above comparison to highlight the difference in the mode of operation between the 'dual state' of Nazi Germany and the dualistic rule of the Chinese communist regime. In Nazi Germany, the prerogative of the Nazi Party was achieved by first empowering the state office, namely, the Reichskanzler occupied by Hitler, and then using that office to enact laws and statutes to create further prerogatives to the Nazi Party and its programs. In the process, the sovereignty of the state system was kept potent as the primary seat of power, and the party system served simply as an electoral platform and an internal communication channel. In contrast, in China, the composition of the dualistic rule represents the opposite approach: in law the Party subjugates itself to the constitutional order of the state, not the other way around; the Party keeps the sovereignty of the state intact de jure but castrates the latter de facto in actual operation. The actual subjugation of the state is achieved by creating a separate seat of power, namely, the Party, outside of the state structure, and then chaining the state to the Party through a series of organisational instead of legislative arrangements.

7.2.2 'Mono-organisational Society'

The 'mono-organisational society' is a concept developed by T. H. Rigby to describe the political–social ecology of the Soviet Union (USSR). The concept evolved from Rigby's earlier efforts to characterise societies based on how coordination of human activities is achieved. According to Rigby, coordination is a problem characteristic of human societies because 'societies arise from the possibility of achieving ends by combined efforts which cannot, or cannot as well, be achieved by individual efforts' (Rigby 1964: 539). Any combination of effort produces a problem of coordination, including the organisation of a society. Hence, Rigby distinguished three types of societies, each of which is dominated by one particular mode of coordination: traditional societies dominated by custom, market societies dominated by contract and organisational societies dominated by command (Rigby 1964: 540).

Around a decade later when he contributed a chapter to Robert C. Tucker's edited volume on Stalinism (Rigby 1975), Rigby prefixed 'organisational' with 'mono', presumably to sharpen the contrast between communist and non-communist industrial societies. In Rigby's updated description, he describes a society as mono-organisational when nearly all of its social activities are coordinated by hierarchies of appointed officials under the direction of a single overall command (Rigby 1975: 53). In order to set it apart from the Weberian bureaucracy, Rigby addresses three distinctively mono-organisational characteristics of the Soviet system. First, unlike Weberian bureaucratic systems, the Soviet system installs parallels of party and governmental hierarchies that allow party institutions to 'guide and check' the work of governmental and non-governmental agencies without supplanting the latter (Rigby 1975: 55). Second, the totality of demands of the single command requires the introduction to the system of a measure of decentralisation of decision-making, which fosters substantive rationality at the expense of Weberian formal rationality (Rigby 1975: 55–6). Third, the salience of the use of campaigns as the dominant mobilisational method creates regular 'anomalies' that depart from the 'mechanistic' operation of classic rule-following Weberian bureaucratic systems (Rigby 1975: 55).

As can be predicted, post-1949 Chinese society shares all the mono-organisational features that Rigby ascribed to the USSR. In fact, if we replace all the references to the USSR in Rigby's conceptual analysis with the PRC, one would accept the description readily. However, Rigby's analysis, despite its accurate description, is limited in depth because he failed to recognise the profoundness of the duality of communist regimes' parallel organisational infrastructure and how this duality helps increase the institutional capacity of the communist party to govern a vast state in changing environments.[3]

[3] The author is aware of the popular view that the fall of the Soviet Union and its satellite states was evidence of the opposite of the postulation made above: the lack of institutional capacity of the communist party to govern a modernizing state. Although the fall of the

7.2.3 Party-State as a Dual-Organisation

To put it simply, the essence of the Leninist institutional framework in China is its Party-state construct, where the Party and the state are institutionally integrated. It means that Party institutions are embedded in state institutions, but the two are not fused. Instead, the Party and the state remain self-contained: in the Party system, all Party institutions are subject to the Party normative system, where all Party institutions are established and organised according to the Party Charter, and all Party activities are regulated by Party disciplines and Party rules; in the state system, all state institutions are established and organised according to the Constitution, and state activities are regulated by state laws, which are enacted by people's congresses (not the Party) and enforced by people's courts comprised of judges elected by the people's congresses (again, not the Party). Simultaneously, the two systems are integrated into a grid that grants the Party direct access to state decision-making processes.

This gridded Party-state structure consists of two key components: regimentation and the interlocking of decision-making bodies. Regimentation refers to the hierarchical design of all Party and state institutions as well as of each single post within them. Regimentation is critical in establishing a web of chains of command, which are relied upon to channel and, more importantly, to enforce instructions from the apex of the Party to the lowest level where the potency of the central authority begins to attenuate as the chain of command extends and scatters to cover an extensive territory. The well-studied ranking system is the embodiment of regimentation. The system has borrowed some core concepts from the Soviet *nomenklatura*, but it also bears indigenous features of the bi-millennial Chinese imperial ranking system and hence remains as 'eclectic' as the Chinese state itself.

The second institutional arrangement of the gridded Party-state structure is the interlocking of Party and state decision-making bodies, or what is called the 'interlocking directorate' (Shambaugh 2000). Here, what needs to be stressed is that the Party interlocks its decision-making bodies with those of the state, not only by appointing individual Party officials to take key offices of all state institutions but also by planting

Soviet Union is too complex an issue to be discussed here, it is necessary to mention here that the author holds the opinion that the Soviet Union fell not because the Party-state system broke it but because the Soviet leader delinked the party and the state. Chinese leaders reversed the delinking attempts in the aftermath of 1989 and consolidated the Party-state structure thereafter. The regime remains resilient.

Party-groups in the decision-making bodies of these institutions, through which the Party can latch onto the state in a more structured and consolidated manner.

Through regimentation and the interlocking of decision-making bodies, the Party subjects the state to a subordinate status. The superiority of the Party is not established in state laws that provide the Party a privileged status above the state or the state law. Instead, it is achieved through the regimentation and the interlocking of Party and state decision-making bodies via the Party-groups. Since members of the Party-groups are not ordinary government employees but key decision-makers holding executive offices in the state institutions concerned, to have the Party-groups answer to the Party is to have the state answer to the Party.

7.2.4 *Administration of Control*

Unlike other authoritarian regimes with political parties, the Party as an institution collectively exercises monopolistic control over the state. However, such a monopoly is not achieved through constitutional safeguards but through administrative arrangements. Specifically, the Party's control over the state links two seats of power, each of which is self-contained and commands a matching multi-layered sub-structure that is used to centralise decision-making from geographically divided regions and locales. The Party, from its own seat of power, constructs and maintains a bureaucratic system of its own, which mirrors that of the state. Once the parallel structure is put in place, the Party has at its disposal two approaches to administer control over the state.

The first is the shared-control approach. This is achieved by first installing Party-groups in the decision-making bodies of all state institutions. Members of the Party-groups constitute the absolute majority of the decision-making bodies of the state institutions they inhabit. They perform state functions but answer to the Party. Then the Party delegates a great magnitude of authority to state institutions by roughly demarcating Party matters and state matters and reserves the power to intervene if any matter of importance catches its attention. Such intervention is carried out through the Party-groups located at the backstage of a bifurcated state decision-making process (Li 2015). Their activities are regulated through Party regulations and exempted from external scrutiny by the state legal system. As required by Party regulations, the Party-groups are bound to report their activities to their supervising Party organisation and are responsible for translating and converting any Party instruction given to them into state decisions. Once converted into state decisions, the Party instruction gains authority and legality from the seat of power of the state. With the shared-control approach, the Party's actions are taken under the name of relevant state institutions, whose activities are at least nominally subject to the scrutiny of the state legal system.

The shared-control approach is employed for two types of affairs. The first type involves actions that can be legitimated only by the popular-sovereignty-based state authority, for instance, the use of violence and other types of coercive measures, or the appointments of officials to state offices. The second type involves matters which, in isolation, are of little or negligible interest to the Party in order to retain its monopolistic rule. But these matters can be of interest when they aggregate or coalesce and hence require routinised regulatory attention. Under the shared-control approach, the Party delegates a lot of regulatory competence to the state institutions concerned and exercises its control in a selective and mostly ex post fashion.

The second is the exclusive-control approach. Whilst under the shared-control approach, the Party lets the state run business at the front end and controls the outcome at the back in a selective and ex post manner. Under the exclusive-control approach, the Party controls both the procedure and outcome of the affairs throughout the process.

Two types of affairs fall into the exclusive jurisdiction of the Party. The first type of affairs that warrant exclusive-control concerns the application of 'internal' regulatory measures on Party members and/or Party institutions. Such internal measures include both cautionary and punitive sanctions which are not penal in name but some of which may assume a factual penal capacity in practice when being used as triggers to start prosecutorial procedures. When the Party proclaims exclusive authority over Party affairs, its jurisdiction over these affairs is justified on grounds of the voluntary acceptance of the terms of membership (which include acceptance to the Party's disciplinary procedures and measures) when a Party member joins the Party, the same as the terms of contract when one joins a fitness club or updates the service contract with a telecommunications provider. However, the difference is the fact that the Party is not a private club but 'the government behind the government'; and unlike a private contract, which cannot deprive a service user of the protection provided by public law, the Party's exercise of power is kept outside of public law and is largely immune from external scrutiny.

The second type of affairs that fall under the exclusive jurisdiction of the Party has two features. First, these affairs are of critical importance to the Party, so much so that they could not be regulated under the shared-control approach. Second, to regulate these affairs, the Party has to invoke state authority because they are beyond the scope of the Party's jurisdictional reach, either because the person or institution under regulatory scrutiny is not a Party member or institution or because the action to be taken can only be legitimated by invoking state authority and popular sovereignty. To deal with these circumstances, the Party devised the office-sharing practice or 'one office two plaques/hats' to allow the Party to exercise exclusive control over the affairs concerned and at the same time to borrow the legal authority from the state office that the Party adjoins or 'the hat of which it wears'. As will be shown in Section 7.3, this practice of office-sharing has become a vital device for the Party in the latest reform of its disciplinary system, legalising its actions and upgrading its control over newly politicised spheres.

7.3 Building the Party's Disciplinary Regime

The development of the Party's disciplinary regime is a good illustration of various approaches with which the Party exercises control over state affairs. As will be shown, the Party has primarily relied on its own authority to initiate disciplinary investigations, thus retaining exclusive control over its entire process. The need for exclusive control over disciplinary activities remains essential for the Party to preserve the potency of its chain of command. The Party applies the shared-control approach and invokes state authority primarily for the legitimation of the use of coercion. However, in the earlier years of the PRC's history, the need for legitimation was narrowly understood by the Party, which sought state authorisation only in cases where the conviction was certain and the punishment was publicly announced. The use of coercion prior to conviction – in particular, in the process of investigation – was authorised by the Party alone as a matter of political expediency. It was only after decades of state-building that the use of coercive measures by the Party in its disciplinary investigations became a matter of concern due to its legitimacy deficiency, which was discordant with the Party's commitment to a law-based governing regime. It was against this backdrop that the new NSC was established in 2018.

7.3.1 1949–54: One Regime, Two Systems

When the PRC was founded in 1949, the Party, being debilitated after decades of wars, introduced a politically inclusive Constitution and operated side by side with a coalition government that at the time consisted of a number of other political parties and social forces (Li 2015). In the earlier years of the PRC, the Party placed as much effort in Party-building as it did in state-building. In 1949, the Party installed its own disciplinary institution, the Central Commission of Discipline and Inspection of the Party (CCDI), alongside the Central People's Supervision Commission (PeoSC), which was established under the coalition government. Even before 1949, the CCDI, as an internal disciplinary body, had been a constitutive part of the Party; however, it was rarely in full operation due to the Party's minimal need for specialisation in administrative affairs (Li 2016). Immediately after the establishment of the PRC in 1949, the Party Centre[4] passed an edict to set up the CCDI, mirroring the control commission of the USSR. It was also expected to help preserve the secrets of the state and the Party because of concerns about the pluralistic political environment in which it was embedded at that time, which was highlighted by Mao's edits of the draft of the said edict (with Mao's edits in bold):

> The Party has established itself as the ruling party nationwide, **democratic coalition governments have been or will be established across the nation, the volume of collaborative affairs between the Party and non-Party members is increasing day by day**. Against this backdrop, in order to better implement the Party's political line as well as various **concrete** policies and **to preserve confidential information of the Party and the nation**, to strengthen the organisational and disciplinary characters of the Party, to connect closely with the masses and to overcome bureaucratism, to ensure the correct implementation of **all** Party decisions, the Central Party decided to establish the discipline and inspection commissions at the central and all other levels.
>
> (Centre 1949)

At that time, the CCDI was a very small organisation, compared with what it has become today. Members of its decision-making body, including the director, worked only part-time for the CCDI and were appointed, instead of being selected through an electoral process (Centre 1949). The CCDI had only one office, with few staff members (Politburo

[4] The Party Centre officially refers to the highest collective decision-making body of the Party, including the National Party Congress (NPC) and the Central Committee (CC). However, they are congregations that are in session very briefly and cannot perform routine decision-making, whilst the Politburo and the Politburo Standing Committee, as permanent executive bodies of the CC, are the de facto Party Centre. In this article, 'Party Centre' refers to the latter two, unless specified otherwise.

1950). Although the Party commanded that regional and local Party committees should also set up Commissions of Discipline and Inspection (CDIs) under its wing, the goal was not fully actualised because the Party's institutional infrastructure was not fully built, especially in the newly 'liberated' regions where the Party's presence was recent and its power base not established. For instance, CDIs had no presence at the grassroots level and barely maintained a presence at the basic level of the administrative structure, that is, in urban districts and rural counties (Province A 1953). This meant that the CDIs had no agents of their own to conduct disciplinary investigations. Instead, they functioned more like sanctioning boards based on evidence sent to or passed on to them by other institutions. Moreover, the sanctioning power of the Party was very tightly centralised in the hands of the Party committee at the county level and above.[5]

While the disciplinary institution was still in the making, the Party nevertheless launched a great number of punitive and often violent political campaigns during this time. These campaigns were carried out primarily by Party Committees, the central nervous system, as it were, of the Party. Relying on mass mobilisation to identify targets and to induce, very often through coercion, confessions and/or witness statements as evidence to establish the guilt of the targets, these campaigns were most forceful in eradicating opposition to the Party, silencing dissent and, most importantly, establishing the Party Centre as a seat of power independent from that of the state. State authority was invoked only when serious punishment, especially the death penalty, was to be meted out, in which case a written guilty verdict and sentence would be issued by the people's tribunals upon instructions of the Party (County A 1960). In these cases, courts enjoyed little autonomy since Party committees were regularly and directly involved in the determination of guilt and sentencing.

In the meantime, on the state side, the PeoSCs and their offices at various administrative levels were nominally the disciplinary institutions charged with monitoring the performance of public employees and holding them accountable for any unlawful or derelict conduct. Constituted on a pluralist political basis, the PeoSC had a high percentage of non-Party representation – more than 40 per cent of its 20 commissioners

[5] According to local archives, a village Party-cell (*zhibu*) or a general Party-cell (*zongzhi*) of a work unit did not even have the remit to apply light sanctions, such as warnings, to party members under its administration.

were non-Party members, including its director. The activities of these supervision offices were confined to civil servants in the administrative branches and to non-Party members only. And their function seemed more in the nature of the later specialised letter-and-visit offices and not to conduct investigations (Party Centre 1952).

7.3.2 1955–66: Party-Building without the State

During its first five years in power, the Party relied primarily on Party committees as the driver of its many coercive campaigns. These campaigns, despite their triumphant success, as measured by overachieved targets, also exposed the primitivity of the disciplinary system of the Party at that time. First of all, there was a long backlog of cases. Part of the problem was attributable to the shortage of staff to process the cases and part to the mandatory chain of approval, which prolonged the decision-making process. Zhu De, the then director of the CCDI (1949–55), had even proposed to merge the CDI and PeoSC offices so that their managerial and operational resources could be optimised (Database 2006). The second problem was the excess of punitive enforcement, including the excessively widened scope of investigation and the excessive application of penal punishment, especially the death penalty. To counter these problems, the Party replaced the CCDI with the Central Party Supervision Commission (CPSC) and a series of institutional changes which I outline below.

First came a change in the constitutive method of the Party's disciplinary institution. Instead of using the mechanism of appointment, members of each Party Supervision Commission (PSC) were now to be elected by Party delegates in their constituency. Although elections in the Party were never free and were always subject to close control from the top down, the change of constitutive approach, however, conferred on the PSC the perception of having democracy-based legitimacy, which appointed offices do not enjoy. It also gave the commission a special status that allowed it to encroach upon the autonomy of other organisational components of the Party, which was, decades later, manifest in the anti-corruption campaign in 2012–17 (Li 2019).

Second came the expansion of the Party's competence to discipline non-Party members. Before the establishment of the PSC, the competence of the CDIs was confined to Party members. Although in practice such confinement may not have been fully complied with, given the lack of a record of activities of the PeoSC, a division between Party and state disciplinary institutions was nevertheless upheld in principle. After the Anti-Rightist campaign (1957), which purged nearly all critics outside of the Party, the role of state authority in the overall institutional development of the disciplinary regime was further weakened. In 1959, the Party disassembled all state supervisory offices. In 1962, the Party installed its own supervision outposts in the ministries and committees under the state Council and in lower-level governments (Centre 1962).

Thus, without any legislative manoeuvring and disguise, the Party overstepped its jurisdictional boundary and finally devoured the state arm of the disciplinary regime (Jiang 2017). After its inauguration, the PSC was responsible for carrying out all political campaigns of the Party, including the socialist reconstruction of the ownership of productive materials, the Anti-Rightist campaign, the eradication of hidden anti-revolutionists, the rural Three-Anti campaign, the people's commune, the Great Leap Forward and the socialist education campaign (the Four Eradications movement). All these campaigns were launched with the issuance of a Party resolution, which carried the binding power to dictate actions of Party institutions that had been established at all administrative levels. The Party barely invoked state authority except towards the end of a campaign, when cases that were about to be concluded with criminal punishment were sent to the courts.[6]

Third, a significant expansion of staffing occurred. As mentioned earlier, under the previous CDI regime, disciplinary activities were constrained by staff shortages (Database 2006). Upon authorisation from the Party Centre, staffing of the PSCs doubled nationwide between 1955 and 1956 (Anonymous 1957). After a series of intraparty purges in the late 1950s, the PSCs shrank in staffing but soon had their numbers replenished upon a new initiative issued in 1962 to strengthen supervision institutions (Wang 1962). The magnitude of the PSC expansion is extraordinary considering the severity of fiscal challenges that the country was

[6] For instance, in the notorious Anti-Rightist campaign, the Party issued multiple directives to guide its agents' actions on all aspects of the campaign, including the pace of the campaign, the scope of investigation and the standards to identify and classify 'rightists', and so on. The state legislature was involved only when a new form of punitive measure, education through labour, was introduced upon Mao's instruction at the Qingdao Conference in 1957 (Centre 1957). See also, *Guanyu huafen youpai fenzi de biaozhun de tongzhi* (Notice on the Standard of Classifying the Rightists) (Mao Zedong's 1957 Speech at the Qingdao Conference [Transcript]. In *Selected Works of Mao Zedong*, Renmin Publishing House, p. 456). Another example is the Three-Anti and Five-Anti campaigns, which were carried out prior to the promulgation of the Anti-Embezzlement Directive.

facing at that time. As a result, the new PSCs were to be headed by the deputy-secretary of the corresponding Party committee, assisted by a full-time deputy director and an office of a number of full-time agents, which sets a contrast against the previous CDIs, many of which were one-person offices (Province A 1955; 1956). At the same time, the PSCs also established their presence at townships, work units and other grassroots-level places where the previous CDIs had never managed to reach. The manpower infusion meant that, unlike the previous CDIs, the PSC was no longer a sanctioning board but an enforcement agency with the capacity to conduct inspections and to investigate disciplinary violations themselves.

Fourth came the increasing delegation of disciplinary power. As mentioned earlier, under the previous regime, grassroots-level Party organisations had no sanctioning power. Under the new regime, grassroots-level Party organisations could apply light sanctions (warnings), and the power to apply severe sanctions (removal from posts, probation pending expulsion) was delegated to basic-level (township or work unit) Party committees (Commission 1957).

Fifth, having gained a new mandate and manpower, the PSCs began to establish greater vertical integration. At the onset of their establishment, the PSCs were required to answer to the PSC at the next higher level instead of to a corresponding Party committee (CCP 1955). In the following year, however, a new amendment of the Party Charter reversed the practice. Apparently, Central Party authorities were concerned that the PSCs, untied from their corresponding Party committees, would start to work on their own initiative instead of implementing the core programs adopted by the Party (Anonymous 1960; Province A 1960). But central authorities were also aware that if they tied the PSCs to their corresponding Party committees, it would limit their capacity to check on the latter. As a measure of adjustment, the central Party authorities gave the PSC at the superior level the authority to check and to advise on the work of the lower PSCs.[7] Later, in 1962, the Party further strengthened vertical control by permitting local PSCs to skip the corresponding Party committee and to report disciplinary violations directly to

[7] The Party amended the Party Charter in 1956 and changed the nature of the relationship between Party Committees and their corresponding supervision commissions from being advisory to supervisory. At the same time, the amended Party Charter mandated that the superior supervision commissions had the authority to inspect and advise on the work of lower supervision commissions in their territorial jurisdictions.

the PSC at the higher level and all the way up to the Party Centre (Centre 1962).

7.3.3 1966–78: The Anti-establishment Phase

On the eve of the Cultural Revolution, the Party's disciplinary system had grown significantly in terms of its institutional strength and capacity. Compared with the limited presence and obscure status of its predecessor (the CDI), the PSC had established itself as a powerful enforcement agency of the Party and played an indispensable role in the implementation of the political campaigns launched by the Party beginning in 1955. These campaigns were mostly coercive, directed at a wide range of targets and encompassing both rural and urban populations. In these campaigns, the PSCs served as a 'taming instrument' (Centre 1962) and performed the function of identifying and punishing those who dared to defy, question the Party's policies or express different opinions at the time. On the other hand, the PSCs also served as the Party's ombudsmen, handling complaints, tempering radical conduct and rectifying mistakes (Centre 1962). During this time, the normative system of the Party also started to take shape. A number of regulations were issued to standardise disciplinary practices. Conferences were held periodically, where PSC cadres across the country gathered together to exchange experience and to receive instructions on the latest policies and directives.

It is therefore not surprising that not long after the Cultural Revolution had begun and a mass-driven anti-establishment movement (Walder and Lu 2017) had started, the PSC itself became a target. In 1969, upon the receipt of a formal request from Kang Sheng, who performed a background investigation of members of the Central Party Supervision Commission, the Party Centre dissolved the PSCs nationwide on the ground that 80 per cent of the CPSC committee members and half of its staff members were traitors, spies and anti-revolutionary revisionists, according to Kang Sheng's investigation (CCDI 1980).[8]

Between 1966 and 1976, the function of the PSCs was performed by 'special-case examination groups' (SCEG) (*zhuan'an'zu* 专案组). Unlike the PSCs, whose activities included not only case-investigation but also policy implementation, political education and handling of grievances,

[8] During the investigation, fourteen out of fifteen CPSC standing committee members were brutally treated, six of whom died in custody.

the SCEG was a special task-force that carried out investigations of named targets, mostly high-ranking officials (Schoenhals 1996). And unlike the PSC, the operation of the SCEG had no internal institutional oversight and enjoyed an even wider magnitude of freedom to use coercion as the method of investigation (Schoenhals 1996). The SCEGs frequently drafted staff from military or para-military institutions and the public security organs to conduct interrogations. During this chaotic period, state legal institutions, including the courts and the procuratorates, were managed by ad hoc military offices. Party committees were replaced by revolutionary committees. And state authority was completely disengaged from the operation of disciplinary actions of the Party during this time.

7.3.4 1978–2017: State-Building

From the mid-1970s, the Party started to gradually restore its own institutions that had been dissolved at the peak of the Cultural Revolution. In 1978, the Party resurrected the CDI as its specialised disciplinary institution. The CDI inherited most of the institutional features of the previous PSC, including its constitutive method (though elections) and its vertical structure. The new CCDI was also rejuvenated by a significant expansion, with the number of committee members doubled compared to the peak time of the previous CPSC (CCDI 2013). Systematic institutional expansion followed. By the mid-1980s, regional and local CDIs had been established not only at all administrative levels but also in grassroots Party organisations (CCDI 1983). At the same time, a great number of Party rules and directives were introduced to regulate disciplinary activities and standardise disciplinary practices.

However, the CCDI did not assume the extra-Party jurisdiction that the PSC had been mandated to exercise. Instead, the one-regime, two-systems practice was restored as the Party restored the Ministry of Supervision (MoS) in 1986. In 1993, the CCDI started to 'share offices' with the MoS, which means that the operation of Party and state disciplinary activities was integrated under the CCDI, but the institutional identity of the MoS was kept separate from that of the CCDI. This way, the Party could borrow state authority from the MoS to legalise disciplinary actions against officials who were not Party members and hence fell outside the disciplinary competence of the Party. During this process of institution-building, the method of disciplinary investigation also changed. Having borne witness to and been victimised by the terror of mass campaigns in the 1960s, newly rehabilitated Party leaders decided to abandon the use of mass mobilisation as an enforcement tool to achieve policy objectives (Centre 1980; Ye 2005). Legitimate use of violence thus became monopolised in the hands of specialised enforcement agencies of the Party-state.

Meanwhile, as a key component of the state-building program, great efforts had been invested in constructing a new and holistic state legal system, covering all law-related fields, including legislation, adjudication, prosecution, lawyering and legal education. The development of this comprehensive state normative system, despite its structural flaws and limits, nevertheless significantly changed the landscape of the Party's disciplinary regime.

First, the landscape changed with the growth of specialised disciplinary investigative institutions of the state. Almost in sync with the resurrection of the CDI, the restoration of people's procuratorates also started in the late 1970s. As the result of an arrangement to even the workload between different legal institutions, the procuratorates were then mandated to conduct investigations of certain types of cases, which previously had been the jurisdiction of the public security organs (Lv 1992). These cases were primarily crimes committed by public employees. Since a great proportion of public employees have Party membership, the jurisdictional overlap between the procuratorates and the CDIs became inevitable. It meant that the procuratorates, as state institutions, were entitled by law to carry out investigations of crimes committed by Party members independently from the CDI. For investigations carried out by the procuratorates, the Party could exercise control only selectively and indirectly through the shared-control approach as an effort to preserve the nominal autonomy of state authority.

Second came the recognition of the need for authorisation of the use of coercion in criminal investigations. Nearly three decades of state-building efforts, roughly from 1982 to 2012, witnessed a significant increase of awareness among the legal professions as well as the general public of due process protection in criminal investigations. This increased awareness is attributable to a number of factors. First, legislative efforts were made to improve rights protection in criminal procedural law, however restricted and flawed. Second, there developed an unprecedented expansion of legal education, which has in turn improved the level of professionalisation of law enforcement agencies. And third, the Party strategically adopted and actively promoted the 'rule of law' program, which was upheld as the new political philosophy and principle of governance of the Party-state. It is against these pronounced efforts of the Party to elevate state authority and to preserve the autonomy of the state that the legitimacy of CDI-authorized use of coercion as an investigative method was called into question in the two decades preceding the Xi Jinping era.

7.4 Post-2017 Party-Building through the State: The National Supervision Commission

When Xi Jinping came to power in 2012, the state had expanded significantly after over three decades of state-building activities. The expansion of the state is manifested by the degree of specialisation of state institutions and the development of a comprehensive and self-contained state legal system that has nearly all the essential components of a developed legal system. We would assume that a natural outcome of this expansion in state institutions would be a growing expectation and demand for more independence and autonomy. Also concomitant to this expansion we could assume a widening distance between the Party and the state. However, as mentioned earlier, when the Party manages public affairs through state institutions, it can only do so *via* the shared-control approach, namely, to influence decision-making in state institutions indirectly, selectively and very often ex post. This situation constituted a predicament for the Party and reached a crescendo by the time that Xi Jinping came to power.

Being placed at such a critical juncture, the new Party General Secretary Xi Jinping chose to strengthen instead of weaken the Party's control over the state because of the fear that further distancing of the Party from the state could trigger a domino effect and cause the collapse of the Party-state in the same way as occurred in the former USSR. It was against this backdrop that Xi launched his signature anti-corruption campaign, which was unprecedentedly impactful in duration, depth and scale. However, during the campaign the attention of all observers was drawn to the fallen 'tigers' and the exposed high-profile corruption scandals, and few had anticipated what would come after. It was only at the end of the nearly five-year anti-corruption campaign that the Party rolled out its series of reform packages to narrow the gap between the Party and the state. Among these reforms, the one concerning the reorganisation of the disciplinary regime best illustrates the trajectory of the evolution of the Party's administration of control over state affairs.

Under the Party's disciplinary regime, the power to initiate and conduct disciplinary investigations is the most critical element in all its activities because it shapes the outcome of whatever disciplinary procedures follow. As mentioned earlier, with the establishment of the PSC (1955–66), the Party had monopolised the power to investigate accusations of disciplinary violations of any civil servant with or without Party membership. In the post-1978 period, this monopoly was broken when the Party started the state-building process. This process was characterised by the Party-sponsored elevation of state authority and its instrumental promotion of an autonomous state legal system under the banner of the rule of law, which created a second seat of power, the state. It meant that state institutions could obtain legality for their actions independently because of authorisation by state laws. Although the Party still retained its control over the state through a number of administrative devices, the newly gained autonomous status of the state was nonetheless potent enough to mark boundaries of Party activities.

This post-1978 change of condition that occurred in the state-building process began to have an impact on the Party's control over the administration of the disciplinary regime in two aspects. First was the loss of direct disciplinary investigative power over non-Party members. The immediate consequence of the Party's instrumental introduction of a claim to popular sovereignty as a source of legitimacy was the demarcation of jurisdictional boundaries between the Party and the state. So far, the Party had based its exercise of jurisdiction on the voluntary subscription to Party rules through the registration of Party membership. This meant that the Party had no direct jurisdiction over any individual who was not a Party member. This may not have been a decisive loss of control for the Party given the dominance of Party members in public offices. However, as the state continued to expand, an increasing number of non-Party members was employed to work in public institutions, and their activities were not monitored by the Party as directly and as closely as were the activities of those who bore Party membership. The Party found a solution to this issue in the form of office-sharing, which was to pair the Party disciplinary office (CCDI) with that of the MoS of the state, and to allow the former to share both the operational resources and legal authorities of the latter. However, the practice did not solve all the problems because the authority of the MoS was limited in at least two aspects. First, the MoS was mandated only to monitor the performance of civil servants, who constitute only a small portion of the population working in public institutions. Second, the MoS, as a division under the state Council, is inferior in rank and not authorised to monitor those members of the top echelon of the political elites.

Second was the loss of the exclusive power to conduct intraparty disciplinary investigations. As mentioned above, the Party's promotion of the state as an autonomous seat of power, however instrumental in motivation and constrained in practice, nevertheless gave the law and enforcement agency of the state and the procuratorates, in particular after the establishment of its anti-corruption units, the mandate to investigate corruption-related crimes, regardless of the membership status of the suspect (Chen 2015). Even though in practice procuratorates were required to share investigative leads and coordinate their investigative activities with the local CDIs, which they often did, this did not change the fact that the Party no longer enjoyed exclusive power to investigate disciplinary violations committed by Party-members (Li and Wang 2019). In the post-Mao state-building period, as corruption continued to grow both in scale and intensity, the institutional capacity and reach of the procuratorates also expanded. The more powerful and resourceful the procuratorates grew, the more difficult it became for the Party to control the investigative process and to shape its outcomes.

Third, the legality of coercive investigative measures used by the Party came to be increasingly challenged. Beginning in the early 1990s, the CDIs were authorised by the Party to apply coercive measures to investigate corruption-related disciplinary violations committed by public officials. These measures include solitary confinement of suspects for a sustained duration of time (infamously known as *shuanggui*), search and seizure, and freezing and confiscation of assets (Sapio 2008; Li 2016). None of these measures obtained any form of authorisation from the state and hence were often challenged for their illegality. Tension regarding the legality of *shuanggui* intensified as the Party revved up its declared commitment to a law-based governing approach as an essential ingredient of its new political philosophy. The Party was thus pushed into a corner. On the one hand, under the rule-of-law rhetoric, it became more and more difficult for the Party to continue to use coercion, which is a prerogative of designated state agencies according to the constitutional order that the Party had declared to uphold. On the other hand, as corruption become more parochial and hidden, primarily taking the form of bribery, the Party became dependent upon *shuanggui* in order to solicit confessions from suspects, which were then used as evidence of guilt in courts. Without *shuanggui* the Party's entire disciplinary regime would be rendered toothless and impotent.

It was against this backdrop that the Party rolled out its 'supervision institutional reform' at the triumphant end of the five-year anti-corruption campaign in 2017. The reform would not only legalise the Party's coercive investigative measures but also allow the Party to annex the anti-corruption units of the procuratorates under the wing of the CCDI, which was bound to meet resistance from both legal critics and the procuratorates. To mitigate the resistance, the reform was first introduced in the form of tentative pilot programs in three provinces and barely caught much attention from critics and observers. This testing of the waters lasted one year before the Party announced its successful conclusion and started to implement the reform nationwide at the end of 2017. Implementation was carried out in the form of an enforcement campaign, where instructions were sent directly to the first-in-commands of Party committees of all administrative levels, who were tasked to carry out the reform plan like a military mission in a matter of three months (Anonymous 2018). Without much suspense, the NSC was inaugurated in March 2018 on schedule, marking the pinnacle of the success of the reform.

Authorised by the newly promulgated Supervision Law, together with a new constitutional amendment, the NSC now enjoys a much higher constitutional status than the previous MoS and has become an autonomous branch of the state that equals the state legislature, the state Council, the Supreme Court (SPC) and the Supreme Procuratorate in rank. The new commissions have absorbed the mandate as well as human resources of three important anti-corruption units of the procuratorates – the Anti-Embezzlement and Bribery Bureau, the Bureau of Anti-Dereliction and Rights Infringement and the Crime Prevention Bureau Concerning Public Duty-Related Offenses. The supervision commissions are mandated to conduct investigations of a wide range of public employees and are also authorised by the state legislature to exercise all the coercive measures that were previously used extra-legally in investigations by the Party's disciplinary institution, the CDIs. And in line with the previous office-sharing practice between the CCDI and the MoS, the supervision commissions now share all their operational resources and legal authorisations with the CDIs. This means that the reform has achieved three profound objectives in one strike: to reclaim the Party's exclusive control over the entire process of investigation of disciplinary violations of Party members, to expand the scope of the Party's investigative power to public employees who are not Party members and to legalise the Party's application of coercive measures in its disciplinary investigations.

The reform has more or less refurbished the CCDI, giving it the widest scope of power that was enjoyed by its predecessor, the PSC, from

1955 to 1969. However, what distinguishes the PSC then from the CCDI-NSC now is that in the old regime the Party strengthened its power by devouring the state whilst in the current regime the Party has learned to reinforce or re-establish its control over the state by a process of 'regurgitation', namely, to first nurture the state and then compel the state to offer its resources to the Party through the device of office-sharing. In this manner, the Party manages to enhance the potency of the chain of command originating from its own seat of power while still retaining a minimal measure of structural coherence of the state system. Such structural coherence is necessary to uphold state authority, which has become an indispensable component of the overall regulatory regime of the Party-state, especially in the governance of civil affairs and private sectors that do not require the Party's micro-management.

7.5 Conclusion

In this chapter, I examined the mechanics of the 'operational weapon' of the CCP and how such mechanics define the mode of operation of China's Party-state. Specifically, I pointed out that China's Party-state operates from two seats of power, one of the Party itself and one of the state. This feature of duality is not reflected in the 'mono-organisation' depiction of the Leninist system put forward by T. H. Rigby. I also identified that in China the Party constituted an independent seat of power that operated outside of the constitutional order. This characteristic differentiates China's Party-state from the Nazi regime and the latter's associated 'dual state' model presented by Ernst Fränkel. To further illustrate the mode of operation of China's Party-state, I identified two base-types of administration of control by the Party: the exclusive approach and the share-approach (with state institutions). Based on this classification, I historicised the methods with which the Party controlled the process of disciplinary investigations within and beyond the Party from 1949 till the present. Such a historical comparison allows me to demonstrate the advantages of having dual seats of power in authoritarian governance and the centrality of the use of administrative tools to simultaneously engineer legitimacy and preserve political monopoly. This historical analysis also provides the necessary context to understand the significance, both practically and conceptually, of the introduction of the NSC, which will surely remain an important component of the legacy of the Xi Jinping era.

References

Anonymous. 1957. Di er ci quanguo dang de jiancha huiyi gongzuo zongjie caogao (Concluding summary of the 2nd conference of national party supervision work [draft]). File number: CS-IMG-0624-0631.

1960. Quansheng jiancha gongzuo huiyi jingshen de huibao, chuanda zhongyang shujichu dui jiancha gongzuo de zhishi (Report on the spirit of the provincial supervision conference regarding the central secretariat's instructions on supervision work). File number: CS-IMG-0452-0463.

2018. Sanshiyi sheng qu shi jiancha weiyuanhui lingdao banzi quanbu chansheng (Supervision commission leading bodies established in all 31 provincial regions nationwide). *People's Daily Oversees Edition*.

Blumer, H. 1952. The organizational weapon: a study of bolshevik strategy and tactics. *Americal Sociological Review* 17, 630–31.

CCDI. 1980. Guanyu wei zhongyang jiancha weiyuanhui chedi pingfan huifu mingyu de qingshi baogao (Request to rehabilitate and completely rectify the wrongful disciplinary action against members of the Central Supervision Commission), submitted by the CCDI on 15 December.

1983. Guanyu dang de jilv jiancha xitong jiaqiang jijian duiwu jianshe de zanxing guiding (Provisional Rules on completing the party's disciplinary system and strengthening the disciplinary personnel construction work).

2013. Zhongyang jilv jiancha weiyuanhui lishi yange (Historical development of the CCDI). *CCP News Database*, available at: http://cpc.people.com.cn/n/2013/0904/c75234-22804679.html.

CCP. 1955. Guanyu chengli dang de zhongyang he difang jiancha weiyuanhui de jueyi (Decision on the establishment of Central and Local Party Supervision Commissions), issued on 31 March by the Congregation of National Delegates Conference of the CCP.

CCP News. 2006. Zhu De: zhongjiwei diyi shuji (Zhu De: First Secretary of CCDI Part 3). Zhongguo gongchandang xinwen (CCP News Database). Available from: http://cpc.people.com.cn/GB/64162/64172/64915/5093286.html.

Centre, Party. 1949. Zhongguo gongchandang guanyu chengli zhongyang ji ge ji dang de jilv jiancha weiyuanhui de jueding [Decision on the establishment of the central and local committees of discipline and inspection], issued in November.

1957. Guanyu huafen youpai fenzi de biaozhun de tongzhi (Notice on the Standard of classifying the rightists).

1962. Guanyu jiaqiang dang de jiancha jiguan de jueding (Decision to strengthen Party Supervision Organs), issued by the 8th Central Committee at its 10th Plenary Meeting.

1980. Guanyu dangnei zhengzhi shenghuo zhunze (Principal guidelines regarding intra-Party political life).

Chen, Lei. 2015. Zhongguo jiancha jiguan fantanju de lailongqumai (The historical background of the establishment of the anticorruption bureaus in the procuratorates in China). *Jiancha ribao* (Procuratorate' Daily), 3 February. Available from: http://newspaper.jcrb.com/html/2015-02/03/content_178373.htm.

Commission, Central Party Supervision. 1957. Zhongyang jiancha weiyuanhui guanyu chufen dagnyuan de pizhun quanxian de guiding (Rules on the competence to approve disciplinary decisions against party-members), issued on October 16. File number: CS-IMG-0675.

County A, Party Supervision Commission. 1960 *Case deliberation records. File number FJSC-0092-1960.*

Fränkel, E. 2017. *The Dual State: A Contribution to the Theory of Dictatorship (with an Introduction by Jens Meierheirich).* New York [u.a.]: Oxford University Press.

Jackson, R. H. 1945. Chapter V. Opening address for the United States. *Nazi Conspiracy and Aggression.*

Jiang, Laiying. 2017. Guojia jiancha tizhi gaige de shijian yu duice (Historical lessons of and solutions regarding national supervision system reform). *Journal of National Administrative College*, 10–16.

Li, Li. and Wang, Peng. 2019. from institutional interaction to institutional integration: the national supervisory commission and China's new anti-corruption model. *The China Quarterly* (advanced online view doi:10.1017/S0305741019000596), 1–23.

Li, Ling. 2015. 'Rule of law' in a party-state – a conceptual interpretive framework of the constitutional reality of China. *Asian Journal of Law and Society* 2, 93–113.

2016. The rise of the discipline and inspection commission, 1927–2012: anticorruption investigation and decision-making in the Chinese communist party. *Modern China* 42, 447–82.

2019. Politics of anticorruption in China: paradigm change of the party's disciplinary regime 2012–2017. *Journal of Contemporary China* 28, 47–63.

Li, Ling. and Zhou, Wenzhang. 2019. Governing the 'constitutional vacuum': federalism, rule of law, and politburo politics in China. *Chinese law and society review* 4.

Lv, Jiao. 1992. Woguo jiancha jiguan jizhen gongzuo de lishi yange (Historical development of the conduction of criminal investigation by the procuratorates). *Jiancha lilun yanjiu* (Procutorial Theory Research), 83–7.

Mao, Zedong. 1957. Speech at the Qingdao conference (transcript). *Selected Works of Mao Zedong*. Renmin Publishing House, p. 456.

Osakwe, C. 1985. The four images of soviet law: a philosophical analysis of the soviet legal system. *Texas International Law Journal* 21, 1–37.

Party Center, Huabei Bureau. 1952. Guanyu chuli renmin laixin jiejian renmin qunzhong gongzuo de zhishi (Directives on the work of processing people's letters [of complaints] and visits), issued in November. Available from: www.marxists.org/chinese/reference-books/chineserevolution/195303/1.htm.

Politburo. 1950. Zhongyang jilv jiancha weiyuanhui gongzuo xize (CCDI Operational Rules).

Province A, Discipline and Inspection Commission of. 1953. X tongzhi zai zhongong sichuan shengwei di yi ci jilv jiancha gongzuo huiyi shang de fayan (Speech of Commorade X at the 1st conference of discipline and inspection work of the Party Committee of Province A). File number: FJDC-0007-1953-038.

Province A, Party Supervision Commission of . 1955. Guanyu chengli jianwei zuzhi jigou wenti de dafu (Reponses to inquiries regarding the establishment of Party supervision commission). File number: FJSC-@0014-1955-@025.

1956. Dang de di yi ci quanquo jiancha gongzuo huiyi de chuanda baogo (Relaying report of the 1st National Conference of Supervision Work of the Party). File number: FJSC-0035-1956-0001.

1960. Guanyu jiancha gongzuo de yijian (Opinions regarding the supervisory work of the year of 1960). File number: FJSC-0087-1960-040-00044.

RGBL. 1935. *Reichsgesetzblatt*.

Rigby, T. H. 1964. Traditional, market, and organizational societies and the USSR. *World Politics* 16, 539–57.

1975. Stalinism and the Mono-organizational society. In R. C. Tucker, ed. *Stalinism: Essays in Historical Interpretation*. New York: W. W. Norton & Co., pp. 53–76.

Sapio, F. 2008. Shuanggui and extralegal detention in China. *China information* 22, 7–37.

Schoenhals, M. 1996. The central case examination group, 1966–79. *The China Quarterly* 145, 87–111.

Selznick, P. 1952. *The Organizational Weapon – A Study of Bolshevik Strategy and Tactics*. New York: McGraw-Hill Book Company.

Shambaugh, D. L. 2000. The Chinese state in the post-Mao era. In D. L. Shambaugh, ed., *The Modern Chinese State*. New York: Cambridge University Press, pp. 161–87.

Sharlet, R. 1975. Stalinism and soviet legal culture. In R. C. Tucker, ed., *Stalinism: Essays in Historical Interpretation*. New York: W. W. Norton & Co., pp. 155–79.

Walder, A. G. and Lu, Q. 2017. The dynamics of collapse in an authoritarian regime: China in 1967. *American Journal of Sociology* 122, 1144–82.

Wang, Congwu. 1962. Wang cong wu tongzhi zai quanguo dang de jiancha gongzuo huiyi shang de zongjie jiyao (Concluding summary speech delivered by comrade Wang Cong Wu at the national supervision work conference on 11 Dec.).

Ye, Qing. 2005. Lun zhongguo gongchandang yu qunzhong yundong moshi de yunzuo (The party and the operation of the mode of mass campaign). *Party History Research and Teaching* 74–83.

8

Disorientation for the New Era

Intraparty Regulations and China's Changing Party-State Relations

SAMULI SEPPÄNEN*

8.1 Introduction

This essay engages with a curious political and cultural moment in Xi Jinping's China. In the past few years, the Chinese Communist Party (CCP or Party) leadership has aimed at increasing the Party's power within the Chinese state and society, in some instances merging Party organs with state organs. Such reforms, it seems, aim to strengthen the Party's political leadership over Chinese society at the expense of formal legal and bureaucratic processes. One milestone in this development was the establishment of the National Supervision Commission (NSC) through an amendment of the People's Republic of China (PRC or China) Constitution (*Zhonghua renmin gongheguo xianfa* 中华人民共和国宪法) in March 2018.[1] The establishment of the NSC was meant to improve the efficiency of the Party's anti-graft campaign and to 'place the political before anything else' in discipline inspection (Xinhua News Agency 2017). Although the new PRC Supervision Law (*Zhonghua Renmin Gongheguo Jianchafa* 中华人民共和国监察法) comprises some procedural safeguards to prevent rights abuses by its staff members, the NSC has been established as a non-judicial organ, whose actions appear to be outside the purview of China's judicial organs. The heightened political nature of the new discipline supervision system supposedly allows anti-corruption investigators to 'see the 'forest' for 'the trees', that is, to better assert the underlying causes of corruption than was the case before (Xinhua News Agency 2017).

* Associate Professor, The Chinese University of Hong Kong, Faculty of Law. I thank Rogier Creemers, Ryan Manuel, Meng Ye, Ryan Mitchell, Teemu Ruskola, Ewan Smith and Sue Trevaskes for their comments on this project.

[1] For a more detailed discussion on the NSC see Ling Li (Chapter 7).

The establishment of the NSC can be seen, therefore, as an example of the Party's project to limit the purview of China's formal judicial system in favour of the Party's own 'political' discipline inspection methods. At the same time, however, the establishment of the NSC has been promoted as 'an important institutional tool to realise law-based governance' (Lu 2018). The NSC has been established through a constitutional amendment and a statute, whereas the Party's previous internal discipline inspection methods existed in a 'zone of lawlessness', as Flora Sapio (2010: 8) has noted. Moreover, institutional reforms extending the Party organs' powers into the formal legal system have coincided with efforts to establish a more coherent system of intraparty regulations within the CCP (Catá Backer and Wang 2014: 333–8; Zhang Xiaodan 2017: 392–3). Improving the Party's internal regulations was part of the legal reform program, which the Party launched in 2014, calling particular attention to links between state law and intraparty regulations (CCP Central Committee 2014).

Some Chinese and foreign scholars and experts have understandably experienced these developments as confusing – a Western diplomat in Beijing called them outright 'crazy'.[2] On the one hand, Party leaders appear to be intent on limiting law-based governance and expanding the scope of holistic, self-consciously 'political' discipline supervision methods; on the other hand, the Party leaders seek to provide a legal framework for the Party's discipline inspection methods and regulate Party members' uses of power more closely through a system of intraparty regulations. These two aims appear to be motivated by conflicting approaches to rule-based governance. Party leaders seem to be dissatisfied with formal legal processes in their project to control corruption, and yet they are building rule-based processes within the Party in order to control corruption.

It may be possible to impose (what may first appear as) a coherent narrative upon the Party's simultaneous efforts to limit formal legal and bureaucratic processes and to regulate Party cadres' uses of power through formal rules. According to such a narrative (which I call the 'commonsense account' or 'narrative'), Chinese leaders seek to enhance their personal power by systematising the Party's internal governance

[2] Interview S, Beijing (June 2018) (notes on file with author). See, also, Deng (2018: 60) (noting that 'with regard to the role of the rule of law in the new [discipline inspection] system, it is not easy to understand what is really going on'). Compare with Zhang Xiaojun (2019: 5).

procedures and by diminishing the role of politically suspect or ignorant legal professionals in the discipline inspection processes. Party leaders are, according to this account, interested in constraining Party members' abuses of power through rules, without, however, limiting their own power through the same rules. Internal regulations and discipline inspection processes are a more convenient means for achieving these two aims than legal processes because Party leaders are better able to control them. This narrative, therefore, imagines intraparty regulations and Party discipline as a reasonably coherent system of governance – as a form of 'rule-by-regulations' – which applies the logic of rational bureaucracy to the governance of both state and Party organs, without evoking the ideals of the rule of law or even the rule by law. When governing through intraparty regulations, Party leaders are not accountable to courts nor do they have to make use of nominally 'legal' institutions.

Although incomplete, the commonsense narrative is a plausible enough explanation for some of the motivations of the Party leadership. It is telling that President Xi Jinping has described Party discipline in seemingly Weberian (Weber 2001: 123) terms as a 'cage' (*longzi* 笼子) which constrains Party cadres' uses of power (Xinhua News Agency 2013). Nevertheless, the commonsense narrative overlooks the complications in establishing even a non-legal regulatory system within a Marxist-Leninist one-party state. In particular, it fails to account for the tension between (1) dictatorial interventions, which are deemed necessary because rule-based processes are presumed insufficient for achieving the aims of the dictatorship, and (2) the rule-based (quasi-) bureaucratic processes through which such interventions are meant to take place.

This essay problematises the Party's relationship with rule-based governance and the nature of 'the political' more generally in the Party's governance project.[3] If the Party's political leadership cannot be meaningfully said to be governed, constrained or otherwise constituted by formal state law, should such leadership, nevertheless, be seen as being channelled through, restrained and, indeed, constituted by the Party's own intraparty regulations? Indeed, can intraparty regulations play a more meaningful role in constraining Party cadres' uses of power than formal state law, and if so, what difference does the institutional location of rule application make? Alternatively, should we assume that Party

[3] For Schmitt's concept of 'the political', see Schmitt (1996). For the relevance of Schmitt's political thought in China, see Sapio (2015) and Kroll (2017).

cadres are expected to follow neither formal state law nor the Party's own formal regulations in important (or at least existentially important) matters? In that case, should we understand Party leadership and 'the political', more generally, as a form of human conduct that exists outside all rule-based governance? Indeed, should Party leaders' attempts to cage political power through intraparty regulations be seen as incoherent or even disingenuous goals? If that is the case, how can Party leaders hope to govern a 90-million-member organisation if not through formal rules?

Rather than attempting to answer these questions conclusively, this essay argues that they emerge from the above-mentioned institutional and ideological background of China's one-party system, that is, they are a consequence of an attempt to exercise illiberal political leadership through a 'modern', supposedly rationalist, bureaucracy. Moreover, this essay argues that the questions above follow from a more general confusion about the relationship between rules and 'the political', which is apparent not only in the writings of CCP ideologues but also in the scholarship of their foreign observers (and in this essay).

While this essay is theoretical in its focus, it may be worth acknowledging that China's recent developments may be discussed in a decidedly non-theoretical register. From this perspective, Party leaders' and ideologues' somewhat conflicting statements and policies are consequences of political infighting among Chinese elites. In this conflict, politically centrist and liberal-minded Party members prefer to empower China's professionalised legal institutions rather than the politically chosen staff of the discipline inspection organs. In contrast, employees and supporters of the discipline inspection organs cannot (or do not wish to) dismiss centrist and liberal concerns out of hand and, therefore, end up making contradictory statements about the objectives of the reforms, emphasising both legal and political discipline control methods in their public remarks. Plausible as this explanation may be, it should not be the end of our analysis. It remains for us outsiders (that is, scholars who are not participants in the political campaigns within China) to explain the various ideological motivations at play in China and to consider their implications for legal and political thought beyond the Chinese context.

The remainder of this essay is structured as follows. Section 8.2 provides answers to the above-described questions through what may be called the commonsense narrative on party leadership and the political. According to this narrative, 'the political' is not in conflict or even tension with rule-based governance: it is simply one site of rule application, and only institutionally distinguishable from 'the legal', which is located in judicial organs. Section 8.3 then aims to problematise this narrative by describing the inadequacy of *all* rule-based governance for an illiberal one-party government. Section 8.4 finally describes the nature of 'the political' in the Party's governance project and in attempts to understand Chinese law and politics.

8.2 The Commonsense Account: Rule-by-Regulations

This section seeks to narrate the establishment of the NSC, the increasing marginalisation of judicial organs in the Party's anti-graft campaign, and the Party leaders' focus on intraparty regulations through a single 'commonsense' account of the Party's governance project. This account sees intraparty regulations as a means to enforce the Party leaders' will through what could be called a system of 'rule-by-regulations'. The commonsense narrative follows naturally from the commonly held conception that Party leaders relate to law instrumentally (hence its commonsense nature). Just as is the case with instrumentalist conceptions of the Party's approach to law (Tamanaha 2004: 92–3; deLisle 2015: 24; Ringen 2016: 84–5), Party leaders can be said to use intraparty regulations as a means to achieve political objectives, without intending to be bound by these regulations. This view sometimes comes up in discussions with (liberal-leaning) Chinese scholars and foreign China observers, but it is admittedly mostly a strawman. As far as I am aware, the commonsense account discussed here is not advanced in scholarship on Chinese law and politics with regard to intraparty regulations specifically (as opposed to scholarship on formal state law). In China, the mainstream position describes intraparty regulations and laws as binding on the Party leadership, and not only on lower-level Party cadres (Song 2016; Yang 2019: 77–8). For this essay the commonsense account provides, therefore, a convenient rhetorical counterpoint for the critical and deconstructive efforts in Sections 8.3 and 8.4.

With these caveats in mind, it seems helpful to subject certain presumably commonsensical assumptions about the relationship between formal rules and illiberal political leadership to critical evaluation. First of all, underlying the commonsense account is the assumption that the highest political will is ultimately neither constrained nor constituted by laws and intraparty regulations but formed free of such normative restrictions. Party leaders, in other words, use intraparty regulations and discipline inspection mechanisms – such as the newly established NSC – in order to advance their political agendas and to combat political enemies, but the highest political will itself is not constrained by intraparty regulations. Similar observation was made about the institutionalisation of political power in the Soviet Union (USSR). Although the Soviet executive developed various formal structures and procedures – for instance, for selecting its highest leadership – in the final analysis executive power in the USSR remained personalised and unconstrained by laws, Communist Party regulations and other rules (Rigby 1989: 35, 49).

In addition to the assumption that the highest political will is ultimately free of normative restrictions, the commonsense account assumes that political leadership can be exercised through rules within the Party organisation. Under this narrative, CCP intraparty regulations can be seen to effectively constrain lower-level Party members' discretion. To this end, the commonsense account probably needs to describe the Party in Weberian terms as a 'modern' organisation which possesses some elements of a rational bureaucracy. Max Weber (1978: 220–4) famously characterised modern bureaucracies as being built upon a rational legal authority. Weber did not associate legal authority and modern bureaucracies exclusively with formal state law and organs of the state. According to Weber, the Catholic Church, for instance, was a bureaucracy, as was the army and, indeed, the modern political party (Weber 1978: 221–4).[4] From this perspective, the modern political party operates on the expectation, if not the reality, that party members' conduct is effectively regulated by rules which establish hierarchies and specific fields of jurisdiction among them. The adoption of such rules, it may be further noted, is part of the normal rationalisation process of a political party, and a process that could be observed in the USSR (Rigby 1989: 10) and seen today in contemporary China (Zhang Xiaojun 2019: 6, 11).

A starting point for describing the CCP as a Weberian (quasi-) bureaucracy may be found in the Party's Constitution. Article 4 of the CCP Constitution (*Zhongguo gongchandang zhangcheng* 中国共产党章程) sets up 'democratic centralism' as the key organisational principle of the Party. This principle confers on Party members various rights to propose and discuss matters within the Party, while also requiring them to 'firmly uphold' the authority of the CCP Central Committee and Comrade Xi Jinping once the deliberations are over. Below the CCP

[4] See Rogier Creemers's discussion on the religious overtones of Chinese ideology in Chapter 2 in this volume.

Constitution are various intraparty regulations. Intraparty regulations comprise, according to the CCP Regulations on the Formulation of Intraparty Regulations (*Gongchandang dangnei fagui zhiding tiaoli* 中国共产党党内法规制定条例), those adopted by the Central Commission for Discipline Inspection and other central organs, as well as by Party committees in provinces, autonomous regions, and municipalities directly under the Central Government.

The Party leadership has sought to rationalise the system of intraparty regulations during the past two decades (Zhang Xiaojun 2019: 5, 15). For instance, the CCP Central Committee has adopted rules to indicate how Party organs are to identify binding rules and commands. According to Article 31 of the CCP Regulations on the Formulation of Intraparty Regulations, the Party's Constitution enjoys the 'highest degree of effectiveness'. The CCP Central Committee has directed lower-level Party organs to recognise and enforce normatively binding decisions adopted by the leadership of that Party organ which approved the Party organ's establishment as well as other higher-level Party organs.[5] The CCP Central Committee has also established hierarchies between intraparty regulations issued by different Party organs. According to Article 31 of the CCP Regulations on the Formulation of Intraparty Regulations, Central Party regulations are hierarchically higher than the regulations issued by the Party's Central Commission for Discipline Inspection (CCDI), and CCDI regulations are hierarchically higher than the regulations issued by other Party organs. The CCP General Office (*Zhongyang bangongting* 中央办公厅) is tasked with reviewing the compliance of intraparty regulations with the CCP Constitution, higher-level intraparty regulations, the PRC Constitution and the laws.[6]

As part of this rationalisation process, the CCP leadership has sought to ensure that intraparty regulations are drafted as regulatory clauses rather than as general statements on policy or as opinions (the CCP Regulations on the Formulation of Intraparty Regulations). As a general matter, regulatory clauses can take the form of bright-line rules (setting,

[5] CCP Regulations on the Work of Party Units (for trial implementation) (*Zhongguo Gongchandang dangzu gongzuo tiaoli (shixing)* 授权发布:中国共产党党组工作条例（试行）). 16 June 2015. Articles 4, 18. Available from: http://www.xinhuanet.com/politics/2015-06/16/c_1115638059.htm.

[6] CCP Regulations on the Filing of Intraparty Regulations and Normative Documents (*Zhongguo Gongchandang dangnei fagui he guifanxing wenjian bei'an guiding* 中国共产党党内法规和规范性文件备案规定). 1 July 2012. Article 7. Available from: http://dangjian.people.com.cn/n/2013/0528/c117092-21635861.html.

for instance, specific time periods for disciplinary penalties) or flexible, substantive standards (providing, for instance, vaguely-worded standards for Party members' conduct) (Kennedy 1976). Many intraparty regulations are substantive standards, but there are also a number of bright-line rules in intraparty regulations. Chinese scholars suggest that the drafters of these regulations have not always achieved the right balance between rules and standards. A number of intraparty regulations are thought to be too difficult for Party members to follow and understand (Qin 2016: 61; Song 2016: 7). Not all intraparty regulations appear to be accessible to Party members, although many regulations are publicly available (Qin 2016: 61; Song 2016: 7; Zhi 2016: 42).

The commonsense account, therefore, describes intraparty regulations as a system of increasingly rational rules which at least seek to restrict Party members and lower-level Party cadres, without, however, ultimately constraining the highest Party leadership. From this perspective, intraparty regulations can be thought of as the partially concealed plumbing of the Chinese state: decisions emerging from the visible Chinese state organs have been flushed down through parallel Party channels. Under this account, 'the political' is nothing more curious than one institutional site among others. It is the concealed plumbing of the Chinese Party-State, which operates according to the same bureaucratic principles as the visible pipes of the judiciary and other state organs.

The commonsense account provides a plausible explanation for the seemingly contradictory trends behind the establishment of the NSC in March 2018. The new supervision system essentially transfers an important part of law enforcement (at least in the investigative stage) from China's judicial organs into the domain of intraparty discipline (Gan 2018; Horsley 2018; PRC Supervision Law, Article 5). The PRC Supervision Law provides NSC powers to conduct supervision of all public employees exercising public power, vastly increasing the number of people under the Party-led discipline supervision. Under the new law, anybody suspected of occupation-related illegal and criminal activities may be held (*liuzhi* 留置) in a specific place for up to six months. The supervision process is self-consciously extra-legal. Although the PRC Constitution and the PRC Supervision Law direct the supervision commissions to exercise their powers in accordance with the law, Article 127 of the amended PRC Constitution explicitly states that NSC is not subject to interference by administrative organs or public organisations. The new PRC Supervision Law makes no mention of the suspect's right to legal counsel during detention with supervision organs, which is a right under the PRC Criminal Procedure Law (*Zhonghua renmin gongheguo xingshi susong fa* 中华人民共和国刑事诉讼法).

Under the commonsense account, therefore, the new supervision system changes the institutional setting of anti-corruption work from one rule-based system – formal state law – to another (albeit much more rudimentary and imperfect) rule-based system – intraparty discipline. The change of institutional setting can be explained by the Party leaders' motive to increase their political power. By controlling the initial investigation stage in corruption cases in state organs and public institutions through intraparty regulations, Party leaders are better able to guide subsequent prosecution by the state's procuratorate towards or away from specific crimes (Deng 2018: 64–5).[7] Importantly, under the commonsense approach there is no contradiction between the Party leaders' aim to strengthen and rationalise intraparty regulations and their simultaneous project to marginalise the role of formal state law. On the contrary, a rational and effectively enforced system of intraparty regulations can be seen as an important element in the Party leaders' effort to increase the Party's political power.

8.3 Questioning Common Sense

At the first look, the commonsense narrative seems perfectly plausible. Intraparty regulations and the new discipline inspection mechanisms – the concealed plumbing of the Chinese Party-state – enable Party leaders to achieve their objectives more efficiently than would be possible through, say, enacting stricter laws and providing additional resources to judicial organs. The commonsense account may also initially be thought to have considerable theoretical backing beyond the Weberian rationality narrative. It may, for instance, be argued that intraparty regulations are in some foundational way different from *legal* norms and, as such, more useful to the Party leaders' governance project than formal state laws. This argument can claim some support in the unorthodox Soviet legal theorist Evgeny Pashukanis's distinction between legal and technical regulations. Pashukanis (1980: 58–9) argued that 'legal' regulations inevitably reflected capitalist social relations even if they were supposedly socialist. In Pashukanis's view, 'legal' regulations ultimately served private interests, conferring rights to individuals and thereby

[7] It is a different question whether these efforts have been successful (Meng 2019).

provoking disputes between them. 'Technical' regulations, in contrast, were marked by a unity of purpose (Pashukanis 1980: 58–60). The difference between the two forms of regulations depended on whether the rules could be 'considered from the perspective of the same single purpose' (Pashukanis 1980: 58–60). Following Pashukanis's distinction – and ignoring certain inconvenient facts discussed below – intraparty regulations could be seen as a form of non-legal technical regulation, which does not presume antagonisms between private individuals and which is, therefore, a more suitable form of rule-based governance for the Chinese Party-state than inherently capitalist 'laws'.

The commonsense explanation may also be seen to conform to seminal accounts of illiberal legal systems, such as Ernst Fränkel's (2017) critical analysis of the 'dual state' in Nazi Germany. As noted by Ling Li in Chapter 7, Fränkel (2017: 3) distinguished between the 'Normative State', which comprised Nazi Germany's formal state law, and the 'Prerogative State', which stood for the 'political' and which was able to trump the formal state when political leaders so decided. Fränkel (2017: 3) saw no 'law' within the political. The political sphere, according to Fränkel, was 'a vacuum as far as law [was] concerned'. At the same time, Fränkel (2017: 27–8) alluded to political regulations which could 'transfer entire spheres of life from the jurisdiction of the Normative State to the Prerogative State'. Arriving at a synthesis of sorts, Fränkel (2017: 206) argued (in Weberian terms) that the dual state 'combine[d] rational bureaucratic methods with irrational or ... charismatic ones', being irrational at its core. Following Fränkel, one could see the CCP's intraparty regulations as part of the inner-sanctum of the rational bureaucracy of the Chinese Party-state (or, indeed, its concealed plumbing), which enables Chinese leaders to enforce decisions that are ultimately made free of any normative restrictions.

Commonsensical as the above explanations may first appear, they do not describe the complex intertwining of 'the political' and 'the legal' in the Chinese Party-state and in other illiberal governments which follow the one-party model. As Hannah Arendt (1976: 395) observed with regard to totalitarian states, attempting to unravel the relationships between the party and the totalitarian state would have driven even an expert 'mad'. Arendt (1976: 395) further pointed out that this sense of madness was due to the dual existence, or conflict, between the party and the state.

The first step in problematising the commonsense account begins with an observation about the aims of the Party's discipline supervision reform. An explicit aim of these reforms has been to expand the scope of holistic, self-consciously 'political' supervision from Party members to state organ employees (Zhi 2016: 45; Ding and Wang 2018; Lu 2018). Chinese state media has explicitly described the new supervision organs as having a 'political' (*zhengzhi* 政治) rather than 'judicial' (*sifa* 司法) or 'administrative' (*xingzheng* 行政) identity (Xinhua News Agency 2017; Horsley 2018). The project to 'place the political before anything else' (Xinhua News Agency 2017) appears in part to be a consequence of the Party leadership's distrust of legal processes and legal professionals – a point which some politically centrist Chinese legal scholars are eager to make in private conversations.[8] The newly established supervision commissions received part of their staff members from the procuratorates (Li 2019: 62), but these legal professionals now work in a self-consciously extra-legal setting. The personnel policies of these commissions reportedly emphasise the political consciousness and ideological qualities of their staff (Xinhua News Agency 2017). In this sense, the strengthening of the Party's discipline inspection methods aims to ensure that rules are applied by politically trusted persons.

At the same time, the strengthening of the Party's discipline inspection mechanisms also reveals a deeper distrust towards legal processes and – this may be a more controversial observation – towards rules-based governance, in general. To be sure, public statements on the new supervision mechanism stress that these organisations must follow the relevant discipline inspection procedures (Xinhua 2017). It is also true that the Party's leaders wish to be credited for introducing a more rule-based, even legally sanctioned, discipline inspection procedure through the newly established NSC (Lu 2018). The PRC Supervision Law, Article 6, declares that 'the rule of law shall be improved, and power shall be effectively restricted and overseen' through the national supervision system. Xinhua News Agency (2017) has even reported that the new supervision system aims to improve the protection of the rights of the accused.

Yet an aim of these reforms is to facilitate a holistic examination of anti-corruption cases, and to allow Party officials to make anti-graft investigations more politically purposeful than was previously the case. Chinese media has described this change as meaningful. In a Xinhua report on the NSC, for instance, a former procuratorate official noted

[8] Interview K, Beijing (June 2018) (notes on file with author).

that he was 'looking at his job from a more political perspective now' (Lu 2018). According to the news report, the perspective change helps focus anti-corruption investigations on the root causes of corruption. The institutional structure of the new supervision system also supports the use of 'political' (and potentially extra-legal) investigation methods. The functions and the personnel of the NSCs are integrated with the Party's discipline inspection organs. For instance, the commissions use the Party's detention centres for their investigative work (Lu 2018). This suggests that the use of extra-legal investigation methods in Party organs as documented by Flora Sapio (2010: 102–5) and Eva Pils (2018: 38) continues within the new national supervision system.

The national supervision system, therefore, enables discipline inspection officials to disregard, rather than observe, laws more confidently than was the practice previously. Whether discipline inspection staff are also expected to ignore or suspend intraparty regulations is a more complicated question. Here, it is helpful to establish a point of contrast in formal state law. Whereas Party leaders and ideologues appear to consistently hold up the virtue of following the Party's internal regulations, their approach to formal state law is far less consistent. Indeed, it is possible to identify a specific conservative socialist approach to the rule of law which (paradoxically) establishes state law as a formally autonomous system, while also destabilising this autonomy through various means, such as suggestive statements about the 'leadership of the Party' and the inseparability of politics from adjudication (Seppänen 2016: 87–91). Among other things, such speech acts enable the Party leadership to warn judges against expanding the people's courts' powers further into the political domain, while also insisting that the people's courts are independent in the concrete adjudication of cases.[9]

The problem is that, as is the case with formal state law, intraparty regulations do not apply themselves. Intraparty regulations need an agent to interpret them, and it cannot be assumed that this agent shares the same interests as the Party leaders. It is at least theoretically possible that insubordinate Party members interpret intraparty regulations against the Party leaders' perceived or actual interests. For instance, the CCP

[9] The threat of power-grabbing judicial activism in not an unrealistic prospect in a one-party state. In the well-known Qi Yuling case in 2001, the Supreme People's Court (SPC) used constitutional rights for the first time as a source of law, hinting at a more prominent role for constitutional rights in the PRC (Morris 2012). The court later withdrew its own decision (Morris 2012).

Regulations on the Protection of Party Members' Rights (*Zhongguo gongchandang dangyuan quanli baozhang tiaoli* 中国共产党党员权利保障条例) provides various procedural rights for Party members in the discipline inspection process. These rights comprise, among other things, the right of Party members to participate in each other's defence (Article 11) and the guarantee to maintain confidentiality of whistle-blower complaints from the accused Party organisation (Article 19). Moreover, various intraparty regulations (including the CCP Constitution and the CCP Regulations on the Protection of Party Members' Rights) direct Party members to strictly observe the PRC Constitution and laws. According to the Chinese government's submission to the United Nations' human rights monitoring process, these laws protect defendants from making confessions against their will through means such as 'coercion of confession by torture' (United Nations Committee Against Torture 2014: para. 17). In fact, the collection of evidence in the discipline inspection process through threats, coercion and deception is prohibited in intraparty regulations.[10]

Applying these regulations in favour of the core leadership's political foe in the discipline supervision process could be as inconvenient for Party leaders as the politically misguided application of China's rights-conferring state laws in favour of an undeserving criminal defendant. As is the case with formal state laws, it seems likely that intraparty regulations also need to be interpreted creatively and even suspended when 'political' expediency so requires. To be sure, acts of interpretative insurrection within the Party are probably a small concern for Party leaders. It is also true that discipline inspection organs have powers to 'interpret' (*jieshi* 解释) intraparty regulations under the CCP Regulations on the Protection of Party Members' Rights. Such powers probably render the normative force of rights-conferring provisions within intraparty regulations very limited. Nevertheless, the larger point remains. In contrast to Pashukanis's technical regulations, and despite Party ideologues' assumption that intraparty regulations embody the Party's unified will (Song 2016: 39), intraparty regulations generate antagonistic relations between Party members by conferring rights and powers on some cadres and denying them to others.

[10] The CCP Working Rules on Discipline Inspection Organ Supervision and Discipline (for trial implementation) (*Zhongguo gongchandang jilü jiancha jiguan jiandu zhiji gongzuo guize (shixing)* 中国共产党纪律检查机关监督执纪工作规则（试行）), Article 32.

Chinese legal scholars have documented concrete instances in which the interpretation of intraparty regulations has caused friction among Party members and between Party organs and state organs. Liu Song-shan, a professor at the East China University of Political Science and a former Vice-Secretary of the National People's Congress Standing Committee, has examined several aspects of such conflicts. According to Liu (2016: 30), conflicts about the application of intraparty regulation are particularly common in the personnel appointment process in Chinese state organs. Party organs recommend candidates for positions at state organs. Employees of state organs may wish to object to these recommendations, for instance, if they believe that the appointments would not be in the best interests of the state organ. It may also happen that state organ officials, who may themselves be Party members, conclude that the Party organ's decision has been reached in violation of intraparty regulations (Liu 2016: 29–30). As Party members, state officials are expected to follow Party instructions, but as employees of state organs or of state-owned enterprises, Party members are expected to follow formal state law (Liu 2016: 30). Liu believes that such conflicts are not uncommon (Liu 2016: 30).

Intraparty regulations also suffer from the same limitation as formal state laws (and all other rules), being either over-inclusive or under-inclusive for the political leaders' purposes (Schauer 1988). For instance, the above-described rules on the collection of evidence in the discipline inspection process may appear over-inclusive – that is, too strict – in a specific Party cadre's view. Even if it is possible to assume that in the overwhelming majority of cases Party members have no difficulties following intraparty regulations, a Party member still has to decide whether to view Party leadership as a matter of rule application or follow a different political prerogative, and elevate political leadership above all rules, including intraparty regulations. As a consequence, political leadership in a one-party state does not simply manifest itself as the determination of goals, which are then pursued within a rationalist Weberian clockwork. Instead, members of the illiberal government – the 'core' leader himself and the rest of his company – exercise political leadership precisely because rules are presumed to be insufficient for advancing the political project of the illiberal government. At the same time, the real and potential disputes in the application of intraparty regulations in the PRC demonstrate that even internal Party rules create possibilities for misinterpretations, conflicts and resistance (Liu 2016). In sum, intraparty regulations are an imperfect means to enforce the Party leaders' will.

Against this background it does not seem likely that the establishment of the NSC amounts to a transition from one rule-based system – formal state law – to the Party's internal rule-based system. Instead, the change seems to have been motivated by a more generalised aversion towards rules-based governance. From this perspective, the new discipline supervision process facilitates the exercise of political will, unbound by all rules, more effectively in anti-corruption investigations than the previous law-based system, while at the same time seeking to establish a cage of intraparty regulations within the Party itself.

8.4 A Diagnosis

We may now attempt to diagnose the causes for the sense of disorientation mentioned in the introductory part of this essay. To a certain extent, the sense of disorientation is due to the seemingly contradictory words and deeds of CCP leaders and ideologues. On the one hand, Party leaders and ideologues insist that the aim of the reforms is to improve the socialist rule of law (Xu 2017; Ding and Wang 2018). The recent reforms have surrounded previously extra-legal discipline inspection processes with legal scaffolding, and they aim to strengthen Central Party organs' ability to curb illegal conduct. On the other hand, these reforms aim to bring state organs even more squarely within the Party's control, expanding the use of the Party's discipline inspection methods and, it may be assumed, further normalising the use of extra-legal methods in corruption investigations. These two aims – strengthening the rule of law and expanding extra-legal discipline inspection methods – seem contradictory, and yet they emerge from a coherent ideological background. The socialist rule of law is a value in its own right, but legal processes must, nonetheless, be at times suspended in order to move history forward towards ever-higher stages of socialism and communism.

Another potentially confusing aspect of Party leaders' words and deeds concerns their approach to rule-based governance within the CCP (and not merely between the CCP and state organs). On the one hand, the Party leadership appears to be committed to establishing a rationalist rule-based bureaucracy within the Party. As pointed out above, Party leaders and ideologues have made an effort to systemise and institutionalise intraparty regulations, adopting both substantive standards and bright-line rules as part of this project (CCP Central Committee 2014; Song 2016). On the other hand, a central justification for the Party's leadership is that it is non-formalist and non-bureaucratic (Xi 2014; Zhi 2016).

To be sure, non-formalist and non-bureaucratic leadership does not necessarily form a conflict with rule-based restrictions on Party cadres' uses of power. It is possible that even bright-line rules establishing, say, voting procedures and command structures between Party organs succeed in making the Party less formalist and non-bureaucratic, depending on what is meant by these terms. Yet a potential source of confusion remains. If Party leaders truly were concerned about building a regulatory cage to limit Party cadres' abuses of power (Xinhua News Agency 2013), why would they have gone out of their way to establish an organisation that partly stands outside legal regulation and enables a wide use of informal discipline enforcement methods?

An answer may be found in the specific role played by 'the political' in the Party's governance project. 'The political' for Party leaders and ideologists is not just another site for rule application, distinguishable only institutionally from judicial organs, but a privileged sphere of human activity, which falls within the exclusive domain of the Party. This view emerges from the tradition of self-consciously illiberal political thought, which has informed various political projects from nineteenth-century conservative Catholicism to twentieth-century fascism and Marxism-Leninism. Scholars such as Joseph de Maistre (2006), Juan Donoso Cortés (1874) and Carl Schmitt (1996) thought that liberal legal institutions could not replace political leadership, and that political leadership – whether it was exercised by the sovereign monarch, a dictator or some other sovereign agent – had to stand above the law. As Carl Schmitt (2013: xl–xli, 1–2) pointed out, this illiberal tradition is visible in the Marxist-Leninist concept of the proletariat's dictatorship. In Marxism-Leninism, the proletariat's – that is, the Party's – leadership is presumed necessary until society has safely completed its transition to communism. Just as is the case with the dictator's ability to suspend laws in an emergency situation, Party leadership is visible in its practice of suspending the law – and, arguably, the Party's internal rules – when this is deemed necessary.

Complicating this picture is the fact that the 90-million-member Party is not an individual but a (quasi-)bureaucratic organisation which is at least partly constituted by its formal rules. Disorienting as it may be, the tradition of political thought, which has informed the construction of China's Marxist-Leninist one-party state, builds on the premise that all rules may ultimately be subjected to political leadership, whereas the tradition that has informed the construction of the Party bureaucracy presumes that decisions about the exercise of political leadership are made and implemented in a rule-based process. In this political arrangement formal rules both are and are not expendable.

To be sure, paradoxes about rule-based governance and illiberal political leadership are seldom visible in mainstream Chinese scholarship, which generally describes Party leadership, formal state law and intraparty regulations as a single coherent system of governance (Song 2016: 40, 75; Zhang Xiaojun 2019: 7, 10).[11] Nevertheless, it appears that the dichotomy between the political and the legal is institutionalised in Marxism-Leninism. Merging the Party organisation with the formal structures of the state would rid society of a key component of Party leadership, which is presumed crucial for the society's transformation towards communism. Soviet leaders resisted fusing the Party with state structures (Rigby 1989: 10), and, also in contemporary China, the merging of the Party with state organs cannot be completed without ultimately diluting the Party's power. The Party needs separate state organs in order to 'lead' them.

Finally, and perhaps most importantly, the outsider's sense of disorientation in the face of China's changing Party-state relations may be due to a more generalised confusion about of the relationship between rule-based governance and 'the political'. Is 'the political' a sphere in which no rules – legal or non-legal – exist, or can 'the political' be institutionalised through legal or non-legal rules all the way up to constitutional emergencies and, in China, to the commanding heights of Party leadership? Viewpoints differ. 'The political', according to Weber, could be rationalised to a certain extent through bureaucratic processes. While bureaucratic institutions were a means to an end, the determination of the ends themselves escaped rationalisation. The ends were determined in the 'struggle of the Gods', in which the choice between the Gods – the ends – was not warranted through reason (Weber 1946: 152). This is also how the above-described commonsense accounts see 'the political'. Party leaders make use of laws and intraparty regulations to achieve their ends, but the ends themselves are not decided through rule application (say, in the judiciary or in political organisations). In China, politically centrist and liberal-minded Chinese scholars make use of this approach when they deny 'the political' a privileged status and instead seek to constrain it within the cage of formal state law, while also acknowledging potential conflicts between the two domains of

[11] Other Chinese scholarship does, however, acknowledge such conflicts (Liu 2016).

normativity (Qin 2016; Tu 2016; Zhang Qianfan 2019). As mentioned above, there also exists a narrative in China which represses conflicts between intraparty regulations, the rule of law and Party leadership as a matter of principle (Song 2016).

Theorists of and from illiberal legal systems have imagined 'the political' as a space which is defined by the absence of rules even in the context of modern bureaucracies. As pointed out above, Fränkel assumed that 'the political' was devoid of law (while also suggesting that within 'the political' there existed some rules). For Schmitt (1996: 45), 'the political' was not just another location for a Weberian (quasi-) bureaucracy but a defining feature of the 'decisive entity', the state, which transcended all other social groupings and did not answer to legal reasoning. It was futile to attempt to bind 'the political' to a set of rules even in liberal societies (Schmitt 2005: 30). In dictatorships, such an attempt would have been against the very purpose of dictatorial intervention, which was precisely to suspend rules for some higher goal (Schmitt 2013: 117). In contemporary China, Schmitt's views have been reflected in arguments that caution against bureaucratising the Party through formal rules (Jiang 2016; Zhi 2016).

As is the case with Weber's (1946: 152) struggling Gods, choosing sides in this debate does not appear to be warranted by reason. As a consequence, here it must suffice to conclude that the outsider's sense of disorientation in Xi Jinping's China is at least partly a symptom of the tensions within the popular conceptions of 'the political'. On the one hand, it seems plausible that specific decisions about the application of intraparty regulations do not necessarily reflect the Party leadership's current interests or wishes (whatever these may be) but instead are made within the limits and possibilities of the Party's internal regulatory system. In this sense, even the highest political decisions are channelled through, restrained and constituted by rules. On the other hand, it also seems plausible to conclude that, in the final analysis, existential (and not-so-existentially important) decisions within the CCP are not constrained by rules, just as was the case in the USSR (Pakulski: 6–8). This observation, of course, raises a fundamental question about the relationship between rules and 'the political': if rules are not effective 'when it matters', why should we assume that they are ever effective? Is not the decision to follow the rule (rather than the practice of merely citing it) based on something other than the rule itself in each and every instance (Schmitt 2005: 30)?

The commonsense account confines norm-free decision-making to the highest level of political power, suggesting that dictatorial intervention is exercised only by the highest leaders in an otherwise rationalist cage of intraparty regulations. However, as was pointed out in Section 8.3, it seems unlikely that lower-level Party cadres observe all intraparty regulations strictly or that they are even expected to do so. Instead, the ability to suspend intraparty regulations appears to be presumed in these very regulations, given their occasionally idealist nature. In this sense, 'the political' seems to be devoid of truly effective formal rules. Yet, as was seen above, this conclusion is in tension with another plausible view of 'the political', which places the uses of power within the language of governance. Even an illiberal government channels the uses of political power through over- and under-inclusive formal rules which in some way define those uses.

No matter how one chooses to address these questions (and bracketing them may be the easiest approach), it can be noted here that the critique of rule-based governance presents a challenge not only against liberal political thought but also against technocratic illiberal governments. Instead of assuming that the great helmsmen and core leaders exercise political leadership within a rational system of rule-by-regulations, it seems likely that illiberal political leadership is diluted, misinterpreted, muddled and resisted in the jumble of laws, political regulations and various informal practices and suggestive uses of language that make up governments. Of course, the same argument can also be used to justify the need for strong illiberal political leadership.

References

Arendt, H. 1976. *The Origins of Totalitarianism*. Orlando: Harcourt.

Catá Backer, L. and Wang, K. 2014. The emerging structures of socialist constitutionalism with Chinese characteristics: extra-judicial detention and the Chinese constitutional order. *The Pacific Rim Law & Policy Journal* 23, 251–340.

CCP Central Committee. 2014. (R. Creemers and J. Daum, trans.). Decision concerning some major questions in comprehensively moving governing the country according to the law forward. 28 October. Available from: https://chinacopyrightandmedia.wordpress.com/2014/10/28/ccp-central-committee-decision-concerning-some-major-questions-in-comprehen sively-moving-governing-the-country-according-to-the-law-forward/.

CCP Constitution. (Zhongguo Gongchandang zhangcheng), as amended on 24 October 2017. Available from: http://language.chinadaily.com.cn/19thcpcnationalcongress/2017-11/06/content_34191468.htm.

CCP. 2012. Regulations on the filing of intraparty regulations and normative documents (Zhongguo Gongchandang dangnei fagui he guifanxing wenjian bei'an guiding). 1 July. Available from: http://dangjian.people.com.cn/n/2013/0528/c117092-21635861.html.

2012. Regulations on the formulation of intraparty regulations. (Gongchandang dangnei fagui zhiding tiaoli). 26 May, revised on 30 August 2019. Available from: http://www.xinhuanet.com/politics/2019-09/15/c_1124998366.htm.

Regulations on the protection of party members' rights. 25 October. Available from: http://cpc.people.com.cn/GB/33838/2940495.html.

Regulations on the work of party units (for trial implementation). 16 June. Available from: http://www.xinhuanet.com/politics/2015-06/16/c_1115638059.htm.

Working rule on discipline inspection organ supervision and discipline (for trial implementation). 8 January. Available from: http://news.cctv.com/2017/01/20/ARTIQkb2nu3tVFB5qJ5Aoy7Q170120.shtml.

delisle, J. 2015. The rule of law with Xi-era characteristics: law for economic reform, anticorruption, and illiberal politics. *Asia Policy* 20, 23–9.

de Maistre, J. 2006. *The Collected Works of Joseph de Maistre: Electronic Edition.* Charlottesville: InteLex Corporation.

Deng, Jinting. 2018. The National Supervision Commission: a new anti-corruption model in China. *The International Journal of Law, Crime and Justice* 52, 58–73.

Ding, Xiaoxi, and Wang, Qi. 2018. Zai fazhi guidao shang tuijin guojia zhili tixi he zhili nengli xiandaihua: Zhongguo faxuehui fuhuizhang Zhang Wenxian tan xianfa xiugai (Promoting the modernisation of the national governance system and governance capacity on the road towards the rule of law: Zhang Wenxian, vice president of the China Law Society, discusses constitutional amendments). *Xinhua* (Xinhua News), 16 April. Available at http://www.xinhuanet.com/legal/2018-04/16/c_1122691273.htm.

Donoso Cortés, J. 1879. (W. M'Donald, trans.). *Essays on Catholicism, Liberalism and Socialism, Considered in Their Fundamental Principles*. Dublin: M. H. Gill & Son.

Fränkel, E. 2017. *The Dual State.* Oxford: Oxford University Press.

Gan, N. 2018. China's national supervision commission: fresh, bigger fears over reach of new anti-corruption super agency. *South China Morning Post,* 19 July. Available from: www.scmp.com/news/china/policies-politics/article/2155888/fresh-bigger-fears-over-reach-chinas-new-anti-graft.

Guo, Dingping. 2017. The changing patterns of communist party-state relations in China. *The Journal of East Asian Affairs* 31: 65–96.

Hart, H. L. A. 2012. *The Concept of Law: 3rd edn.* Oxford: Oxford University Press.

Horsley, J. P. 2018. What's so controversial about China's new anti-corruption body? *The Diplomat*, 30 May. Available from: https://thediplomat.com/2018/05/whats-so-controversial-about-chinas-new-anti-corruption-body/.

Jiang, Shigong. 2016. Cong xingzheng fazhiguo dao zhengdang fazhiguo: dangfa he guofa guanxi de falixue sikao (From an executive rule-of-law state to the party's rule-of-law state: a legal theoretical analysis of the relationship between party law and state law). *Zhongguo falü pinglun* (China Law Review) 11(3), 35–41.

Kennedy, D. 1976. Form and substance in private law adjudication. *Harvard Law Review* 89, 1685–778.

Kroll, C. 2017. Reading the temperature curve: Sinophone Schmitt-fever in context and perspective. In Kai Marchal and Carl K. Y. Shaw, eds., *Carl Schmitt and Leo Strauss in the Chinese-Speaking World: Reorienting the Political*, Lanham: Lexington Books, pp. 103–19.

Li, Ling. 2019. Politics of anticorruption in China: paradigm change of the party's disciplinary regime 2012–2017. *Journal of Contemporary China* 28, 47–63.

Liebman, B. L. 2014. Legal reform: China's law-stability paradox. *Daedalus* 143, 96–109.

Liu, Songshan. 2016. Quanli jiguan xingshi zhiquan zhong de dangnei fagui yu guojia falü (Intraparty regulations and the law in the exercise of authority by organs of power). *Zhongguo falü pinglun* (China Law Review) 11(3), 28–34.

Lu, H. 2018. China focus: supervision law gives legal teeth to China's graft-busting agency. *Xinhua News Agency*, 20 March. Available from: www.xinhuanet .com/english/2018-03/20/c_137053224.htm.

Meng, Ye. 2019. Judicial (dis-)empowerment and centralisation efforts: institutional impacts of China's new Supervision Commission. (Unpublished manuscript on file with author).

Morris, R. J. 2012. China's Marbury: Qi Yuling v. Chen Xiaoqi: the once and future trial of both education & constitutionalisation. *Tsinghua China Law Review* 2, 274–316.

Pakulski, J. 1986. Bureaucracy and the Soviet system. *Studies in Comparative Communism* 19, 3–24.

Pashukanis, E. 1980. *Pashukanis: Selected Writings on Marxism and Law*. London: Academic Press.

Pils, E. 2018. *Human Rights in China: A Social Practice in the Shadows of Authoritarianism*. Cambridge: Polity.

PRC Constitution. 2018. Zhonggua renmin gongheguo xianfa (Constitution of the People's Republic of China), as amended on 11 March 2018. Available from: www.gov.cn/guoqing/2018-03/22/content_5276318.htm.

PRC Criminal Procedure Law. 2012. Zhonghua renmin gongheguo xingshi susong fa (PRC Criminal Procedure Law), as amended on 14 March 2012. Available from: www.gov.cn/flfg/2012-03/17/content_2094354.htm.

PRC Supervision Law. 2018. Zhonghua renmin gongheguo jianchafa (PRC Supervision Law). 20 March 2018. Available from: www.npc.gov.cn/npc/xinwen/2018-03/21/content_2052362.htm.

Qianhong, Qin. 2016. Lun dang nei fagui yu guojia falü de xietiao xianjie (Coordinating intraparty regulations and state law). *Xueshu Qianyan* (Frontiers) 5, 50–95.

Rigby, H. 1989. The Soviet political executive, 1917–1986. In A. Brown, ed., *Political Leadership in the Soviet Union*. Bloomington: Indiana University Press, pp. 4–53.

Ringen, S. 2016. *The Perfect Dictatorship: China in the 21st Century*. Hong Kong: Hong Kong University Press.

Sapio, F. 2010. *Sovereign Power and the Law in China*. Leiden: Brill.

2015. Carl Schmitt in China. *The China Story* , 7 October 2015. Available from: www.thechinastory.org/2015/10/carl-schmitt-in-china/.

Schauer, F. 1988. Formalism. *Yale Law Journal* 97, 509–48.

Schmitt, C. 1996. *The Concept of the Political*. Chicago: University of Chicago Press.

2005. *Political Theology: Four Chapters on the Concept of Sovereignty*. Chicago: University of Chicago Press.

2013. *Dictatorship*. Oxford: Polity Press.

Seppänen, S. 2016. *Ideological Conflict and the Rule of Law in Contemporary China: Useful Paradoxes*. Cambridge: Cambridge University Press.

Smith, E. 2018. *The Unwritten Constitution in Britain and China*. Ph.D. dissertation, Oxford University. (On file with author).

Song, Gongde. 2016. *Danggui Zhi Zhi (Governance through Intraparty Regulations)*. Beijing: Falü chubanshe (China Law Press).

Tamanaha, B. Z. 2004. *On the Rule of Law: History, Politics, Theory*. Cambridge: Cambridge University Press.

Tu, K. 2016. Dang nei fagui yu guojia falü gongchu zhong de liang ge wenti (Two problems regarding the coexistence of intraparty regulations and state law). *Zhongguo Falü Pinglun* 11(3), 47–51.

United Nations Committee Against Torture. 2014. CAT/C/CHN/5. 3 April 2014. Available from: https://undocs.org/CAT/C/CHN/5.

Weber, M. 1946 (H. H. Gerth and C. W. Mills, trans.). *From Max Weber: Essays in Sociology*. New York: Oxford University Press.

Weber, M. 1978. (E. Fischoff, trans.) *Economy and Society: An Outline of Interpretive Sociology: Volume I*. Berkeley: University of California Press.

Weber, M. 2001. (T. Parsons, trans.). *The Protestant Ethic and the Spirit of Capitalism*. London: Routledge.

Xi, Jinping. 2014. *The Governance of China*. Beijing: Foreign Language Press.

Xinhua News Agency. 2013. Xi Jinping: Ba quanli guan jin zhidu de longzi li (Xi Jinping: Shutting power into the cage of a system). *Xinhuawang* (Xinhua online), 22 January. Available from: www.ccdi.gov.cn/ldhd/gcsy/201307/t20130710_114955.html.

2017. Jiji tansuo shijian xingcheng baogui jingyan guojia jiancha tizhi gaige shidian qude shixiao: Guojia jiancha tizhi gaige shidian gongzuo zongshu

(Actively exploring practice, forming valuable experiences, obtaining practical results from the pilot program for national supervision system reform: summary of the pilot work on the reform of the national supervision system). *Xinhuawang* (Xinhua online), 5 November. Available from: www.xinhuanet.com/2017-11/05/c_1121908387.htm.

Xu, X. 2017. Gongchandang ji zai falü zhi zhong, ye zai falü zhi xia, hai zai falü zhi shang (The Communist Party is in the middle of the law, under the law, and above the law). *China Digital Times*, 16 April. Available from: http://bit.ly/2sUBn04.

Yang, Fan. 2019. The role of CPC regulations in Chinese judicial decisions: an empirical study based on published judgments. *The China Review* 19(2), 69–97.

Zhang, Q. 2019. Constitutional conundrums under the party-state. *China Heritage*, 2 May. Available from: http://chinaheritage.net/journal/the-professor-a-university-the-rule-of-law/.

Zhang, X. 2017. Rule of law within the Chinese party-state and its recent tendencies. *Hague Journal on the Rule of Law* 9 (2), 373–400.

2019. The historical track of internal regulations of the Communist Party of China ruled by law. *China Legal Science* 7, 3–30.

Zhi, Zhenfeng. 2016. Dang nei fagui de zhengzhi luoji (The political logic of intraparty regulations). *Zhongguo falü pinglun* (China Law Review) 11(3), 42–6.

9

Technologies of Risk and Discipline in China's Social Credit System

ADAM KNIGHT

It has been more than fifteen years since work towards the design and construction of a social credit system (*shehui xinyong tixi* 社会信用体系) began in earnest. Over that time, much has changed in terms of how social credit is both conceptualised and applied. What began as a central plan for the specific provision of financial credit has evolved into a highly decentralised collective of thousands of different initiatives unified by an abstract ideological goal, namely the promotion of honesty and credibility (*chengxin* 诚信) across all walks of life. This chapter charts the development of social credit thought from its origins as a 'technology of risk' in the provision of financial services to its role as a disciplinary technology of regulation deployed in the enforcement of judicial decisions and at the local level in the pursuit of a state-arbitered moral ideal.

9.1 From Zhengxin to Chengxin: Credit with Chinese Characteristics

The social credit system has its roots in China's period of 'reform and opening up' of the 1980s and 1990s. At its inception, social credit was conceived of as an economic tool concerned primarily with the provision of financial credit, or *zhengxin* (征信), in China's nascent market economy.[1] As market conditions eased, the Chinese Communist Party (CCP or Party) made sustained efforts to free up capital for borrowing, lending, investing and spending, as well as to encourage participation in such economic activities among an ever broader share of the population as a stimulant for growth. The expansion of market forces, however, by definition also introduced capital risk, one that had to be mitigated in

[1] For an introduction to early theoretical thought on social credit, including an overview of research carried out by the Chinese Academy of Social Sciences on the subject in the mid-2000s, see Lin (2003), Wu (2009) and Cheng (2010).

order to keep the market functioning. Put simply, financial institutions had to be able to gauge the creditworthiness of their borrowers in order to calculate the risk they were exposing themselves to when making lending decisions.

For this, China took the lead from other more established economies. Credit rating or scoring – the aggregation of an individual's or business's reputation into an easily readable, centralised summary of trustworthiness for assessment by providers of financial services – has long served as the technology used to mitigate such risks in all modern markets (Lauer 2017). The credit industry as we understand it today has its roots in post-bellum America, where newly-formed specialist credit agencies gathered information on merchants' financial reputations and property ownership, as well as their personal lives and habits. This information was textualised into alpha-numeric ratings and published in weighty ledger books for circulation amongst commercial subscribers. Credit scores became a 'technology of risk' employed as a counterbalance to capitalism's 'spasms of creative destruction' (Levy 2012; Bouk 2015; Lauer 2017). The ability to quickly and accurately determine a party's creditworthiness and thereby calculate risk was central to America's economic boom, fuelling the 'engine of enterprise' that powered the country's Gilded Age (Olegario 2016).

The idea of a unified and centralised credit score as a way of stimulating economic activity in China was floated as early as 1989. It wasn't until ten years later, however, that the first concerted steps towards a national credit system were made when, in 1999, Premier Zhu Rongji commissioned the Chinese Academy of Social Sciences (CASS) to launch a research project titled 'Establishing a National Credit Management System' (State Council 1989).[2] CASS sent out teams to study the cases of various Latin American and Asian countries to better understand the functions of credit-giving in emerging economies, laying the groundwork for China's own national credit rating infrastructure. After three years of research, President Jiang Zemin took the project's findings and formally proposed the establishment of a 'social credit system' at the 16th Party Congress in November 2002, the first high-level mention of social credit and, for many, the genesis of social credit political thought (Jiang 2002; Lin 2012).

[2] Legend has it that Zhu Rongji initiated the project after receiving a letter from a female entrepreneur in Shenzhen complaining about the lack of access to credit in the area. See Ma (2012).

In the early years of social credit, the system continued to serve a purely economic role. Responsibility for the design, management and promotion of the social credit system was apportioned in large part to the People's Bank of China (PBoC). The PBoC's first concrete forays into the setup of a credit rating system came in 2004 with the launch of its 'Banking Credit Reference Service Centre' (known simply as the 'Credit Reference Centre' upon its national roll-out in March 2006), China's first independent credit scoring bureau. By mid-2017, the PBoC had collected credit data on 926 million people and 24 million businesses, with over 3.4 million personal credit reports being issued every day (Xinhua 2017). In December 2004, the State Council formed its first 'leading small group' (*lingdao xiaozu* 领导小组) with the aim of building consensus around the construction of a national, centralised commercial and consumer credit reporting system (National People's Congress 2004). A total of 17 government ministries along with the five largest national banks were invited to attend meetings of the *xiaozu*, with the PBoC retaining its leadership of the project as appointed chair. Just over two years later in April 2007, the purview of the *xiaozu* was expanded considerably as it morphed into a new 'Inter-Ministerial Joint Conference on the Construction of the Social Credit System' (State Council 2007). The Joint Conference remains to this day one of the most powerful bodies in the development of broad social credit policy. In its early years, under the continued management of the PBoC, it maintained an explicit focus on financial matters such as taxation, contract enforcement and quality standardisation.

From 2011 onwards, social credit thought began to diverge from its purely economic roots. Behind this was a tacit acknowledgement of the usefulness of a centralised credit 'identity' in the execution of a range of policy goals outside of the sole charge of the PBoC. This shift began at the Sixth Plenum of the 17th Party Congress in October 2011 where, for the first time, reference to the so-called 'four general areas' (*sida lingyu* 四大领域) of social credit were made. These would go on to form the basis of the 2014 Planning Outline (see below) and were cited as part of a broader plenary focus on the development of 'spiritual civilisation' (*jingshen wenming* 精神文明) (Central Committee of the Chinese Communist Party 2011). These 'four areas' of interest – government, commerce, judiciary and society – represented a departure, albeit an as of yet undefined one, for social credit thought away from the purely financial. This shift was further consolidated at the 18th Party Congress in November 2012, with a call to improve moral education as a governance solution, and again at that Congress' Third Plenum in 2013 (Sina News 2011). Beyond such rhetorical advances, perhaps the biggest practical development in this vein came in late 2012, when the PBoC relinquished its monopoly control over the 2007 Joint Conference. The body would now be co-led by the PBoC and China's leading planning agency, the National Development and Reform Commission (NDRC), granting the Joint Conference significantly more power and influence, particularly in areas beyond merely banking.

9.1.1 Central Thinking: The 2014 Social Credit Planning Outline

While judging financial creditworthiness would remain an important function of social credit, the publishing of the 'Planning Outline for the Construction of a Social Credit System (2014–20)' in June 2014 marked a significant milestone in the development of social credit thought (State Council 2014). The Planning Outline represented the government's most comprehensive articulation of its policy thinking to date and to this day still sits at the root of what we now conceive of as social credit.[3] It also marked a significant expansion of what was to be understood as 'credit' (*xinyong* 信用) beyond the remit of the purely economic to also encompass governmental, judicial and societal sincerity. Together, building on the Sixth Plenum of October 2011, these were defined as the 'four general areas' of social credit work. This pivot saw the epistemic potential of the system extended to not only judge the suitability of an individual, government body or commercial entity for credit in the fiscal sense (*zhengxin* 征信) but also to promote honesty and credibility – *chengxin* (诚信) – more generally.

The 2014 Planning Outline provides mainly macro-level guidance on the general direction and goals of social credit between its publication and 2020, rather than a specific roadmap or set of targets to be achieved within that period. At the heart of the Planning Outline lies an elucidation of the 'four general areas' and their relevance to social credit. The policy's economic roots are reflected in an increased push for greater 'commercial sincerity', defined as improving trust within a range of different sectors, including the food industry and ecommerce. Beyond this, the social credit system was to increase transparency in government, as well as enhance 'judicial sincerity' through the sharing of legal

[3] For an excellent summary of the implications and structure of the 'Planning Outline', see Creemers (2018).

information and the implementation of punishments. Finally, 'societal sincerity' was to be improved in areas such as healthcare, labour rights, education, environmental protection and intellectual property. Together, these represented a significant departure in terms of the scope and ideology of social credit policy.

Beyond these top-level guiding principles, much of the early legislative activity in the wake of the 2014 Planning Outline focused on smoothing out the technical barriers to the expansion of a social credit system. Overcoming intra-governmental rivalry and 'narrow departmentalism' (*benwei zhuyi* 本位主义) was certainly one sticking point (People's Daily 2014), but actually being able to collect and process data from multiple ministerial sources was seen as the biggest roadblock to the system's roll-out.[4] To this end, a new 18-digit 'unified social credit code' was launched in June 2015 by the NDRC as a way of enabling different departments to append new information to a business's or individual's social credit record and for that record to be made available across multiple participating ministries (State Council 2015). In parallel with the launch of unified coding, the 'National Technical Committee for the Standardisation of Social Credit Data' was launched in July 2015, comprising 75 members who quickly got on with the task of developing national standards for social credit-related data, publishing a total of 29 instructions on the subject within its first year of existence. In order to further ease the flow and accessibility of information, the 'National Platform for the Sharing of Credit Information' was launched in October 2015 and quickly established itself as the central repository of social credit-related information. In the first three years of its existence, the platform had gathered some 16.5 billion data points from 44 different government departments and ministries and 31 provincial bodies (Zhao 2018). In addition to public data, the platform has relied increasingly on information supplied by private companies. Since the announcement of the 2014 Planning Outline, some 65 commercial and non-governmental organisations, including major banks and technology companies such as Alibaba, Baidu and Qihoo360, have signed social credit-related data-sharing agreements with the central government. The public face of the 'National Platform' is the website 'Credit China', developed in conjunction with Baidu and launched in June 2015. While publishing only a fraction of the total data available on the intra-governmental 'National

[4] For an overview of this and other Chinese media commentary on the social credit system, see Ohlberg, Ahmed and Lang (2017).

Platform', 'Credit China' still acts as a central archive of credit-related legislation, industry information and black lists. By 2018, it had published 140 million data points and was garnering 5 million site visits daily (Credit China 2017).

9.1.2 *Black Lists and Joint Punishments*

First and foremost amongst initial priorities after the publication of the 2014 Planning Outline was the roll-out of a joint system of incentives to encourage compliance across the scheme. At the heart of this policy mechanism was the concept of black-listing. The fundamental idea here was that individuals or commercial entities that fell afoul of one ministry's regulations would have their private information recorded, published and shared with other government bodies for them to apply their own punishments and thus encourage greater levels of legal compliance as a whole. This concept originated as a response to a growing need for the courts to be able to punish and uphold cases in which enforcement was becoming increasingly difficult (*zhixing nan* 执行难) (Clarke 1995). In 2013, the Supreme People's Court (SPC) launched the first of what would become many 'black lists' (*hei mingdan* 黑名单) for individuals or parties that had failed to act on a court order. Under the SPC's plan, judgement defaulters (*shixin beizhixing ren* 失信被执行人) – or *laolai* 老赖 as they have become known colloquially, translating roughly as 'debt-dodger', 'scoundrel' or 'deadbeat' – were to have their information recorded on a black list for a period of two years (or until the issue had been rectified) and for their names to be published online and through the media (Supreme People's Court 2017). Membership on this black list would subject *laolai* to a range of additional sanctions, such as an inability to apply for government subsidies or tender for procurement contracts, as well as limitations on career progress as an employee in the public sector.

This system was absorbed into the social credit system after the publication of the 2014 Planning Outline, with other government bodies encouraged to both contribute data in the form of their own departmental black lists and subject black-listed parties to cross-jurisdictional punishments within their own jurisdictions. Responsibility for the creation, maintenance and use of such a system of shared black lists was expanded away from the SPC to encompass other government ministries and departments in a memorandum of understanding signed by the SPC, NDRC, PBoC and forty-one other bodies in April 2016 (Finder 2016).

This memorandum of understanding (MoU) established the framework within which different departments and ministries would share information on judgement defaulters as well as seven varieties of punishment to which they would be subjected. These categories expanded on the economic and professional restrictions introduced by the SPC in 2013, encouraging government departments to implement additional constraints on a range of private activities. Individuals black-listed on the SPC Judgement Defaulter List were no longer allowed to purchase real-estate or engage in any sort of conspicuous consumption, including visits to luxury hotels, resorts and restaurants. A ban on international trips, as well as travel by high-speed rail or plane, was also introduced, as were restrictions on the ability for a *laolai* to privately educate their children. The 2016 MoU was fleshed out and formalised just two months later with a State Council notice on a system of joint punishments for judgement defaulters as a way of improving societal sincerity, as well as a further set of measures published by the Central Committee General Office in September 2016 (State Council 2016; Central Committee General Office 2016). Together, these documents provide the basis for what has become a hallmark of social credit thought, namely the notion that individuals who 'default in one area will be punished in all areas' (Liu 2018). Social credit's use of joint punishments through the sharing of departmental black lists marked a significant departure from its previous application as a technology in the calculation of risk to one that encouraged judicial discipline and compliance.

The expansion of black-listing in this manner received enthusiastic legislative attention. Building on the State Council's framework, thirty-seven government bodies had by mid-2018 published memoranda of their own detailing how the system of joint punishments would be implemented at the departmental level. These documents follow a standardised format, outlining infringements of which specific existing laws will result in an individual party's black-listing, as well as the punishments to which they will be subjected. One well-developed example of social credit black-listing is the growing 'no fly list', membership in which can be earned through a variety of behaviours seemingly unrelated to the aviation industry (National Development and Reform Commission 2018b). Failure to contribute to social insurance schemes, pay one's taxes on time or pay court fines in full will all result in an individual being unable to take a flight (Daum 2018). Taken in aggregate, the system of black-listing has expanded significantly since its inception. In May 2018, the Public Credit Information Centre published its first monthly analysis of the structure as a whole, revealing that 8.4 million legal or natural persons were at that point black-listed. Approximately 250,000 new additions were being made to these lists every month, 84.9 per cent of which were individuals rather than companies, with 125,000 removed (National Public Credit Information Centre 2018).

Perhaps unsurprisingly, news of curtailed freedoms as a result of black-listing have made headlines in the Chinese media, thrusting this element of the social credit system into the limelight. In March 2018, the Jilin City government published the names of seventeen soldiers who had decided to leave the military and would therefore be black-listed in accordance with the State Council 2016 document outlined above (Jilin City Military Recruitment Office 2018). In addition to an unspecified fine leveraged by the Jilin City Military Recruitment Office, the black-listing of the 17 recruits meant that they were also subjected to restrictions across a wide range of areas, including a ban on high-speed train or air travel, taking out loans, purchasing real-estate or enrolling in any form of education for the next two years (Ni 2018). Three soldiers in Anhui province were fined 30,000 RMB and black-listed for similar offences, resulting in a two-year ban on leaving the country (Xie 2018). In July 2018, several media outlets reported the case of a child in Wenzhou who, having been given a place at a private school in the city, had had their offer rescinded due to the black-listing of their father.[5] This followed a similar story in August 2017 in Quanzhou where a child lost his 80,000 RMB-a-year place at a private school in Xiamen on account of over 80 million RMB of outstanding debt owed by his parents. This case speaks to the *nan* (difficulty) in *zhixing nan* that led to the expansion of social credit in this direction in the first place. Proceedings against the child's parents began in late 2012, when they were first ordered to repay an initial 4 million RMB loan. Several trials later, the then-divorced couple had by 2017 a total of 30 cases open against them. Instructing the child's school to eject them through the joint punishment system followed several other bans on travel, luxury consumption and holidaying, all to no effect (Ji 2017). Not all applications of social credit black-

[5] According to media reports, the father owed 200,000 RMB to a local bank and had been added to a departmental black list for non-payment. The case drew significant attention, with over 30,000 Weibo posts published on the topic, as well as mentions in national media outlets such as China Central Television (CCTV) and *People's Daily*. The father apparently paid what was owed and his child was able to take up his place. For an overview of the incident, see Wade (2018).

listing in this manner have been justified or welcomed. In July 2018, the Foreign Languages School also in Quanzhou announced that it would be checking parents' names against local and national black-lists, and that the children of black-listed parents would no longer be allowed a place at the institution. After some consternation and disbelief on local WeChat groups, the municipal Ministry of Education clarified that it had nothing to do with this restriction, as the school's fees were not deemed high enough at 17,000 RMB per year for it to be classified within the system as conspicuous consumption. The school, however, confirmed that it would be continuing with its policy nonetheless in a somewhat performative and pointlessly punitive demonstration of loyalty to social credit ideals (Zhong 2018).

9.2 The Moral Turn

The expansion of social credit beyond its application as a narrow financial tool must be viewed within the context as not only a solution to the problem of *zhixing nan* (difficult judicial enforcement) but also against the re-insertion of a moralising ideology into political life under Xi Jinping. Beyond its application as a technology of discipline in the resolving of judicial issues, social credit has increasingly been applied in the pursuit of other governance priorities, namely the promotion of a more 'civilised' society, under the banner of improving *chengxin*, or honesty and credibility.

This shift can at least in part be seen as a response to a perceived 'moral crisis' or 'trust deficit' that permeated political and media discourse in the years either side of Xi Jinping's coming to power. A number of high-profile moral scandals circulated in the press at this time, prompting soul-searching nationwide. Among some of the most egregious examples were the cases of Yueyue, a toddler run over twice and ignored by 18 passers-by before someone came to her aid (Sina News 2011); the Good Samaritans who themselves in turn were extorted or sued by the very person they were helping (Branigan 2011); and the embezzlement of charitable donations at the hands of local corrupt officials (iFeng 2008). The causes of this 'moral crisis' have been debated extensively. Some, such as sociologists Fei Xiaotong (1992) and Yun Yuanxiang (2011), have argued that the crisis has its roots in their characterisation of China as an innately low-trust society of kith and kin (*shuren shehui* 熟人社会) bound together by family ties and social networks within a traditional Confucian hierarchy. Due to this insularity compounded by rapid socio-economic changes brought about by the reform period, China has – according to this narrative – experienced a 'moral decay', epitomised by the shocking cases detailed above (Lee 2014; He 2015). Various scholars have attributed this crisis to the collapse of a collective identity and the rise of economic and social individualism, political corruption and anti-liberalism, as well as the effects of extreme inequality and its undermining of individual moral agency (Stenmüller 2013; Ci 2014).

This rhetoric of moral crisis and decay serves a dual purpose with regards to the social credit system; it both legitimises its creators as moral saviours while simultaneously positioning them as absolute arbiters of moral authority. That the CCP might want to 'solve' this perceived trust deficit follows a long tradition of Chinese moral governance, as explored in detail earlier in this book (Lin and Trevaskes Chapter 5). In contrast with rhetorical narratives of 'new' versus 'old' China, many Chinese scholars have highlighted the moralising of the CCP as a continuation of the Confucian 'rule by virtue' (*dexing zhengzhi* 德行政治) that characterised imperial times (Deng 2007; Cai 2010). This model of governance positions the Chinese state as the mediator of what can normatively be considered as moral and immoral, as well as the sole 'moral agent' entrusted with promoting such a vision of society (Thornton 2007). Since the 1980s, the notion of 'moral construction (*daode jianshe* 道德建设) has fused with concepts of 'social engineering' (*shehui gongcheng* 社会工程) to form a morals-driven technocratic tradition that has become a defining characteristic of post-Mao elite politics (Andreas 2009). The resurrection of the spirit of Lei Feng, Mao's model soldier, typifies a model of mythology-based governance that has in recent years seen the CCP insert itself into ever more personal walks of life (Zhang, Kleinman and Tu 2011). In the CCP's view, the answer to this 'moral panic' lies in the creation of what Bakken (2000) has termed an 'exemplary society', an educative and disciplinary culture where virtue is rewarded and ethical wrongdoing is punished in the name of 'human quality' (*suzhi* 素质).

That the CCP might use social credit as a disciplinary technology of regulation to encourage and enforce this 'exemplary society' again follows a pattern of Chinese statecraft that has long sought to divide, rank, subjugate and moralise the Chinese populace. Indeed, parallels can be found across Chinese imperial history: several scholars have drawn comparisons between the *baojia* (保甲) system of collective law enforcement in the Song dynasty and social credit's use of joint punishments and black-listing (Hoffman 2017; Creemers 2018). During the Ming-Qing transition, the *gongguoge* (功过格) or 'Ledgers of Merit and Demerit' were used as a form of practical morality handbook popular among Neo-Confucian elites. These ledgers contained lists of good and bad deeds – each designated a number of heavenly merit and demerit points – as well as steps one could take to earn rewards or avoid punishment. According to Cynthia Brokaw (1991), by the eighteenth century these ledgers had become a 'vehicle for the expression of a complete social vision', an important point of reference as to what behaviour was deemed appropriate within society. The parallels with the lists of positive and negative behaviours found in some iterations of social credit at the pilot city level, such as Rongcheng (see below), are too tempting not to make.

In the contemporary period, the CCP has compartmentalised the Chinese population rhetorically and administratively along various lines as a model of 'divide and conquer' governance. The designation of class (*chengfen* 成分) was a backbone of political ideology in the early Communist period, with the state acting as final arbiter of what was 'good' or 'bad', 'red' or 'black'. This polarisation peaked in the Cultural Revolution with 'bloodline theory' (*xuetong lun* 血统论), the notion that such traits were hereditary (Andreas 2002). 'Black' labels – 'capitalist running dog', 'revisionist', or 'renegade', and so on – were frequently levelled in disputes at both the political and local level. This social stratification was formalised with the introduction of a number of regulatory technologies used to divide and conquer the Chinese population. Whether through its use of the work unit (*danwei* 单位) as a method of collective organisation, through 'community building' (*shequ jianshe* 社区建设) as a tool of middle class self-governance or through the proliferation of personnel files (*dang'an* 档案) as a record of an individual's personal, professional and political history, the CCP has consistently deployed such technologies in the pursuit of its 'socialist governmentality' (Bray 2005; Tomba 2014; Thornton 2018).

Against the backdrop of an increasingly moralised ideology as the answer to a perceived trust deficit and moral decay, the development of the social credit system under Xi Jinping has seen a notable shift in both goals and means. Early efforts to implement a cross-government system of joint incentives focused largely on the punishment of judgement defaulters (*laolai*) and the enforcing of judicial decisions made outside of the social credit system. Put simply, social credit was being applied to fix a specific governance issue in the judiciary. More recently, however, there has been a concerted push towards introducing a more positive – and more abstract – slant to the system in the form of a joint rewards mechanism for red-listed (*hong mingdan* 红名单) individuals and companies who behave in certain heavily moralised ways.

Efforts to emphasise a defined view of 'correct' behaviour through the use of a social credit carrot over a stick have intensified since mid-2018. This has been most clearly evidenced at the local level, with the 'Second Summit for the Construction of City Social Credit' held in June 2018 under the theme of 'credit makes life happier' (*xinyong rang shenghuo geng meihao* 信用让生活更美好), marking somewhat of a sea-change in social credit thought (State Information Office 2018). Under the leadership of the NDRC, the Summit saw the announcement of a new policy of rewards for 'good' behaviour called 'CreditEase+' (*xinyi jia* 信易加). Just as with the system of joint punishments, this policy laid out general areas of potential incentives before devolving actual interpretation and implementation to individual government departments and localities. The June 2018 Summit saw the announcement of five such areas for reward. CreditEase Loans (*xinyi huo* 信易货) would offer access to cheap finance for small and medium-sized businesses. CreditEase Rent (*xinyi zu* 信易租) would provide subsidised or deposit-free office rental for start-ups and small companies as a way of promoting innovation. CreditEase Travel (*xinyi xing* 信易行) would grant free or discounted travel on public transport. CreditEase Approve (*xinyi pi* 信易批) aimed to reduce bureaucracy and would give preferential consideration in applying for government services. Finally, CreditEase Tourism (*xinyi you* 信易游) aimed to make holidaying more comfortable, with discounted services at a range of hotels, restaurants and tourist attractions. In some ways, several of these promotional offers parrot the efforts of pseudo social credit schemes operated by private companies, such as Alibaba's Sesame Credit (Ahmed 2017). The difference here, as with the joint punishments system, however, is the connectedness of the policy's goals, that 'good' behaviour in one area of administrative, commercial or social life should have positive ramifications elsewhere. In the words of Lian Weiliang, deputy director of the NDRC, the CreditEase+ programme aimed to 'create tangible value out of the intangible; to ascribe use to maintaining honesty and to give it feeling' (Zhonghong Wang 2018). A total of 30 cities announced at the City Credit Summit that they would be integrating CreditEase+ rewards into their social credit systems. At the time of writing, at least five cities had announced the launch of Resident Credit Scores (*shimin xinyongfen* 市民信用分) through which CreditEase+ benefits would be administered.[6] While the effects of these more positive incentives are yet to be tested, the shift in rhetoric away from punishment and enforcement towards reward is striking. With the launch of CreditEase+, the system of joint incentives has become not purely an exercise in deterring certain behaviours but also one engaged in actively encouraging others by creating a degree of user 'buy-in' as a way of legitimising the system's existence.

9.3 Local Innovation: Pilot City Credit Schemes

This reliance on cities as a source of innovation in testing new directions for social credit follows a distinctive pattern of piloted Chinese governance. Beyond the rafts of central planning documents and policies outlined above, a core tenet of China's social credit system has been its reliance on local implementation. This delegated form of governance-through-piloting follows on from a long tradition of CCP policymaking, one that emphasises the importance of localised experimentation in testing and refining policies set centrally before applying them nationwide (Heilmann 2018). This delegated model of governance – 'federalism, Chinese style' – has been central not only to the implementation of policy, but to its innovation (Liu and Weingast 2018). Göbel and Heberer (2018) argue that 'in contrast to policy experimentation, where desired policy outcomes are clearly defined, local officials engaging in policy "innovation" need to decode central government documents and directives to assess whether their planned innovation is likely to meet with approval' (283). Under this model, overarching policy roadmaps and targets are set centrally, but the methods and mechanisms of implementation are developed and tested locally and in competition with other localities before being rolled out on a national level. This allows for the continuous policy flexibility that has been so central to China's exceptional and unconventional style of adaptive governance, without the usual checks and balances present in multi-party systems (Heilmann and Perry 2011).

This model of localised piloting as a way of incubating, reviewing and innovating policy has been pivotal to the development of China's social

[6] Each Resident Credit Score announced to date has been given a friendly name for use in public affairs. In Suzhou, the credit scoring system is known as the Osmanthus Score (*guihua*); in Suqian, it is the Western Chu Score (*xichu*); Fuzhou has Jasmine Score (*moli*); in Xiamen, it is an Egret Score (*bailu*); in Shenyang it is the Rose Score (*meigui*).

credit system. Indeed, to paraphrase official rhetoric, policymakers in this area have been advised 'first to test and learn, and innovation will burst forth' (State Information Office 2018). This process of experimentation began in August 2015 when the NDRC and PBoC, co-chairs of the Joint Conference on the Construction of the Social Credit System, reported the launch of 11 pilot model social credit cities (National Development and Reform Commission 2015). Eight months later, another 32 pilot cities were announced. Beyond these 43 official model city-level social credit schemes, including several large municipalities such as Chengdu, Nanjing and Guangzhou, hundreds of other social credit programmes have been implemented across China since 2015, with an increasing impetus towards developing systems at the rural level. The first 'Summit for the Construction of City Social Credit System' held in Hangzhou in July 2017 brought together a number of these schemes in an effort to promote examples of best practice and potential collaboration. A report drawn up after the summit cited data from 653 separate social credit initiatives, all at various stages of development (Xinhua 2017).

With cities innovating based on their own interpretations of the 2014 Planning Outline, the central government has been mindful to keep a close eye on developments. In November 2016, the think tank China Reform Daily, together with Renmin and Peking Universities, was commissioned to carry out a third-party analysis of progress in 20 of the 43 official pilots. These cities were judged according to a strict set of criteria outlined by the NDRC and PBoC and then scored out of 100 with an additional 20 bonus points available for exceptional work (National Development and Reform Commission and People's Bank of China 2016). The evaluation emphasised cross-government collaboration with 0.2 point awarded for each local bureau's participation in the supply of data (up to a maximum of 10 points). A further 0.05 point was given for each system of joint reward or punishment – again, up to a maximum of 12 points in total. Sheer scale does not seem to have been particularly valued, with only 5 points available (one point for every one million data points collected). The importance of connectedness, however, was apparent, with online credit search portals of the kind used by citizens awarded 3 points, and up to 8 further points available to local governments that enabled the search of credit score records across different departments.

This method of comparative analysis was revised in August 2017 to take a far wider range of factors into account in the assessment of local piloting success (National Development and Reform Commission and People's Bank of China 2017). These new 'assessment indices' placed a much greater emphasis on seemingly subjective and abstract criteria, mirroring the ideological turn in social credit policymaking that took place around this time. Eight points were made available for the promotion of *chengxin* culture, up from 2 points under the 2016 regulations, while a further 8 discretionary points were awarded for adherence to the spirit of Xi Jinping Thought. Another big change was that for the first time, cities could also lose points: 0.1 point was docked for each major incident of 'lost trust' (*shixin* 失信) in government affairs over the last 2 years. Another 0.1 point was deducted per percentage point of errors (above 5%) in the collection of public credit information. Armed with a new set of assessment criteria, the NDRC and PBoC commissioned a follow-up survey of 20 city schemes in November 2017. This culminated in the announcement of 12 model city social credit systems in January 2018: Hangzhou, Nanjing, Xiamen, Chengdu, Suzhou, Suqian, Huizhou, Wenzhou, Weihai, Weifang, Yiwu and Rongcheng (National Development and Reform Commission 2018a). A second list of 16 additional model city-level social credit systems was announced in August 2019 (National Development and Reform Commission 2019).[7]

A comparative study of city-level social credit in action across these model schemes and beyond reveals a remarkable degree of variety in terms of both approach and scope. In Wenzhou, credit ranks between A and D are used to dissuade academic fraud and promote quality of work within the scientific research community (Credit China 2019b). In Zhengzhou, both companies and individual drivers in the waste removal industry receive a credit score of between 0 and 100 based on good practice (Credit China 2019a). Companies with a score lower than 60 will neither be able to tender for government contracts nor apply for loans. Drivers with a score of 60 or lower will have their driving licences revoked. In Hohhot, a new government-backed platform, *Xinguanjia* (信管家), provides information on the 'trustworthiness' of domestic workers so as to match them with job prospects (Wei 2019).

Among all city-level social credit schemes, the city of Rongcheng in Shandong province has been held up by the Chinese authorities as the most developed and comprehensive example of social credit thus far. The Rongcheng social credit system has won praise not only for its scale – comprising 'credit dossiers' (*xinyong dang'an* 信用档案) for all 670,000

[7] City-level projects announced as model pilots in August 2019 included Qingdao, Wuhan, Anshan, Shanghai Pudong, Shanghai Jiading, Wuxi, Hefei, Huaibei, Wuhu, Anqing, Fuzhou, Putian, Zhengzhou, Yichang, Xianning and Luzhoul.

of its inhabitants as well as over 50,000 businesses and 142 government departments – but also for its innovation and the totality of its city-wide push for 'model' status. At the 2017 inaugural City Credit Summit in Hangzhou, a study of 361 county-level credit schemes ranked Rongcheng the most developed in China, with the city winning a national prize for innovation (Sohu 2017). Since being named as one of China's 12 model social credit cities in January 2018, numerous media, academic, and government delegations have visited Rongcheng on study tours in an attempt to replicate its success elsewhere in the country (Credit Shandong 2017).

Further extending the delegated piloting that has driven local social credit experimentation, the Rongcheng social credit scheme relies on a devolved system of innovation and implementation. Social credit is administered at three levels of government; the municipal level, the departmental level and the subdistrict level (Credit Rongcheng 2018a). Hundreds of separate social credit systems make up the Rongcheng scheme, each one functioning independently of the other but connected through a unifying ideology and a well-developed system of joint incentives. Rongcheng is one of very few social credit schemes to use a point system, with individuals given a starting score of 1,000 credit points and commercial entities 100 points, both corresponding with an 'A' rating.[8] Since 2016, Rongcheng's Credit Management Office has published an annual catalogue of data categories that should be considered in the calculation of social credit scores. The most recent edition of this catalogue details activities across a broad spectrum of economic and social life, including 150 behavioural categories that can increase an individual or legal entity's credit score and 570 that can decrease it (Rongcheng Social Credit Management Office 2018). Exactly how these categories of behaviour are elucidated and quantified, however, is left up to individual government ministries and localities as they seek to solve their own specific governance issues.

[8] Institutions and commercial entities are given 100 credit points, corresponding with an A rating. Falling below 95 points will result in a B grade, while fewer than 90 points translates into a C. For individuals, the spectrum is much wider. Each citizen of Rongcheng begins with 1,000 credit points – ranked A. As this score increases, citizens can be awarded an AA (1,030–1,049 points) or even an AAA (>1,050 points) rating. Loss of credit points will see an individual ranked B (850–949 points), C (600–849 points) or D (<599 points). See Rongcheng Municipal Communist Party Committee & Rongcheng People's Government (2014).

The devolution of control has resulted in some quite elaborate interpretations of the system. The Rongcheng Ministry of Transport has issued over a dozen directives on the establishment of a social credit system for the city's taxi industry (Rongcheng Ministry of Transport 2016a and 2016b). Under this system, all 205 of Rongcheng's taxi drivers are pooled into groups of 10 cars, with each group headed by one of a 21-strong 'Honest Model Taxi Team' responsible for monitoring the behaviour of other drivers, managing conflicts, and improving overall service (Rongcheng Ministry of Transport 2017). The data gathered on drivers, whether from passengers or their peers, is collated on a monthly basis and converted into a star rating (0–4) that is then displayed in LED lights in the windscreen of each driver's car. By the end of 2017, 145 taxis had the highest 4-star rating, while 59 had 3 stars and only one driver had two. Particularly courteous drivers are referred for city *chengxin* awards; in January 2018, 10 drivers were honoured at an industry ceremony for their model behaviour. According to the Ministry of Transport's own statistics, the system appears to be having an effect, with passenger complaints down 72 per cent and over 2 million RMB's worth of lost property returned by drivers within 12 months of the system's launch (Credit Shandong 2018). In July 2018, the Credit Rongcheng website reported that 15 drivers had donated blood in order to increase their score (Credit Rongcheng 2018b).

The behaviours both rewarded and punished at this decentralised level speak to the highly localised nature of social credit as a tool for solving an increasingly broad range of governance issues. Given its reliance on the kelp industry, it is unsurprising that a significant focus of social credit legislation in Rongcheng has been on the boat industry. Similarly, the detail at the subdistrict and village level around field boundaries and drying one's crops in public spaces are relevant only to those living in site-specific agricultural communities (Gangwan Subdistrict Credit Leading Small Group 2018). Some, such as a loss of 100 credit points for burying a relative in a grave that exceeds the permitted square-footage, boggle the mind as to the low-level scandal that must have transpired before.[9]

9 Other behaviours that are punished severely in the Gangwan Subdistrict of Rongcheng include gambling (-20 points), failure to pay relevant fines after the birth of a child outside of family planning laws (-50), children who neglect their elderly parents, as well as parents who mistreat their children (-50) and abusing one's dog (-10).

9.4 Conclusion

In the decade or more since work on the construction of a social credit system began in earnest, much has changed in the way that social credit is both conceived of and applied. Its evolution from 'technology of risk' and provider of *zhengxin* within China's nascent market economy to technology of discipline in the enforcement of judicial rulings, as well as its use as a promoter of honesty, or *chengxin*, and application to an increasingly diverse range of governance issues, speaks to two broad trends.

The first notable shift in the application of social credit has been one from the centre to the periphery. Social credit's development and roll-out has been a prime example of the importance of localised piloting and experimentation in Chinese policymaking over the mass campaigns of times gone by. The publishing of the 2014 Planning Outline heralded a new direction in social credit thought, laying out a roadmap for the system's development over the coming five years. Crucially, however, the Planning Outline omitted any real detail as to how social credit ought to be implemented. This was to be left to an ever greater number of ministries, leading groups and municipalities. In doing so, the central authorities have allowed for innovation on a remarkable scale, with the administration of social credit varying wildly by jurisdiction. Connected by a guiding logic centred around the use of shared black-listing and red-listing but otherwise largely left open to interpretation, this has allowed local and departmental authorities to apply social credit systems to a wide range of specific governance issues far beyond its original purpose. In turn, this has created healthy competition between municipalities and officials looking for Beijing's acknowledgement, while also providing a useful feedback mechanism for central government on local issues.

The second shift in social credit's development has been a conceptual one: from concrete tool to abstract ideal. At its inception, social credit was designed as a specific device for the fulfilment of a specific goal. As in systems elsewhere in the world, China's credit infrastructure was established with the aim of mitigating risk in the country's increasingly market-driven economy. The scope of social credit was expanded dramatically from 2011 onwards, as the NDRC and by extension the State Council saw other, broader applications for the country's credit system beyond the purely economic. The first major development in the broadening of social credit's purview was the adoption of the SPC's system of black-listing as a means of enforcing judicial decisions across multiple jurisdictions. The idea here was to systematically punish decision defaulters through the deployment of black lists as disciplinary technologies with the goal of encouraging compliance with existing laws. In the intervening years, however, the meaning of social credit has expanded through localised experimentation and a creeping political idealism to include rafts of benefits, material or otherwise, as reward for 'good' behaviour: carrots to the black lists' sticks. What began as a narrow policy goal has developed into an increasingly broad and abstract series of initiatives to promote the ideological spread of *chengxin* culture. This progression has mapped neatly onto the re-insertion of ideology more broadly under Xi Jinping that has been so widely and thoroughly discussed in this book.

This positive turn in social credit thought can in part be seen as an attempt to legitimise a system that arguably benefits the state more than the average citizen: difficult questions around privacy, data protection and access to justice are more easily avoided. It would be simple to dismiss *chengxin* sloganeering as mere propaganda, but separating manufactured consent from 'real' independent opinion among ordinary citizens is increasingly difficult in contemporary China (Brady 2008; Johnson 2019). Creating user 'buy-in' for the social credit system as a whole through localised incentives against a backdrop of media-propagated moral panic does seem to be having an impact: initial survey work done on attitudes to social credit has shown a strong degree of popular support for the system (Kostka 2019). The promotion of a more abstract set of policy goals – *chengxin* behaviour – over concrete initiatives such as the provision of financial credit must be understood as part of the Party-state's broader paternalistic aspirations. The CCP has long viewed itself as the sole moral arbiter of what is right and wrong; social credit provides one more disciplinary technology it can leverage to expand and consolidate its rule over an increasingly broad swathe of social life.

References

Ahmed, S. 2017. Cashless society, cached data: security considerations for a Chinese social credit system. *The Citizen Lab*, 24 January. Available from: https://citizenlab.ca/2017/01/cashless-society-cached-data-security-considerations-chinese-social-credit-system/.

Andreas, J. 2002. Battling over political and cultural power during the Chinese cultural revolution. *Theory and Society*, 31(4), 463–519.

2009. *Rise of the Red Engineers: The Cultural Revolution and the Origins of China's New Class.* Palo Alto: Stanford University Press.

Bakken, B. 2000. *The Exemplary Society: Human Improvement, Social Control, and the Dangers of Modernity in China.* Oxford: Oxford University Press.

Bouk, D. 2015. *How Our Days Became Numbered: Risk and the Rise of the Statistical Individual.* Chicago: University of Chicago Press.

Brady, A. 2008. *Marketing Dictatorship: Propaganda and Thought Work in Contemporary China.* Lanham: Rowman & Littlefield.

Branigan, T. 2011. China's good samaritans count the cost of their altruism. *The Guardian*, 8 September. Available from: www.theguardian.com/world/2011/sep/08/chinas-good-samaritans-count-cost.

Bray, D. 2005. *Social Space and Governance in Urban China.* Palo Alto: Stanford University Press.

Brokaw, C. 1991. *The Ledgers of Merit and Demerit: Social Change and Moral Order in Late Imperial China.* Princeton: Princeton University Press.

Cai, Xiang. 2010. *Geming/ Xushu: Zhongguo Shehuizhuyi Wenxue Wenhua Xiangxiang 1949–1966* (Revolution/Narration: The Literary and Cultural Imagination of Chinese Socialism, 1949–1966). Beijing: Peking University Press.

Central Committee General Office. 2016. Guanyu jiakuai tuijin shixin beizhixing ren xinyong jiandu, jingshi he chengjie jizhi jiangshe de yijian (Opinions on the acceleration of the construction of a system for the credit supervision, warning and punishment of judgement defaulters subject to supervision), issued 25 June. Available from: www.xinhuanet.com/politics/2016-09/25/c_1119620719.htm.

Central Committee of the Chinese Communist Party. 2011. Guanyu shenhua wenhua tizhi gaige de jueding (Decision on the deepening of cultural structural reform), issued 25 October. Available from: www.gov.cn/jrzg/2011-10/25/content_1978202.htm.

Cheng, Minxuan. 2010. *Xinyong de Jingjixue Fenxi* (Economic Analyses of Credit). Beijing: China Social Sciences Press.

Ci, Jiwei. 2014. *Moral China in the Age of Reform.* Cambridge: Cambridge University Press.

Clarke, D. 1995. The execution of civil judgments in China. *The China Quarterly*, 141.

Credit China. 2017. 'Xinyong zhongguo' wangzhan 2.0 ban zhengshi shangxian yunxing ('Credit China' 2.0 edition officially goes live online), 16 October. Available from: www.creditchina.gov.cn/toutiaoxinwen/201710/t20171016_57943.html.

2019a. Henan Zhengzhou chutai san daxin zhenggoujian xinyong pingjia tixi (Zhengzhou, Henan issues three major credit evaluation systems for government construction), 4 June. Available from: www.creditchina.gov.cn/hangyexinyong_824/zonghedongtai/zhengfubumen/201906/t20190604_157574.html.

2019b. Zhejiang Wenzhou: chengxin guanli fugai keyan quan liucheng shixing siji keyan xinyong dengji guanli (Wenzhou, Zhejiang: four levels of credit rating management implemented for management of honesty across entire process of scientific research), 17 July. Available from: www.creditchina.gov.cn/home/lianhejiangchegn/201907/t20190716_162110.html.

Credit Rongcheng. 2018a. Rongchengshi tuixing 'sanji zhengji, sanceng pingji' xinyong pingjia yunxing jizhi (Rongcheng promotes implementation of system of 'three collects' and 'three ranks'), 4 May. Available from: www.rccredit.gov.cn/rccreditweb/web/cont_97d5e445f604433ab6141be9262b8659.html.

2018b. 15 ming chuzuche siji wuchang xianxue 6000 haosheng (15 Taxi drivers give 6 litres of blood voluntarily), 9 July. Available from: www.rccredit.gov.cn/web/cont_7788019dd6f04923a11cf99b10934661.html.

Credit Shandong. 2017. Guonei xinyong tixi jianshe zhuanjia xuezhe juji rongchengshi yanjiu 'rongcheng moshi' tuiguang 'rongcheng jingyan' (National experts on the construction of a credit system assemble in Rongcheng to research the 'Rongcheng model' and promote the 'Rongcheng experience'), 25 December. Available from: www.creditsd.gov.cn/101/67910.html.

2018. Rongchengshi chuzuche, zhe yi zu zu shuju zu yi rang nin 'fangxin zuo' (Recent data from Rongcheng taxis will make you 'ride with ease'), 31 January. Available from: www.creditsd.gov.cn/101/69158.html.

Creemers, R. 2018. China's social credit system: an evolving practice of control. Working Paper. Available from: https://ssrn.com/abstract=3175792.

Daum, J. 2018. Who did China ban from flying? *China Law Translate*, 21 March. Available from: www.chinalawtranslate.com/en/who-did-china-ban-from-flying.

Deng, Xiaomang. 2007. *Zhong Xi Wenhua Bijiao Shiyi Jiang* (Eleven Lectures On East-West Cultural Comparisons). Changsha: Hunan Educational Press.

Fei, Xiaotong. 1992. *From the Soil: The Foundations of Chinese Society* (G. Hamilton and W. Zheng, trans.). Berkeley: University of California Press.

Finder, S. 2016. Supreme people's court & 43 other central institutions commit to punishing judgment debtors. *Supreme People's Court Monitor*, 27 April. Available from: https://supremepeoplescourtmonitor.com/2016/04/27/supreme-peoples-court-43-other-central-institutions-commit-to-punishing-judgment-debtors/.

Gangwan Subdistrict Credit Leading Small Group. 2018. Rongchengshi gangwan jiedao shequ jumin xinyong guanli shishi banfa (shixing) (Trial regulations on community resident credit management in Gangwan Subdistrict, Rongcheng) (On file with author).

Göbel, C. and Heberer, T. 2018. The policy innovation imperative: changing techniques for governing China's local governors. In V. Shue and P. Thornton, eds., *To Govern China: Evolving Practices of Power*. Cambridge: Cambridge University Press.

He, Huaihong. 2015. *Social Ethics in a Changing China: Moral Decay or Ethical Awakening*. Washington, DC: Brookings Institution Press.

Heilmann, S. 2018. *Red Swan: How Unorthodox Policy Making Facilitated China's Rise*. Hong Kong: The Chinese University Press.

Heilmann, S. and Perry, E. 2011. *Mao's Invisible Hand: The Political Foundations of Adaptive Governance in China*. Cambridge: Harvard University Press.

Hoffman, S. 2017. Programming China: The communist party's autonomic approach to managing state security. *MERICS China Monitor*, 12 December. Available from: www.merics.org/sites/default/files/2017-12/171212_China_Monitor_44_Programming_China_EN__0.pdf.

iFeng. 2008. Fanxinshe: zhongguoren danxin fubai qinshi shankuan (AFP: Chinese people are afraid that corruption is corroding charitable funds). *iFeng Finance*, 30 May. Available from: http://finance.ifeng.com/hwkzg/200805/0530_2180_570189.shtml.

Ji, Weiwei. 2017. Qianxia 8000 wan juze bu huan song erzi shang guizu xuexiao mei nian xuefei 8 wan (80 million RMB in debt and unable to send son to 8,000 RMB luxury school). *Sina Fujian*, 23 August. Available from: http://fj.sina.com.cn/news/s/2017-08-23/detail-ifykcypq4318133.shtml.

Jiang, Zemin. 2002. Jiang Zemin tongzhi zai dang de shiliu da shang suo zuo baogao quanwen, quanmian jianshe xiaokang shehui, kaichuang zhongguo tese shehuizhuyi shiye xin jumian (Comrade Jiang Zemin's report from the 16th party congress of the Chinese communist party: new aspects on the comprehensive construction of a moderately prosperous society and launch of socialism with Chinese characteristics), issued 8 November. Available from: www.fmprc.gov.cn/web/ziliao_674904/zyjh_674906/t10855.shtml.

Jilin City Military Recruitment Office. 2018. Jilinshi guanyu dui 17 ming jufu bingyi renyuan de chengchu cuoshi (Jilin city punishment measures against 17 soldiers who refused to serve), issued 12 March. Available from: https://mp.weixin.qq.com/s/Owe-OPqCEBKQB1RnuI78tA.

Johnson, I. 2019. China, where state pomp comes with real feeling. *The New York Times*, 3 October. Available from: www.nytimes.com/2019/10/03/opinion/china-national-day-.html.

Kostka, G. 2019. China's social credit systems and public opinion: explaining high levels of approval. *New Media & Society*, 21(7), 1565–93.

Lauer, J. 2017. *Creditworthy: A History of Consumer Surveillance and Financial Identity in America*. New York: Columbia University Press.

Lee, Haiyan. 2014. *The Stranger and the Chinese Moral Imagination*. Palo Alto: Stanford University Press.

Levy, J. 2012. *Freaks of Fortune: The Emerging World of Capitalism and Risk in America*. Cambridge: Harvard University Press.

Lin, Junyue. 2003. *Shehui Xinyong Tixi Yuanli* (Principles of a Social Credit System). Beijing: China Fangzheng Press.

2012. Shehui xinyong tixi lilun de chuancheng mailuo yu chuangxin (Fabric and innovation of social credit system theory). *Credit Reference* 1(3), 1–12.

Liu, Lizhi, and Weingast, B. 2018. Taobao, federalism, and the emergence of law, Chinese style. *Minnesota Law Review*, 102(4), 1563–90.

Liu, Xiuhao. 2018. Li Keqiang: jianli hei mingdan zhidu, rang shixinzhe quan shehui cunbu nanxing (Li Keqiang: establish a system of black lists to make it difficult for the untrustworthy to take even a single step across society). *The Paper*, 10 June. Available from: www.thepaper.cn/newsDetail_forward_2185603.

Ma, Peigui. 2012. Huang Wenyun: zhongguo xinyong tixi jianshe diyi ren (Huang Wenyun: first person in the construction of china's credit system). *Yuandian Credit*, 9 September. Available from: http://yuandiancredit.com/h-nd-198.html.

National Development and Reform Commission & People's Bank of China. 2015. Quanguo shoupi chuangjian xinyong tixi jianshi shifan chengshi queding (Decision on the first national list of model cities for the construction of credit system), issued 11 August. Available from: www.gov.cn/xinwen/2015-08/11/content_2910920.htm.

2016. Shehui xinyong tixi jianshi shifan chuangjian chengshi pinggu cankao zhibiao (2016 nian ban) (Indices for the assessment of model cities in the construction of a social credit system [2016 Edition]), issued 28 September. Available from: https://credit.wuhan.gov.cn/xywh/imgcd/5549813355859240.pdf.

2017. Shehui xinyong tixi jianshi shifan chuangjian chengshi pingshen cankao zhibiao (2017 nian ban) (Indices for the assessment of model cities in the construction of a social credit system [2017 Edition]). *On file with author.*

National Development and Reform Commission. 2018a. Shoupi shehui xinyong tixi jianshe shifan chengshi mingdan gongbu (First list of model cities in the construction of a social credit system announced), issued 9 January. Available from: www.ndrc.gov.cn/xwzx/xwfb/201801/t20180109_873409.html.

2018b. Guanyu zai yiding qixian nei shidang xianzhi teding yanzhong shixinren chengzuo minyong hangkongqi tuidong shehui xinyong tixi jianshe de yijian. (Opinions on the proportional limiting of seriously untrustworthy persons from taking civil aircraft for a fixed period of time, and promoting the establishment of the social credit system), issued 2 March. Available from: www.ndrc.gov.cn/zcfb/zcfbtz/201803/t20180316_879624.html.

2019. Di er pi shehui xinyong tixi jianshe shifan chengshi mingdan gongbu (Second list of model cities in the construction of a social credit system announced), issued 12 August. Available from: www.ndrc.gov.cn/zcfb/zcfbtz/201908/t20190813_944514.html.

National People's Congress. 2004. Guanyu zhengdun he guifan shichang jingji zhixu qingkuang de baogao (Report on the reorganisation and standardisation of order in the market economy), issued 27 December. Available from: www.npc.gov.cn/wxzl/gongbao/2005-02/24/content_5337659.htm.

National Public Credit Information Centre. 2018. Shixin hei mingdan yuedu fenxi baogao (Black list monthly analytical report), issued 21 May. Available from: www.gov.cn/fuwu/2018-06/21/content_5300120.htm.

Ni, Xueying. 2018. Duo di jiang jufu bingyizhe naru zhengxin 'hei mingdan' (Multiple locations add soldiers refusing military service to credit 'black lists'). *Xinjingbao* (Beijing News), 19 March. Available from: www.bjnews.com.cn/news/2018/03/19/479533.html.

Ohlberg, M., Ahmed, S. and Lang, B. 2017. Central planning, local experiments: the complex implementation of China's social credit system. *MERICS China Monitor*, 12 December. Available from: www.merics.org/sites/default/files/2017-12/171212_China_Monitor_43_Social_Credit_System_Implementation.pdf.

Olegario, R. 2016. *The Engine of Enterprise: Credit in America*. Cambridge: Harvard University Press.

People's Daily. 2014. Chulihao xinyong jianshe de 'sidui guanxi' (The 'four essential relationships' of attaining credit success), 8 August. Available from: http://politics.people.com.cn/n/2014/0808/c70731–25426246.html.

Rongcheng Ministry of Transport. 2016a. Rongchengshi chuzuche hangye xinyong guanli zanxing guiding (Provisional rules on the credit management of the Rongcheng taxi industry).

2016b. Chuzu keyun xinyong guanli shishi xice (Detailed implementation of credit management for passenger taxis).

2017. Chuzu keyun congye renyuen xinyong guanli kaohe banfa (Assessment methods for credit management of employees in the passenger taxi industry).

Rongcheng Municipal Communist Party Committee & Rongcheng People's Government. 2014. Rongchengshi shehui faren he ziranren zhengxin guanli shixing banfa (Trial regulations for Rongcheng municipal credit management of legal and natural persons). Available from: www.creditsd.gov.cn/101/987.html.

Rongcheng Social Credit Management Office. 2018. Shehui xinyong xinxi zhengji mulu (Social credit information collection catalogue). On file with author.

Sina News. 2011. Liang sui nütong zao liang che nianya (Two-year-old girl run over by two cars). Available from: http://news.sina.com.cn/z/ntzny/.

2011. Zhongyang yaoqiu kaizhan daode lingyu tuchu wenti zhuanxiang jiaoyu he zhili (Central committee calls for development of morals to give prominence to issues concerning education and governance), 25 October. Available from: http://news.sina.com.cn/c/2011-10-25/234523361299.shtml.

Sohu. 2017. 'Rongcheng xinyong' shanyao hangzhou gaofeng luntan ('Credit Rongcheng' dazzles Hangzhou summit). 21 July. Available from: www.sohu.com/a/158878230_759511.

State Council. 1989. Guowuyuan pizhuan guojia jishu jianduju deng bumen guanyu jianli qiye, shiye danwei he shehui tuanti tongyi daima biaoshi zhidu baogao de tongzhi (Notice on the national administration of technology supervision report concerning the establishment of unified score system for industry, professions and community organisations). Available from: www.ybja.gov.cn/32004/32006/2658/2664/201410/MIT897.shtml.

2007. Guanyu shehui xinyong tixi jianshe de ruogan yijian (Guiding opinions on the construction of a social credit system), issued 2 April. Available from: www.gov.cn/zwgk/2007-04/02/content_569314.htm.

2014. Guowuyuan guanyu yinfa shehui xinyong tixi jianshe guihua gangyao (2014–2020 nian) de tongzhi (State council notice on the planning outline for the construction of a social credit system [2014–2020]), issued 14 June. Available from: www.gov.cn/zhengce/content/2014-06/27/content_8913.htm.

2015. Guanyu zhuanpi fazhan gaige wei deng bumen faren he qita zuzhi tongyi shehui xinyong daima zhidu jianshe zongti fang'an de tongzhi (Notice on a general plan for the national development and reform commission and other departments to construct a system of unified social credit numbers for legal persons and other organisations), issued 11 June. Available from: www.gov.cn/zhengce/content/2015-06/17/content_9858.htm.

2016. Guowuyuan guanyu jianli wanshan shouxin lianhe jili he shixin lianhe chengjie zhidu jiakuai tuijin shehui chengxin jianshe de zhidao yijian (Guiding opinions on the improvement of a system for joint reward of the trustworthy and joint punishment of the untrustworthy so as to accelerate the construction of societal sincerity), issued 12 June. Available from: www.gov.cn/zhengce/content/2016-06/12/content_5081222.htm.

State Information Centre. 2018. *Zhongguo Chengshi Xinyong Zhuangkuang Jiance Pingjia Baogao 2018 Nian* (Monitoring and Analysis Report on the Status of China Credit Cities 2018). Beijing: China Economic Press.

Steinmüller, H. 2013. *Communities of Complicity: Everyday Ethics in Rural China.* New York: Berghahn.

Supreme People's Court. 2017. Guanyu gongbu shixin beizhixing ren mingdan xinxi de ruogan guiding (Provisions for the publishing of names of judgement defaulters subject to supervision), issued 28 February. Available from: www.chinacourt.org/law/detail/2017/02/id/149233.shtml.

Thornton, P. 2007. *Disciplining the State: Virtue, Violence, and State-Making in Modern China.* Cambridge: Harvard University Press.

2018. A new urban underclass? making and managing 'vulnerable groups' in contemporary China. In V. Shue and P. Thornton, eds., *To Govern China: Evolving Practices of Power.* Cambridge: Cambridge University Press.

Tomba, L. 2014. *The Government Next Door: Neighbourhood Politics in China.* Ithaca: Cornell University Press.

Wade, S. 2018. College rejection threat highlights social credit. *China Digital Times*, 20 July. Available from: https://chinadigitaltimes.net/2018/07/college-rejection-threat-highlights-social-credit-blacklists/.

Wei Jingyu. 2019. Jiazhen fuwu ruhe kexin you kexin? Huhehaote tuichu 'xin guanjia' (How can housekeeping services be credible and heartfelt? Hohhot launches 'trust manager'). *Renminwang* (People's Daily online), 12 July. Available from: http://sn.people.com.cn/BIG5/n2/2019/0712/c378296-33137876.html.

Wu, Jingmei. 2009. *Xiandai Yinyong Xue* (Modern Credit Studies). Beijing: China Renmin University Press.

Xie, Yinzong. 2018. Anhui san nanzi jufu binyi bei liewei shixin renyuan: fakuan, liang nian bu de chuguo chujing (Three soldiers refusing service in Anhui deemed untrustworthy: subject to fine and unable to travel abroad for two years). *The Paper*, 19 March. Available from: www.thepaper.cn/newsDetail_forward_2033296.

Xinhua. 2017. *Zhongguo Chengshi Xinyong Jianshe Nianbao 2016–2017* (Annual Report on Construction of China City Credit 2016–2017). Beijing: Xinhua Press.

2017. Zhongguo renmin yinhang: jinrong xinyong xinxi jichu shujuku yi shoulu 9.26 yi ziranren xinxi (People's Bank of China: basic data collected on 926 million natural persons for financial credit). *Xinhuawang* (Xinhuanet), 20 June. Available from: www.xinhuanet.com/fortune/2017-06/20/c_1121179605.htm.

Yun, Yunxiang. 2011. The changing moral landscape. In A. Kleinman et al., eds., *Deep China: The Moral Life of the Person*. Berkeley: University of California Press.

Zhang, E., Kleinman, A. and Tu, W. 2011. *Governance of Life in Chinese Moral Experience: The Quest for an Adequate Life*. Abingdon: Routledge.

Zhao, Zhanhui. 2018. Xinyong shehui lailin, ni zhunbei haole ma (The credit society is coming: are you ready). *Renmin ribao* (People's Daily), 4 June. Available from: http://paper.people.com.cn/rmrb/html/2018-06/04/nw.D110000renmrb_20180604_1-09.htm.

Zhong, Yuhao. 2018. Quanzhou yi sili xuexiao: fumu renhe yifang shi shixin beizhixing ren de, ju jiena xinsheng (Private school in Quanzhou: children of parents deemed untrustworthy on any front to be refused admission). *The Paper*, 7 July. Available from: www.thepaper.cn/newsDetail_forward_2246485.

Zhonghong Wang. 2018. Lian Weiliang zai dier jie zhongguo chengshi xinyong jianshe gaofeng luntan de jianghua (Lian Weiliang's speech at the second summit on the construction of city social credit). *Zhonghong Wang* (Zhonghong net), 10 June. Available from: www.zhonghongwang.com/show-124-97129-1.html.

GLOSSARY OF CHINESE TERMS

(Political, Ideological and Philosophical Concepts and Slogans)

B

biaotai 表态 – performative loyalty

buduan cong shengli zou xiang shengli 不断从胜利走向胜利 – continuous advance from victory to victory

C

chengxin 诚信 – honesty and credibility

D

dang de jingshen 党的精神 – the Party spirit

dang de lingdao he shehui zhuyi fazhi shi yizhi de 党的领导和社会主义法治是一致的 – the Party's leadership and socialist rule of law are compatible

dang de sixiang 党的思想 – Party thought

dang de shiye zhi shang 党的事业至上 – the supremacy of the Party's cause

dang jia zuo zhu 当家做主 – the people are masters of their own domain

dang shi lingdao yiqie de 党是领导一切的 – the Party leads over everything

dang yao guan dang 党要管党 – the Party must constrain the Party itself

dangzheng fenkai 党政分开 – separation of the Party and government

dangzhang 党章 – Party constitution or charter

defa hezhi 德法合治 – combining law and morality in governing

dezhu xingfu 德主刑辅 – granting moral rules primacy over penal codes

dingceng sheji 顶层设计 – top-level design
dingyu yizun 定于一尊 – concentrated in one single authority

F

fa li qing yu yiti 法、理、情于一体 – integrating the stipulations of law, common understandings and public emotions
falü shi chengwen de daode, daode shi neixin de falü 法律是成文的道德，道德是内心的法律 – law is moral virtue put down in words, and moral virtue is law borne in people's hearts
fang jin zhidu de longzili 放进制度的笼子里 – to contain within the cage of the [legal] system
fazhi 法治 – rule of law
*fazhi guojia*法治国家 – a nation governed by rule of law
fenfa youwei 奋发有为 – striving for achievement
fuqiang 富强 – material prosperity and strength

G

gaige kaifang 改革开放 – reform and opening up
gongchandang de lingddao 共产党的领导 – the Party leadership

H

hexin 核心 – core
huayu quan 话语权 – discourse power

J

jiaqiang dang dui quanmian yi fa zhi guo de lingdao 加强党对全面依法治国的领导 – strengthening the CCP's leadership over comprehensively 'governing the nation in accordance with the law'
jianyi yongwei 见义勇为 – Good Samaritan behaviour
jingshen wenming 精神文明 – spiritual civilisation
jiuguo 救国 – save the nation
junshi heyi 君师合一 – a saintly moral figure who, by virtue of his very position as ruler, becomes the nation's moral teacher

L

li 礼 – ritual and proper custom / decorum and ritual proprieties

li 理 – natural law (built on the presumption that all of nature, including human/social nature, is fundamentally rational and ordered)

lifa hezhi 礼法合治 – governing through a combination of propriety and law

liangfa 良法 – benevolent laws

lilun fabao 理论法宝 – theoretical magic weapon

liangfa shanzhi 良法善治 – benevolent laws and good governance

liangge yibainian douzheng mubiao 两个一百年斗争目标 – 'Two Centenaries Struggle Objective'; achieving moderate prosperity by the centenary of the Party's founding in 2021; achieving full development by the centenary of the PRC's establishment in 2049

liangxing weixian 良性违宪 – benign constitutional violation

lingdao xiaozu 领导小组 – leading small groups

liuzhi 留置 – to be held/detained in a specific place

M

meiyou gongchandang jiu meiyou xin Zhongguo 没有共产党就没有新中国 – without the CCP, there would be no New China

minquan 民权 – civil liberties

*minsheng*民生 – the people's welfare

Q

qinlao jiejian 勤劳节俭 – hardworking and frugal

R

renmin 人民 – the people

renmin liyi zhi shang 人民利益至上 – to regard as supreme the people's interests

S

sange daibiao 三个代表 – the Three Represents

sange zhishang 三个至上	– the Three Supremes doctrine
sanmin zhuyi 三民主义	– Three Principles of the People
shehui chengxin 社会诚信	– honesty and credibility as a social ethos/process
shehui xinyong tixi 社会信用体系	– social credit system
shehuizhuyi hexin jiazhiguan 社会主义核心价值观	– socialist core values
shijie pubian shiyongxing 世界普遍适用性	– universal applicability
shishi qiushi 实事求是	– seeking truth from facts
si xiang jiben yuanze 四项基本原则 –项	the Four Basic Principles
sifa fubai deng luanju 司法腐败等乱局	– judicial corruption and other chaos
sige quanmian 四个全面	– the Four Comprehensives
sixiang 思想	– thought/ a body of thought
suzhi 素质	– ideological and political qualities

T

tao guang yang hui 韬光养晦	– hiding strength and biding time
tie de jilü 铁的纪律	– iron self-discipline
tifa 提法	– an officially accepted usage for a particular term; (literally) the method [*fa*] of putting a point across [*ti*])

W

wei renmin fuwu 为人民服务	– serve the people
weida fuxing 伟大复兴	– grand rejuvenation
wenming xingwei 文明行为	– civilised behaviour

X

Xi Jinping xin shidai zhongguo tese shehui zhuyi sixiang 习近平新时代中国特色社会主义思想	– Xi Jinping Thought on Socialism with Chinese Characteristics for a New Era (also known as Xi Jinping Thought)
xianfa falü zhi shang 宪法法律至上	– the supremacy of the Constitution and law
xianzheng 宪政	– constitutional government (Sun Yat-sen's term for constitutional governance)
xiangxin dang 相信党	– trust the Party
xiaoqin jinglao 孝亲敬老	– reverence for parents and the elderly

xiaokang 小康	– moderate prosperity
xiaokang shehui 小康社会	– a moderately prosperous society
xinxing zhengdang zhidu 新型政党制度	– new-style political Party system
xuexixing zhengdang 学习型政党	– a learning Party

Y

yide zhiguo 以德治国	– governing the country by moral virtue
yifa zhiguo 依法治国	– governing the nation according to law
yi yan tang 一言堂	– the hall of one voice
yixian zhiguo 依宪治国	– governing the country according to the Constitution
youxuexing 优越性	– the superiority (of a system)
youji tongyi 有机统一	– organic unification
youfa keyi, youfabiyi, zhifabiyan, weifabijiu 有法可依，有法必依，执法必严，违法必究.	– There must be laws to go by, the laws must be observed and strictly enforced, and law-breakers must be prosecuted.
yundongshi zhili 运动式治理	– campaign-style governance

Z

zhengfa weiyuanhui 政法委员会	– political legal committee
zhengque de sixiang 正确的思想	– the correct thought/thinking
zhidao sixiang 指导思想	– guiding thought
zhili nengli 治理能力	– governance capacity
zhongguo moshi 中国模式	– China model
Zhonghua minzu 中华民族	– the Chinese people
Zhonghua minzu weida fuxing de Zhongguo meng 中华民伟大族复兴的中国梦	– Chinese Dream of the Great Rejuvenation of the Chinese Nation
zhonghua wenhua jingshen 中华文化精神	– the 'Chinese cultural spirit'
zunchong yingxiong 尊重英雄	– reverence for heroes

INDEX

Lightning Source UK Ltd.
Milton Keynes UK
UKHW020810201022
410776UK00023B/375